Treasures for Scholars Worldwide

浙江省档案馆藏
中国旧海关瓯海关税务司与海关总税务司署往来机要函

Semi-official Correspondence Between Wenchow Commissioners and the Inspectorate General of Customs in Zhejiang Provincial Archives

主　　编 | 赵　伐　周彩英

本册编译 | 何习尧

5

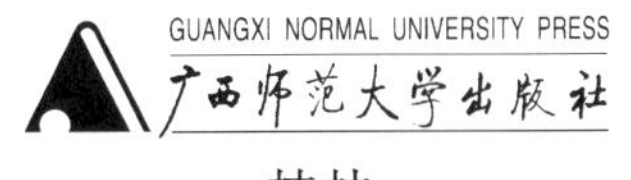

·桂林·

提 要

本册收录了浙江省档案馆藏 1927 年至 1928 年瓯海关税务司与海关总税务司署总税务司及代理总税务司、造册处税务司、总务科等税务司的往来机要函(亦称半官函)。信函如包含有附件,则用符号( )或将附件名称列在该信函标题之后。为简化每封信函的标题起见,信函的责任者与受文人只写人名的中文译名,其英文原名、职务、供职单位集中在以下表中列出。

姓名	职务
安格联(F. A. Aglen)	海关总税务司署总税务司
易纨士(A. H. F. Edwardes)	海关总税务司署代理总税务司
岸本广古(II. Kishimoto)	海关总税务司署代理总务科税务司
卢立基(L. dc. Luca)	海关总税务司署造册处税务司
白立查(E. A. Pritchard)	海关总税务司署署襄办汉文秘书科副税务司
魏尔特(S. F. Wright)	海关总税务司署秘书科税务司
裴纳玑(E. Bernadsky)	瓯海关税务司
吴兆熊	瓯海关暂代税务司
铃木藤藏(T. Suzuki)	瓯海关代理税务司

Contents
目　录

1927 年

1 月 12 日，魏尔特致裴纳玑：告知收到其第 383 号机要函（L060-001-0185-052） ………… 3

1 月 13 日，裴纳玑致安格联：汇报闽系军队完全离开、日常生活逐渐恢复、撤离军队与共军在处州府交战传言、就受损火柴物主申请免征保结事件尚未回复海关监督并请示应如何办理等（S/0 384）（L060-001-0185-055） ………… 4

1 月 19 日，裴纳玑致安格联：汇报浙江省革命军抵达温州情况及相关举措、达兴号轮船遭军警先于海关部门检查、华丰号轮船赴镇海载剩余军队来温（附浙江海陆军省防军司令部布告）（S/0 385）（L060-001-0185-057） ………… 7

1 月 26 日，裴纳玑致安格联：汇报孙传芳军队逼近、各路武装力量盘踞、富人官员逃至上海、银行关门、夜晚戒严、水路搜查逮捕、对进口货物额外征收税款等（附对在温外国居民就现状的提醒）（S/0 386）（L060-001-0185-059） ………… 13

1 月 29 日，裴纳玑致安格联：汇报国民革命军第二方面军要求清空教堂入驻、建国军第一路遣散、水上警察继续戒严搜查、更换厘金局和烟酒局官员、美国传教士及家人撤离等（S/0 387）（L060-001-0185-062） ………… 21

2 月 12 日，裴纳玑致易纨士：汇报各轮船去向、新监督工作情况、英美籍传教士撤离、军队及中外军舰动向、征兵情况等，并表示对海关在华既得利益的担忧（S/0 388）（L060-001-0185-068） ………… 24

2 月 16 日，裴纳玑致易纨士：汇报各轮船去向、国民革命军第十七军提出确保本地外籍居民、在温州的传教士及家人撤离情况等（S/0 389）（L060-001-0185-070） ………… 33

2 月 17 日，易纨士致裴纳玑：告知收到其第 385 号机要函，就达兴号轮船事件询问抗议结果（S/0）（L060-001-0185-058） ………… 36

2 月 17 日，易纨士致裴纳玑：告知收到其第 386 号机要函，就是否应该给国民革命军任命的海关监督发放薪金的肯定回复、就额外征收进口税事件要求瓯海关不卷入纷争、保持中立交由海关监督处理（S/0）（L060-001-0185-061） ······ 37

2 月 17 日，易纨士致裴纳玑：告知收到其第 387 号机要函，通知放行相关有撤离请求的外籍海关职员(S/0)（L060-001-0185-063） ······ 39

2 月 18 日，易纨士致裴纳玑：告知收到其第 384 号机要函，就受损火柴免征保结费事件告知尚无任何新消息（S/0）（L060-001-0185-056） ······ 40

2 月 26 日，裴纳玑致易纨士：汇报各轮船军舰去向、海关监督人员变动、新任浙江省政府总督蔡元培前来、当地民间运动及物价等（S/0 390）（L060-001-0185-075） ······ 41

3 月 5 日，裴纳玑致易纨士：就 3 月份税收的汇率作解释、汇报按国民党要求降下五色旗并升起国民政府旗帜、海盗和各轮船军舰情况、公安局设立及人员任命情况、抵制洋货反英运动等事件（附瓯海关帮办吴兆雄给税务司的备忘录）（S/0 391）（L060-001-0185-077） ······ 50

3 月 10 日，裴纳玑致易纨士：汇报温州发生的系列暴动和对海关的抗议及与监督就此事的沟通情况（附瓯海公报上刊登关于反英运动群众侮辱常关职员的致歉言论）（S/0 392）（L060-001-0185-079） ······ 61

3 月 21 日，裴纳玑致易纨士：汇报杭州关邮政司请求财政补助、海关缺乏职员、各轮船军舰去向、十七军司令部和公安局关于粮食问题的声明等事件（S/0 393）（L060-001-0185-081） ······ 69

3 月 23 日，裴纳玑致卢立基：就年度统计表将于月底送达说明原因并致歉（L060-001-0185-083） ······ 80

3 月 26 日，易纨士致裴纳玑：就华盛顿会议对进口货物征收附税款规定要求海关不直接参与征收并说明操作细则（S/0 Confidential）（L060-001-0185-095） ······ 81

3 月 28 日，易纨士致裴纳玑：告知收到其第 390 号机要函、就 50 里开外常关收税权被夺取表示可抗议及就温州现状详细汇报的感谢、对海关运行未遭受重大影响感到庆幸（S/0）（L060-001-0185-076） ······ 85

3 月 31 日，裴纳玑致易纨士：汇报温州部分政府职员成立工会、各轮船军舰去向、英领馆撤侨、中国银行恢复半营业等、询问是否给予为海关提供引水服务的水手奖励等（附瓯海关给温州外籍居民转发英领馆密电）（S/0 394）（L060-001-0185-087） ······ 86

4 月 4 日，易纨士致裴纳玑：告知收到其第 391 号机要函，就升起国民政府旗帜的许可（S/0）（L060-001-0185-078） ······ 95

4 月 4 日，易纨士致裴纳玑：告知收到其第 392 号机要函，对其汇报的温州暴动事件中海关总体上未受影响及海关监督可以信任表达庆幸（S/0）（L060-001-0185-080） ······ 96

4 月 6 日，裴纳玑致易纨士：汇报温州侨民撤离事宜、抵制洋货和排外及收回海关运动、部分海关职员自愿与税务司留守海关等事件（附瓯海关给温州外籍居民转发英领馆密电）（S/0 395）（L060-001-0185-091） ······ 97

4 月 12 日，裴纳玑致易纨士：汇报抵制洋货运动、外籍居民撤离情况、中华基督教会建立、中国银行恢复营业、税务司无法按时休假、瓯海关资金转移情况等（S/0 396）（L060-001-0185-096） …… 108

4 月 12 日，易纨士致裴纳玑：就瓯海关所发电报要求与英领事商讨撤侨事宜并作相关指示（L060-001-0185-100） …… 115

4 月 18 日，易纨士致裴纳玑：告知收到其第 393 号机要函、要求尽可能多地将钱汇往上海（L060-001-0185-082） …… 116

4 月 19 日，裴纳玑致易致纨士：汇报税务司转交职权给吴兆熊、瓯海关职员在危急时刻的表现值得称道、日法军舰抵达、反英的共产党员被捕、海关外籍职员撤离等（S/0 397）（L060-001-0185-102） …… 117

4 月 20 日，吴兆熊致易纨士：汇报已就职、所有外籍职员撤离、海关人手短缺和常关现状、地方军队不侵犯中外居民规定、反英运动等事件（S/0 398）（L060-001-0185-103） …… 123

4 月 23 日，吴兆熊致易纨士：汇报谢绝监督派职员协助海关工作、拒绝财政部要求以海关现金作军费、海盗活动及军事冲突、当地反帝反封建运动、温州全城戒严等（S/0 399）（L060-001-0185-105） …… 129

4 月 25 日，吴兆熊致易纨士：汇报海关监督试图用无中生有的借口干涉海关事务及应对办法（S/0 400）（L060-001-0185-107） …… 134

4 月 26 日，易纨士致裴纳玑：告知收到其第 394 号机要函、说明就提供引水服务水手的奖励已下发训令（L060-001-0185-088） …… 136

4 月 26 日，易纨士致裴纳玑：告知收到其第 395 号机要函、询问给予温州法籍居民去日本护照合理性及对瓯海关给予侨民撤离帮助和坚持留守表达敬意（L060-001-0185-092） …… 137

4 月 28 日，吴兆熊致易纨士：汇报海关监督的情况、请示在紧急情况下可否寻求日本炮舰庇护、已汇出绝大部分钱款、温州再次张贴反帝海报、劳工组织重组等（S/0 401）（L060-001-0185-112） …… 139

5 月 2 日，吴兆熊致易纨士：汇报监督暂不要求海关上交所收关税、监督要求免除一批土豆的常关税、给引水水夫发放报酬、劳工联盟反对资本家等情况（S/0 402）（L060-001-0185-114） …… 143

5 月 5 日，易纨士致吴兆熊：就辞退部分海关杂役等底层员工以削减开支说明操作原则（S/0）（L060-001-0185-120） …… 149

5 月 6 日，吴兆熊致易纨士：汇报海关监督态度转变、海关关税汇解、查获鸦片销毁、询问职员夏季制服和管理津贴、被捕的共产党员押解杭州、胡鼎仁担任温州地方长官等情况（S/0 403）（L060-001-0185-116） …… 151

5 月 7 日，裴纳玑致易纨士：就瓯海关破例为经日本赴沪的温州法籍居民发放签证的原因作解释（S/0）（L060-001-0185-093） …… 156

5 月 9 日，易纨士致吴兆雄：告知收到其第 396 号机要函、就海关职员推荐儿子担任职位表示否决和税款汇解事宜作指示（S/0）（L060-001-0185-097） …… 158

5 月 9 日，易纨士致吴兆熊：告知收到其第 398 号机要函、就其接替职位和良好态度给予肯定（L060-001-0185-104） …… 160

5 月 11 日，易纨士致吴兆熊：告知收到其第 399 号机要函、指示应如何应对监督的干涉并肯定其对外班员工的管理（L060-001-0185-106） …… 161

5 月 13 日，吴兆熊致易纨士：汇报监督已将 1 至 3 月 50 里外常关税收移交海关、常关及海关 4 月税收数额、灯塔建立、药店商人们针对苛刻规定抗议等（S/0 404）（L060-001-0185-118） …… 162

5 月 14 日，易纨士致吴兆熊：告知收到其第 400 号机要函、就对海关现金的处理办法作指示（L060-001-0185-108） …… 168

5 月 14 日，易纨士致吴兆熊：告知收到其第 401 号机要函、就之前电报遗失部分的增补及要求尽力维持海关运转、告知已增派职员前往（S/0）（L060-001-0185-113） …… 169

5 月 21 日，易纨士致吴兆熊：告知收到其第 402 号机要函、说明在应对海关监督时应遵循之原则（L060-001-0185-115） …… 170

5 月 21 日，吴兆熊致易纨士：汇报将研究裁减底层员工、询问含磷火柴事件应如何处理、陈梅豪申请接任海关医员、共产党和劳工组织被强制解散、日法军舰离开等（S/0 405）（L060-001-0185-121） …… 171

5 月 24 日，易纨士致吴兆熊：告知收到其第 403 号机要函、就税款汇解和新制服作指示（L060-001-0185-117） …… 175

5 月 26 日，吴兆熊致易纨士：就税收报告中的翻译错误致歉、汇报当地军队动向、法籍修女返回、3 名藏有共产党文件的学生被处决、商办轮船招商总局安排一周两班次轮船等事件（S/0 406）（L060-001-0185-123） …… 176

5 月 27 日，裴纳玑致易纨士：汇报瓯海关关医表明可随其他外籍员工返岗及申请 3 个月假期（S/0）（L060-001-0185-125） …… 179

5 月 31 日，吴兆熊致易纨士：汇报反英集会情况、海关职员被非正当传唤情况、平阳周荫人武装力量暂时被击退、全城仍旧戒严、运大号轮船遭遇海盗下落不明等事件（S/0 407）（L060-001-0185-129） …… 180

6 月 1 日，吴兆熊致易纨士：汇报当地的游行示威情况及准予员工半天假期、此前查获鸦片案的后续法律纠纷、当地部队动向、海盗劫掠轮船等（S/0 408）（L060-001-0185-131） …… 185

6 月 3 日，吴兆熊致易纨士：汇报《新瓯潮》按要求修改报道、税款汇解情况、军警搜查有共产党倾向的学生、国民党反共同时提倡反帝反封等（S/0 409）（附《新瓯潮》剪报）（L060-001-0185-133） …… 187

6 月 6 日，易纨士致吴兆熊：告知收到其第 404 号机要函、乐见瓯海关税收增加（S/0）（L060-001-0185-119） …… 191

6 月 10 日，吴兆熊致易纨士：汇报 5 月关税详情、通过监督就海关职员被非正当传唤提出抗议、员工情况、几起海盗抢劫及海战、当地抵制日货及劳工联盟情况、周荫人的武装力量占领处州等事件（S/0 410）（L060-001-0185-135） …… 192

6 月 13 日，吴兆熊致易纨士：就洋广局要求厘金由洋广局人员征收请示应对措施（S/0 411）（L060-001-0185-151） …… 200

6 月 17 日，易纨士致吴兆熊：告知收到其第 407 号机要函、批准反英活动期间关闭海关半天及就海关职员被非正当传唤事件赞同其应对方式（S/0）（L060-001-0185-130） …… 202

6 月 17 日，易纨士致吴兆熊：告知收到其第 408 号机要函、认为《新瓯潮》的虚假宣传最好不予理睬（S/0）（L060-001-0185-132） …… 203

6 月 17 日，易纨士致吴兆熊：告知收到其第 409 号机要函、赞许其要求报纸更正和税款汇解的相关举措（S/0）（L060-001-0185-134） …… 204

6 月 17 日，吴兆熊致易纨士：汇报装有发动机夹板船的归类、海关与鱼贩的协定、平阳匪患现状、劳工和学生反日活动、浙江省烟草专营法规导致店铺停业抗议等事件（S/0 412）（L060-001-0185-153） …… 205

6 月 20 日，易纨士致吴兆熊：告知收到其第 406 号机要函、肯定其工作表现（S/0）（L060-001-0185-124） …… 208

6 月 20 日，易丸士致裴纳玑：告知收到 5 月 27 日的机要函、表明暂时不任命瓯海关关医（S/0）（L060-001-0185-126） …… 209

6 月 20 日，易纨士致吴兆熊：就海关及下属船只应该悬挂何种国旗作说明（L060-001-0185-159） …… 210

6 月 23 日，吴兆熊致易纨士：汇报洋广局寻求海关帮助以增加厘金征收、两名职员再次被传唤、客船与民船相撞、温州地方长官改换、打击海盗等情况（S/0 413）（L060-001-0185-155） …… 212

6 月 29 日，吴兆熊致易纨士：汇报 5 月的税收汇款、就船只碰撞事件扣留民船的证照、与鱼贩签署协定、已故浙江省省长夏超葬礼、本地烟草商继续抗议等（S/0 414）（L060-001-0185-157） …… 217

7 月 4 日，易纨士致吴兆熊：告知收到其第 405 号机要函、就火柴一案作指示及表明暂时搁置海关医员接替问题（S/0）（L060-001-0185-122） …… 221

7 月 4 日，易纨士致吴兆熊：告知收到其第 411 号机要函、指示若监督书面要求则将对邮包的厘金征收权交予洋广局并汇报（S/0）（L060-001-0185-152） …… 222

7 月 5 日，吴兆熊致易纨士：汇报海关及下属船只已悬挂国民党旗帜、海关和常关月度税收情况、米价上涨当局进口大米缓解局势、抵制日货活动、烟草商抵制烟草专营政策等情况（S/0 415）（L060-001-0185-160） …… 223

7 月 6 日，易纨士致吴兆熊：告知收到其第 410 号机要函、对税收情况表示满意并就外班华员的薪酬作相关指示（S/0）（L060-001-0185-150） …… 227

7月6日，易纨士致吴兆熊：告知收到其第412号机要函、认同其与鱼贩签定协议（S/0）（L060-001-0185-154） …… 229

7月7日，吴兆熊致易纨士：汇报听说南京国民政府财政部拟收回50里外常关税收（S/0 416）（L060-001-0185-162） …… 230

7月8日，易纨士致吴兆熊：告知收到其第413号机要函、赞同其对于洋广局要求海关协助厘金的应对方式（L060-001-0185-156） …… 232

7月11日，吴兆熊致易纨士：汇报温州反英反日排外运动高涨、海关监督试图占据海关关产、询问关税自主和废除厘金的进展情况、请示是否应对十字绣手帕征税（S/0 417）（L060-001-0185-166） …… 233

7月15日，吴兆熊致易纨士：请示在无关医的情况下如何应对疫情、汇报当地抵制日货和反日游行、警署长被捕、《瓯海公报》关于海关的虚假宣传等事件（S/0 418）（L060-001-0185-137） …… 238

7月15日，易纨士致吴兆熊：告知收到其第414号机要函、赞同其就船只碰撞事件采取的举措（S/0）（L060-001-0185-158） …… 242

7月19日，易纨士致吴兆熊：告知收到其第415号机要函、乐见瓯海关税收增加（S/0）（L060-001-0185-161） …… 243

7月20日，吴兆熊致易纨士：汇报海关监督借南京国民政府名义干涉海关关税（S/0 419）（L060-001-0185-142） …… 244

7月26日，易纨士致吴兆熊：告知收到其第417号机要函、就抵制日货运动和劳工联盟要求强调海关应保持中立（S/0）（L060-001-0185-136） …… 247

7月26日，吴兆熊致易纨士：汇报监督企图干预税收事宜的进展、国民政府准备于8月1日起开始征收附加税、警察勒令学生离开其占据的教会学校、当地反帝情绪高涨等（S/0 420）（L060-001-0185-149） …… 248

7月29日，吴兆熊致易纨士：对关税自主后海关存废担忧、因当地反帝情绪高涨申请调任其他海关（附《申报》关于海关华员拥有关税自主的报道）（S/0 421）（L060-001-0185-168） …… 251

8月1日，吴兆熊致易纨士：汇报海关监督占据海关和常关并开始征收附加税、请示关税自主政策生效后应如何应对、寻求强有力支援（附《申报》关于财政部裁撤国内通过税的报道）（S/0 422）（L060-001-0185-173） …… 255

8月5日，吴兆熊致易纨士：就海关监督欲借故损毁海关信誉以便监管海关并逐渐蚕食海关职权、商人借故滋事等（S/0 423）（L060-001-0185-178） …… 260

8月8日，易纨士致吴兆熊：告知收到其第419号机要函，就海关监督干涉关税事件表明应严正抵制（S/0）（L060-001-0185-143） …… 264

8月9日，易纨士致吴兆熊：告知收到其第420号机要函、告知已让江海关税务司介入以解决监督干涉海关职权的问题、关税自主问题暂无定论、说明十字绣手帕应缴纳常关税（S/0）（L060-001-0185-167） …… 265

8 月 9 日，吴兆熊致易纨士：汇报计划在收回海关游行当天关闭海关、监督继续占据海关关产、要求监督继续移交 50 里外常关关税、厘金废除将导致浙江省上万人失业等（S/0 424）（L060-001-0185-182） …… 266

8 月 11 日，易纨士致吴兆熊：告知收到其第 421 号机要函、就海关监督威胁海关和关税自主的应对措施作回复（S/0）（L060-001-0185-169） …… 268

8 月 15 日，易纨士致吴兆熊：告知收到其第 422 号机要函、表明暂时无法就关税自主政策做出具体指示（S/0）（L060-001-0185-174） …… 269

8 月 15 日，吴兆熊致易纨士：汇报海关税收减少、北洋政府军队南下、国民党政府忙于关税自主和废除不平等条约宣传等（S/0 425）（L060-001-0185-184） …… 270

8 月 16 日，吴兆熊致易纨士：汇报海关监督亦不确定关税自主政策是否能够成功推行（S/0 426）（L060-001-0185-186） …… 274

8 月 17 日，易纨士致吴兆熊：告知收到其两封机要函、就其编号错误要求改正（S/0）（L060-001-0185-179） …… 276

8 月 19 日，易纨士致吴兆熊：告知收到其第 423 号机要函、就海关监督蚕食海关职权问题寄希望于梅乐和的努力及南京国民政府垮台（L060-001-0185-180） …… 277

8 月 23 日，吴兆熊致易纨士：认为关税自主政策或因南北方交战而搁置破产、与监督就十字绣征税的争议、监督不再于 50 里外常关征收附加税、厘金将恢复征收等（S/0 427）（L060-001-0185-190） …… 278

8 月 25 日，易纨士致吴兆熊：告知收到其第 424 号机要函、鼓励其保持乐观并说明关税自主可能被推迟（S/0）（L060-001-0185-183） …… 283

8 月 27 日，吴兆熊致易纨士：汇报收到消息 50 里内常关税及附加税保持不变、海关监督重复征税、由于上海爆发霍乱将抗染防疫条例运用于上海船只等（S/0 428）（L060-001-0185-192） …… 284

8 月 29 日，易纨士致吴兆熊：告知收到其第 425 号机要函、说明关税自主政策宣告破产、对瓯海关职员未受江海关煽动表示满意（S/0）（L060-001-0185-185） …… 288

9 月 2 日，吴兆熊致易纨士：汇报监督宣布常关税和附加税征收依旧及船钞降低至原来的四分之一、监督处于无管辖状态并骚扰客商和侵占空余办公地点等（S/0 429）（L060-001-0185-194） …… 289

9 月 9 日，吴兆熊致易纨士：汇报关税征收情况、监督暂未进一步侵占海关关产、监督胡乱征税的举报信、防疫条例运用于上海船只、军舰误开火等事件（S/0 430）（L060-001-0185-196） …… 296

9 月 14 日，吴兆熊致易纨士：汇报调整办公室以缓解和海关监督的冲突、职员申请事假、国民党规定信封上印“打倒帝国主义”字样等（S/0 431）（L060-001-0185-198） …… 299

9 月 20 日，吴兆熊致易纨士：汇报南京国民政府下令要求监督不得干涉海关、烟草局和军人搜查抵达轮船是否携带无印花的烟草、部分外籍传教士不配合防疫检查、当局为压榨商人对其出口日本货物不予放行等（S/0 432）（L060-001-0185-202） …… 303

9 月 21 日，易纨士致吴兆熊：告知收到其第 427 号机要函、就关税自主政策破产、厘金恢复征收作指示与说明（S/0）（L060-001-0185-191） …… 308

9 月 21 日，易纨士致吴兆熊：告知收到其第 429 号机要函、就海关监督干涉海关职权、侵占海关关产作相关指示（S/0）（L060-001-0185-195） …… 309

9 月 27 日，吴兆熊致易纨士：汇报反对监督侵占海关关产、据传周凤岐被捕、卸烟草的舢板船与海关职员因罚款发生冲突、日本货船顺利载货返航等（S/0 433）（L060-001-0185-204） …… 311

9 月 29 日，吴兆熊致易纨士：汇报监督征税员的越职行为、请示对于运输的旧家具是否征税、为海关图书馆申请经费、大批军队途经温州、渔政局设立等（S/0 434）（L060-001-0185-206） …… 314

9 月 30 日，易纨士致吴兆熊：告知收到其第 430 号机要函、希望商人对海关的友好态度能继续维持（S/0）（L060-001-0185-197） …… 319

10 月 3 日，易纨士致吴兆熊：告知收到其第 431 号机要函、认可其调整办公室的举措（S/0）（L060-001-0185-199） …… 320

10 月 7 日，吴兆熊致易纨士：汇报海关监督下属的越职行为引起大众抵制、9 月税收增加、派海关职员入住海关闲置宿舍情况、相关船只来往去向及军队运输等（S/0 435）（L060-001-0185-208） …… 321

10 月 11 日，易纨士致吴兆熊：告知收到其第 432 号机要函、强调船长有责任让所有乘客都接受防疫检查（S/0）（L060-001-0185-203） …… 325

10 月 13 日，吴兆熊致易纨士：汇报给海关监督越职行为抗议信的回复情况、商人对海关有良好印象、海关监督不同意在船只上装无线设备、码头货物堆积等（S/0 436）（L060-001-0185-210） …… 326

10 月 19 日，吴兆熊致易纨士：就同意自己调任至粤海关的感谢及工作接替情况、对相关职员的赞扬、收到海关监督越职事件的抗议信回复等（S/0 437）（L060-001-0185-211） …… 330

10 月 22 日，易纨士致吴兆熊：告知收到其第 433 号机要函、批准相关开支申请（S/0）（L060-001-0185-205） …… 333

10 月 22 日，易纨士致吴兆熊：告知收到其第 434 号机要函、就旧家具征税与否及海关图书馆经费申请作相关指示（S/0）（L060-001-0185-207） …… 334

10 月 22 日，易纨士致吴兆熊：告知收到其第 435 号机要函、就其在海关监督越职中采取的行为表示赞同（L060-001-0185-209） …… 336

10 月 22 日，吴兆熊致易纨士：汇报自己卸任及移交职权给铃木藤藏、海关监督态度友好（S/0 438）（L060-001-0185-212） …… 337

10 月 22 日，铃木藤藏致易纨士：汇报自己接任瓯海关代理税务司（S/0 439）（L060-001-0185-213） …… 339

11 月 4 日，铃木藤藏致易纨士：汇报庄智涣接替徐乐尧担任海关监督、前海关医员 Stedeford 短暂返回、本地除张贴有反对渔政局海报外一切无恙（S/0 440）（L060-001-0185-215） …… …… 340

11 月 10 日，易纨士致铃木藤藏：告知收到其第 439 号机要函、确认其就职（S/0）（L060-001-0185-214） …… 342

11 月 18 日，易纨士致铃木藤藏：告知收到其第 440 号机要函、希望其与新监督相处融洽（S/0）（L060-001-0185-216） …… 343

11 月 21 日，铃木藤藏致易纨士：就监督庄智涣暂离、6 月起监督拒绝将 50 里外常关税移交海关、管理船舶事务所、禁烟局和鸦片专卖处成立、煤油税提高、大火焚烧寺庙、共产党员遭逮捕枪决、孙中山生辰纪念活动等（S/0 441）（L060-001-0185-217） …… 344

11 月 26 日，铃木藤藏致白立查：就发现的未登记账单说明详细情况（S/0）（L060-001-0185-223） …… 350

12 月 6 日，白立查致铃木藤藏：就其未登记账单要求以公文请示（S/0）（L060-001-0185-224） …… 352

12 月 7 日，铃木藤藏致易纨士：汇报监督庄智涣返回并寻求海关协助征收附加税、鱼贩和商人抵制渔政局、鸦片专卖处停业、本地 11 月 26 日到 12 月 4 日戒严等（S/0 442）（L060-001-0185-225） …… 353

12 月 12 日，易纨士致铃木藤藏：告知收到其第 441 号机要函、就管理船舶事务所成立要求不予介入（S/0）（L060-001-0185-218） …… 358

12 月 20 日，铃木藤藏致易纨士：汇报何家猷接任海关监督、由中国银行征收附加税且须印有相关字样收讫规定、海关监督拒交 50 里外常关税款、海盗洗劫村落扣押人质等（S/0 443）（L060-001-0185-227） …… 359

12 月 21 日，易纨士致铃木藤藏：告知收到其第 442 号机要函、就附加税征收要求参考江海关做法（S/0）（L060-001-0185-226） …… 363

1928 年

1 月 4 日，易纨士致铃木藤藏：告知收到其第 443 号机要函、就附加税征收要求设法让监督不使用瓯海关字样的收讫、就海关监督拒交 50 里外常关税款说明暂时难以改变现状（S/0）（L060-001-0185-228） …… 367

1 月 6 日，铃木藤藏致易纨士：汇报 1927 年海关及常关税收情况、新瓯海关监督何家猷就任、监督告知美孚和亚细亚及德克萨斯三家石油公司之外其余所有煤油进口需至补征局受检并交税等（S/0 444）（L060-001-0186-001） …… 368

1 月 17 日，易纨士致铃木藤藏：告知收到其第 444 号机要函、要求对煤油进口缴补征税一事让监督自行处理（S/0）（L060-001-0186-002） …… 370

1 月 20 日，易纨士致铃木藤藏：要求尽快提供当地有关附加税征收的详情（L060-001-0186-005） …… 371

1 月 28 日，铃木藤藏致易纨士：汇报给海关监督提前发放津贴、拒绝监督让海关征收邮包附加税之要求、春节期间天气潮湿、少数商人及银行家破产等（S/0 445）（L060-001-0186-003） …… 374

2 月 10 日，易纨士致铃木藤藏：告知收到其第 445 号机要函、要求后续不得给海关监督提前发放津贴（S/0）（L060-001-0186-004） …… 376

2 月 11 日，铃木藤藏致易纨士：随函附寄温州附加税征收详情报告、汇报海关机构重组相关讨论、两艘日舰由福州抵达停靠后前往台湾、中国内地会的神职人员陆续抵达等（S/0 446）（L060-001-0186-006） …… 377

2 月 23 日，易纨士致铃木藤藏：告知收到其第 446 号机要函、要求就海关机构重组一事不要向监督表态（S/0）（L060-001-0186-007） …… 380

2 月 24 日，铃木藤藏致易纨士：汇报监督何家猷调迁杭州主管煤油税补征局并由贝祖祥接替、海门遭遇土匪抢劫情况、瑞安小客轮发生沉船事故、申请向三等一级稽查员 Sia Liang 发放署副监察员同等薪酬、更多教会人士返回温州等（S/0 447）（L060-001-0186-008） …… 381

3 月 8 日，易纨士致铃木藤藏：告知收到其第 447 号机要函、要求就监督更换一事以正式公文汇报、说明三等一级稽查员 Sia Liang 的薪酬事宜将于后续考虑（S/0）（L060-001-0186-009） …… 384

3 月 12 日，铃木藤藏致易纨士：汇报新监督贝志翔到任、贝志翔要求海关协助向商人兜售附加税债券和新印花税票、更多教会人士返回温州、三十二军的 800 名士兵由汕头至温州暂驻准备参加北伐等（S/0 448）（L060-001-0186-010） …… 385

3 月 27 日，铃木藤藏致易纨士：汇报同意印花税票局派代表在海关办公、商人仍使用旧印花税票、监督告知财政部要求转口税由在货物发出的海关缴纳但瓯海关尚未就此采取行动、三十二军士兵已离开、1 艘法舰由宁波抵达停驻后前往镇海等（S/0 449）（L060-001-0186-012） …… 389

4 月 3 日，易纨士致铃木藤藏：告知收到其第 448 号机要函、要求就印花税票事宜不介入华商总会与当局之间的纠纷（S/0）（L060-001-0186-011） …… 391

4 月 17 日，铃木藤藏致易纨士：汇报监督要求海关停止为温州洋广货捐征收局对邮包代征厘金但税务司拒绝、轮船在老鼠山遭遇海盗袭击、水警巡船在三浦湾与海盗激战、收到监督来信告知杭州关已停止代征厘金要求瓯海关效仿等（S/0 450）（L060-001-0186-014） …… 392

4 月 23 日，魏尔特致铃木藤藏：告知收到其第 449 号机要函（S/0）（L060-001-0186-013） …… 398

4 月 26 日，铃木藤藏致易纨士：汇报已将邮包厘金代征权转交给浙江邮包税局、就免除本国及外国香烟子口半税和常关税与监督的交流情况、监督转发关务署指令要求将中文确定为海关办公语言等（S/0 451）（L060-001-0186-018） …… 399

5 月 5 日，易纨士致铃木藤藏：告知收到其第 450 号机要函、要求停止对邮包代征厘金但继续征收关税（S/0）（L060-001-0186-015） …… 402

5 月 11 日，铃木藤藏致易纨士：汇报英美烟草公司经纪同意缴纳除统税外的其他由海关收取的税、监督转告财政部通知要求商人进出口货物时需额外交两份申请、二等监察长 Broderick 到任、申请新增一名苦力、除部分当地人士赴山东参加反日抗议外局势平静等（S/0 452）（L060-001-0186-024） …… 403

5 月 17 日，魏尔特致铃木藤藏：告知收到其第 451 号机要函（S/0）（L060-001-0186-019） …… 407

5 月 25 日，易纨士致铃木藤藏：告知收到其第 452 号机要函、询问新增一名苦力是否确有必要（S/0）（L060-001-0186-025） …… 408

5 月 25 日，铃木藤藏致易纨士：申请授权为外班职员图书馆发放年度拨款、当地学生发动抵制日货情况等（S/0 453）（L060-001-0186-026） …… 409

6 月 8 日，铃木藤藏致易纨士：说明因海盗猖獗引水员对在白岩修建栖息所并不热心、已通知二等一级税务员谢辉准备调职至蒙自关、已与监察长商议好暂不新增苦力、当地局势稳定仍有 1 艘日舰停靠等（S/0 454）（L060-001-0186-028） …… 412

6 月 11 日，易纨士致铃木藤藏：告知收到其第 453 号机要函、同意为外班职员图书馆发放年度拨款但要求以正式公文申请（S/0）（L060-001-0186-027） …… 415

6 月 28 日，易纨士致铃木藤藏：告知收到其第 454 号机要函、同意暂不在白岩修建引水员栖息所（S/0）（L060-001-0186-029） …… 416

6 月 29 日，铃木藤藏致易纨士：汇报收到监督通知对美孚、亚细亚及德克萨斯三家公司已缴特税的煤油不再收取子口半税及常关税、将与外班人员讨论停止订阅部分刊物事宜、监督赴南京参会、因茶叶贸易停滞当月税收较去年下降、停驻的日舰更替等（S/0 455）（L060-001-0186-030） …… 417

7 月 4 日，易纨士致铃木藤藏：告知在未收到政府进一步指示之前暂时对由宁波经内河运往温州的洋糖保持税收优惠（S/0）（L060-001-0186-033） …… 420

7 月 13 日，易纨士致铃木藤藏：告知收到其第 455 号机要函、认为其在三家公司的煤油税收事宜上处理得当（S/0）（L060-001-0186-031） …… 421

7 月 13 日，铃木藤藏致易纨士：汇报帮办谢永钦到任并到总务课任职、帮办戚报元将调全常关、监察长 Broderick 请病假、关员对新政府将要如何管理海关表示担忧、与商办轮船招商局新任经理张一鸣交谈情况等（S/0 456）（L060-001-0186-035） …… 422

7 月 21 日，易纨士致铃木藤藏：告知收到其第 451 号和 452 号机要函、就已交统税的香烟免征常关税一事要求其向监督有策略地打听其意见（S/0）（L060-001-0186-042） …… 424

7 月 31 日，铃木藤藏致易纨士：汇报监督通知免除土布常关税及自己的应对方式、监督已由南京返回、监察长 Broderick 复岗等（S/0 457）（L060-001-0186-038） …… 427

8 月 3 日，魏尔特致铃木藤藏：告知已收到其第 456 号机要函（S/0）（L060-001-0186-036） …… 429

8 月 13 日，易纨士致铃木藤藏：告知收到其第 457 号机要函、要求执行免除土布常关税并以正式公文汇报（S/0）（L060-001-0186-039） …… 430

8 月 17 日，铃木藤藏致易纨士：汇报监督要求执行财政部关于已交统税的货物免除常关税的政策及自己的应对方式、对政府推行统税政策对海关税收的侵蚀表示担忧、洋广局在商办轮船招商局码头开设分局监视海关验货员工作等（S/0 458）（L060-001-0186-043） …… 431

8 月 24 日，铃木藤藏致易纨士：汇报监督要求已缴纳统税的麦麸免除出口税并询问易纨士对此事所持态度、政府又准备对箔类征收统税等（S/0 459）（L060-001-0186-045） …… 435

9 月 3 日，秘书科致铃木藤藏：告知已收到其第 458 号机要函（S/0）（L060-001-0186-044） …… 438

9 月 8 日，岸本广吉致铃木藤藏：告知收到其第 459 号机要函、要求执行已缴纳统税的麦麸免除出口税政策（L060-001-0186-046） …… 439

9 月 11 日，铃木藤藏致易纨士：汇报当地成立与日本断绝经济关系协会分会、台风过境但所幸未造成大的损失、监察长 Broderick 申请 6 个月长假等（S/0 460）（L060-001-0186-047） …… 440

9 月 29 日，铃木藤藏致易纨士：汇报台风二次登陆、新轮船将投入上海至温州航线使用、烟草特税局与煤油特税局合并、当地抵制日货等情况（S/0 461）（L060-001-0186-049） …… 442

10 月 3 日，魏尔特致铃木藤藏：告知已收到其第 460 号机要函（S/0）（L060-001-0186-048） …… 444

10 月 15 日，秘书科致铃木藤藏：告知收到其第 461 号机要函（S/0）（L060-001-0186-050） …… 445

10 月 23 日，铃木藤藏致易纨士：汇报查抄大量谎报为进口货物的国内机制货物详情、当地发生火灾、上海至温州航线轮船投入使用等（S/0 462）（L060-001-0186-051） …… 446

11 月 7 日，岸本广吉致铃木藤藏：告知收到其第 462 号机要函，就查抄谎报为进口货物的国内机制货物一案指出其在与监督沟通上的不当之处（S/0）（L060-001-0186-052） …… 449

11 月 7 日，铃木藤藏致易纨士：汇报日本抵制协会反对向日本出口木炭相关事宜及海关监督贝志翔赴上海出席特别金融会议（S/0 463）（L060-001-0186-053） …… 451

11 月 22 日，铃木藤藏致易纨士：汇报查抄机制棉质货物、商人请愿收取机制货物扣押举报费、因抵制日本活动由上海驶往香港的“Cassum”号轮船燃料供给不足、禁止木炭出口日本及禁止日本船只进口事宜等（S/0 464）（L060-001-0186-055） …… 453

11 月 28 日，易纨士致铃木藤藏：要求其发送年度税收电报（S/0）（L060-001-0186-057） …… 460

11 月 30 日，秘书科致铃木藤藏：告知已收到其第 463 号机要函（S/0）（L060-001-0186-054） …… 461

12 月 6 日，秘书科致铃木藤藏：告知已收到其第 464 号机要函（S/0）（L060-001-0186-056） …… 462

12 月 18 日，铃木藤藏致易纨士：汇报当地暂停向日本出口木炭、“Cassum”号安全抵达香港、为 500 吨级以上的中国船舶安装无线电设备、中国邮政局温州分局已被降级、对二等监察长 Broderick 二次长假申请的意见等（S/0 465）（L060-001-0186-058） …………………… 463

12 月 28 日，卢立基致铃木藤藏：告知已收到其第 465 号机要函（S/0）（L060-001-0186-059） …………………… 466

1927 年

·42]

INSPECTORATE GENERAL OF CUSTOMS,

PEKING, 12 Jan. 1927

Sir,

I am directed by the Inspector General
rm you that your S/O Letter No. 383,
31st December, has been duly
d.

Yours truly,

Stanley F. Wright

Personal ~~Private~~ Secretary.

rnadsky, Esquire,

WENCHOW.

CUSTOM HOUSE,

No. 384. Wenchow 13th January 1927 281

INDEXED

Dear Sir Francis,

[Situ]ation at [Wen]chow.

1st January. Practically all the soldiers from Fukien have left Wenchow. This military movement-evacuation cost this city $ 120 thousand, which were paid to the military Head Quarters by the Chamber of Commerce and the Bank of China. The city life is gradually coming to its normal state.

Tu-chün of Fukien Chou Yin-jen (周蔭人), who arrived here together with the soldiers from Fukien, left Wenchow for Shanghai by S.S. "Tah-hsin".

2nd January. Japanese Gunboat Uji left for Formosa.

3rd January. The Chief of Police Ma Chên-chung (馬振中) resigned and left Wenchow for

FRANCIS AGLEN, K. B. E.,
Inspector General of Customs,
PEKING.

290

for Shanghai. The Taoyin appointed the Magistrate Yü Wên-yao (余文焰) to fill the vacancy for the time being in addition to his own post.

5th January. The survivors 217 men and 116 women of the coolies who carried the soldiers' luggage and ammunition from Fukien to Wenchow went back by the S.S. "Gochow" and $ 620 were subscribed for their passages by the Fukien Guild at Wenchow.

8th January. The former Wenchow garrison soldiers, whom the ex-Commander Lü Ho-yin (吕和音) on the approach of the Fukien troops despatched to the interior and left them there uncared for, returned here on the request of the Wenchow Magistrate.

13th January. The normal life of the city of Wenchow has been practically re-established but the middle schools have not been opened yet and the China Merchants Steam Navigation Company's ships have not been running between Wenchow and Shanghai since 11th

December

3

291

December 1926.

Our mail comes via Ningpo.

During the last few days there have been a lot of rumours here about the fighting between the evacuated soldiers and the reds near Ch'ü-chow-fu (衢州府), about the arrival of the evacuated soldiers and the imminent approach here of the reds.

ches containing low phosphorus, cases of: re-ortation of to ce of original pment, authorised G. Despatch No 8/104,761) but not take place. letter to I.G. 380.

On the 5th instant I received a letter from the Superintendent in which he stated that according to the Shui-wu Ch'u instructions he together with the Commissioner of Customs are to investigate and report the case of the damage brought to the cargo by the Wenchow climate, and if the investigation proves that the statement of the petitioners is correct then the bond is not to be enforced and the remaining undamaged part of the matches is to be re-exported to Shanghai. No reply was sent by me to the Superintendent as I am waiting for your instructions.

Yours truly,

E. Bernadsky.

CUSTOM HOUSE, 293

/0 No. 385. Wenchow 19th January 1927

Dear Sir Francis,

ituation at enchow.

16th January. (a) At 9 a. m. about 1,000 soldiers belonging to the Chekiang 1st Division and the Water Police of the Ningpo district in retreat from Marshal Sun's troops were brought here from Chin Hai (鎮海) by:

Hai-Ping (海平)) Water Police vessels.
Hai-Cheng (海靖))
Hsin Pao-shun (新寶順))
Yung-Ping (永平))

Ping-yang (平陽)) regular steam launches between Wenchow and Ningpo, commandeered by the Military.
Yung-chuan (永川))

Nin-teig (寧台).

The local population met the vessels, the soldiers were very friendly and

IR FRANCIS AGLEN, K. B. E.,
Inspector General of Customs,
PEKING.

2.

294

and streets presented quite a different picture to when the retreating soldiers from Fukien province arrived here.

The first steps taken by the newly arrived military authorities were:

(1) The Telegraph Office was put under their censorship.

(2) A proclamation, a copy and translation of which are herewith, was issued.

(3) The Salt Preventive Force (8th Division) was disarmed and the Head of this Force was arrested.

(b) There is a rumour that the Northerners have left Ch'ü-chow-fu (衢州府) front for Ningpo. If this is true then there is nothing left to prevent the Southerners joining the Chekiang 1st Division at Wenchow.

(c) The local gentry and merchants held a meeting and passed a resolution that the Protection and Peace Bureau (保安事務所) established on the arrival of the retreating soldiers

3.

295

soldiers from Fukien be turned into a Revolutionary Troops Entertaining Department (革命军招待处).

17th January. The S. S. Tah-hsing (达 兴) on her arrival from Shanghai was boarded and carefully searched by armed soldiers and police. I sent a letter to the Superintendent requesting him to make an arrangement with the Military that their functions are to take place after ours.

18th January. (a) Four sailing boats arrived here each containing about 50 soldiers also belonging to the Chekiang 1st Division.

(b) The S.S. Hua-feng (华 丰) has been commandeered by the Military and sent to Chin-Hai to embark at that fort the remaining part of the soldiers of the Chekiang 1st Division.

Yours truly,

E. Bernadsky

296

Wenchow S/O Letter No. 385.

ENCLOSURE.

佈告[illegible]　錄浙江海陸軍省防
軍司令部布告、照得本軍之建設、
原爲鞏固省防、保全浙土、貫澈革命
之精神、推倒殘民之軍閥、浙省民六
以來、禍亂迭乘、幾使文物之邦、摧
殘殆盡、民治眞理、蕩然無存、本司
令觸目時艱、義難坐視、今因戰略上
之關係、來駐温屬、整我軍旅、悶我
疆圉、以民意爲依歸、以地方爲己責
、自示之後、凡屬文武官吏諸色人等
、各安職業、毋自驚擾、如有妨害我
軍行動、及擾亂秩序者本司令當執法
以繩、決不寬貸、仰各凜遵毋違、切
切此布、司令官陳其蔚、來偉良、

中華民國十六年一月十六日

Wenchow S/O Letter No. 385.

ENCLOSURE.

TRANSLATION OF JOINT PROCLAMATION ISSUED BY THE CHEKIANG PROVINCIAL DEFENCE NAVY AND ARMY HEADQUARTERS.

Proclamation No. 1.

The formation of the navy and army is with a view to strengthening the provincial defence, protecting Chekiang territory, completing works of revolution and overthrowing militarism. Chekiang has since the 6th year of the Republic of China been repeatedly entangled with wars and dissensions which have nearly destroyed the civilisation of the province. Democracy and citizens' rights have entirely ceased to exist. We, the Commanders, in view of the seriousness of the situation cannot endure any longer to see such a state of affairs continuing. For ths sake of strategy, we have come here to station ourselves in Wenchow and district. The army will be mobilised and the frontier will be strongly fortified. But we shall act in accordance with the public sentiment and we shall make ourselves responsible for peace and order here. It is requested

that

216

that all the civil officials, military officers and all grades of people should from the date of this proclamation go on with their duties as usual and that they should not get into panics. Those who hinder the movement of the troops or break peace and order will be severely dealt with according to law. No mercy shall be shown to them.

(Signed) Ch'en Ch'i-wei (陳 其 蔚)

(") Lai Wei-liang (來 偉 良).

Wenchow, 16th January, 1927. Commanders.

CUSTOM HOUSE, 303

No. 386. Wenchow 26th January 1927.

INDEXED

Dear Sir Francis,

...ation at ...how.

18th January. (a) The Water Police vessels: Hai-cheng (海靖), Hsin Pao-shun (新寶順) and Yung-Ping (永平) left Wenchow for the South.

There is a rumour that the Southern troops will be brought here by them soon.

(b) The Chief of the local police Ma Chen-chung (馬振中) has returned to his position.

19th January. (a) The Tah-hsing Steamer Company received a letter containing instructions from the Commander of the Chekiang 1st Division to stop the S. S. Tah-hsing at the mouth of the Ou river (entrance to Wenchow)

FRANCIS AGLEN, K. B. E.,
Inspector General of Customs.
PEKING.

2.

31.

Wenchow) each time on her way from Shanghai to Wenchow for an examination by the military. This letter was brought to me and then was forwarded to the Superintendent of Customs. The latter stated that he could not do anything in this case. Therefore I explained the situation to the Company and instructed them to produce me a statement signed by the Captain of the ship giving as many details as possible of the search by the military. It is stated in the letter to the Company that the military authorities are going to establish the examination of all ships coming to Wenchow.

(b) A lot of the wealthy people of Wenchow left for Shanghai by S. S. Tahhsing, as the newly arrived military authorities tried to tax them heavily. Together with these refugees fled also the Manager of the Bank of China and the Taoyin, but the departure of the latter has been denied by

3.

302

by his office.

(c) 300-400 persons of doubtful character (most likely bandits) entered the city from the interior and formed here a kind of Revolutionary Force (建國軍第一路) headed by a certain Chang Chao-chen (張兆宸)

(d) The local French missionaries informed the British Methodist Mission that according to the information in their hands the Kuomintang-party at their last meeting at Wenchow which took place a few days ago decided to molest British residents here.

(e) The name of the Revolutionary troops Entertaining Department (革命軍招待處) has on this day been styled as Yung-chia Military Affairs Entertaining Department (永嘉軍事招待處). This change of name took place evidently to smooth the situation in case of the arrival of Marshal Sun's troops here.

20th January. (a) The S.S. Hua-Feng arrived here from Shih-pu (石浦) and brought news that Marshal

303

Marshal Sun's troops were within 40 li distance from Shih-pu, advancing to Wenchow and therefore she could not proceed to Chih-hai.

(b) The Bank of China is closed. The Revenue is collected by the Bank's people but the collection is kept in the Customs' Safe. The reason why the Bank of China has suspended its business is as follows :-

The Chamber of Commerce at Wenchow has at request of the Chekiang army made arrangements with cash exchange shops to subscribe $40,000.00 for the troops. The money is in the form of promissory notes which the local banks finding it difficult to cash. The military on the 19th instant asked the Bank of China to advance the required amount but the Bank refused to do so on the ground that the cash exchange shops and the Chamber of Commerce have denied their promissory notes for the money the Bank advanced to

the

5.

304

the Northen troops. Then the military authorities when they found the Bank rejecting their demand arrested one of the members of the Bank. And as a result the Bank is closed.

(c) The Acting (temporary) Superintendent told me that there is no responsible person at present in charge of the affairs of the city, as there are four independent heads of military forces at Wenchow who claim to be here for the protection of the city, viz., the Chekiang 1st Division, the Water Police, the local Police and the Revolutionery Force.

This last news and also the formation at Wenchow of the Revolutionary Force have been communicated by me to the foreign residents at Wenchow, for their information and to enable them to take precautionary measures.

(d) The Acting (temporary) Superintendent told me also that instructions have been

305

been received by him from the Superintendent of Customs who up to now has been staying in Shanghai to hand over the office to the Southerners if they occupy Wenchow and appoint their candidate as the Superintendent of Customs.

If such change takes place may I issue salary to the new Superintendent ?

21st January. (a) About 200 suspicious persons again entered the city to join so called the Revolutionary Force.

(b) Some of the native banks in Wenchow have suspended their business.

24th January. (a) The Captain of S. S. Yi-Li reported that the ship on her way from Shanghai to Wenchow was stopped by a rifle fired from the fort at the mouth of the Ou river and about 20 armed water police boarded the ship, searched some passengers and three of them were taken off.

On arrival the ship at Wenchow armed soldiers, military police and water

police

306

police about 40 in number boarded the ship and searched passengers and their luggage and took off the ship six passengers; two of them were Northern people and four others were supposed to be Marshal Sun's men.

(b) A mass meeting was held in the city this afternoon at Ku-lou-hsia (鼓 楼 下) and the object was only how to spread propaganda.

25th January. (a) The Magistrate and the Chief of Police jointly issued a notification that the North, East, West and South Gates will be closed every night at 11 p. m. and opened at daybreak and all the other gates closed at 6 p. m. and opened at daybreak.

(b) Mr. Suzuki, the Agent of Mitusui Bussan Kaisha, told me that the military attache at Foochow informed him that 10 thousand Southerners left that city for Wenchow on the 12th instant.

Collection

8.

37

[Co]llection of [Su]rtax on [Imp]ort.

On the 24th instant I received a despatch from the Civil Governor of the Chekiang Province in which he stated that Marshal Sun Ch'uan-fang in accordance with the Washington decision had issued instructions that a surtax on Imports amounting to one-half of the existing Customs Import Duty is to be collected at once.

The Acting (temporary) Superintendent told me that he would be able to discuss the question with me after receiving some more information from Shanghai, where such collection, it seems, has been in force since the 20th instant.

The case will be reported to you officially after I have discussed this matter with the Superintendent.

Yours truly,

B. Bernadsky

CUSTOM HOUSE,

No. 387. Wenchow 29th January 1927 311

Dear Sir Francis,

[S]ituation at [Wen]chow.

26th January. (a) The S. S. Fukuju Maru - the Japanese charcoal steamer on her way to Wenchow was stopped at the moutn of the Ou river by the armed water police. The pilot explained to them that the vessel was a Japanese one and had nothing on board. The police did not board but allowed the ship to continue on her voyage.

(b) Some representatives of the Red troops arrived here and asked the gentry to clear all churches for them to live in. The gentry persuaded them not to insist on churches as there were a lot of other places quite suitable for military quarters but they said that whenever they enter a place they must have churches.

[SIR] FRANCIS AGLEN, K. B. E.,

Inspector General of Customs,

P E K I N G.

2.

312

churches.

(c) The Revolutionary Force (建国军第一路) which had been formed here out of some rather suspicious people has been disarmed. A few dollars were given to each of them and they were ordered by the Commander of the Chekiang 1st Division to leave the city at once.

27th January. (a) Armed soldiers and the water police searched the S. S. Yi-Li prior to her departure and took off three passengers supposed to be Northern men.

Armed soldiers and police boarded S. S. Tah-hsing on her arrival from Shanghai and searched passengers and luggage.

(b) The local Kuomintang party supported by the Chekiang 1st Division has changed the officials in the Likin Office and Wine Tobacco Bureau. They have also taken away the daily collection made by the Salt Gabelle since the 21st instant.

(c) Instructions from the American Consul at Shanghai have been received by the

3.

312

the American missionaries here to send their women and children to a safer place without delay. With regard to men the Consul has left the question of leaving this port to their own discretion, but he reminded them that in future it may be happen that the means of communication will be embarrassed. Therefore some of the missionaries are going to Shanghai by S. S. Tahhsing, (the last ship before the Chinese New Year) but the majority of them and the Customs families as well as the Japanese community are remaining here still.

Yours truly,

E. Bernadsky

CUSTOM HOUSE, 320

No. 388. Wenchow, 12th February, 1927

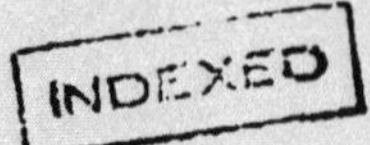

Dear Mr. Edwardes,

[Si]tuation at [Wen]chow.

28th January. The S.S. Hua-feng commandeered since 18th January has been released by the military on payment to them of above $ 2,000.

29th January. The S.S. Meinan - under the American flag - was stopped by armed police at the mouth of the river, but was allowed to proceed after it was known that no passengers were on board. The vessel was not boarded.

30th January. (a) The S.S. Tah-hsing just before her departure for Shanghai was boarded and searched by armed soldiers and police. Nine passengers including two women, being Northern people, were arrested.

(b) The S.S. Yung-chuan, commandeered by

[A]. F. ESWARDES, ESQUIRE,
Acting Inspector General of Customs,
P E K I N G.

2.

321

by the Military, left for Fukien.

(c) A member of the District Assembly here named Wang has been arrested by the Military Authorities for being in communication with the Northerners. A ransom is being demanded.

(d) A despatch from the newly appointed Superintendent of Customs Mr. Liu (刘) has been received informing me of his taking charge of the office. This unpopular man, as I was told, was a Magistrate here 10 years ago and has an intimate knowledge of the place. He is a person who knows definitely who the rich people are and to what extent they can be taxed.

(e) According to the American Consul's advice and in a view of the uncertainty of the situation here 10 missionaries left Wenchow for Shanghai by S.S. Tah-hsing: British subjects - 8 (2 men, 3 ladies and 3 children) and American - 2 ladies.

31st

322

31st January. (a) The Japanese destroyer "Tanikaze" arrived from Formosa. Mr. S. Suzuki, who is the representative of the Japanese community at Wenchow, informed me that this vessel arrived here unexpectedly as he did not ask the Japanese authorities for her.

(b) Mr. Liu, the newly appointed Superintendent of Customs made his official call on me. During our conversation he mentioned probably as a kind of politeness that his tenure of office is only of a temporary nature because the former Superintendent is afraid to come back owing to differences of opinion between them and therefore he must protect the seal. At the end of our interview he expressed his wish to see to-morrow the Assistant-in-charge and the Weiyuan of the Native Customs and asked me to instruct them to call upon him. I promised him to do so.

1st February. (a) The French Gunboat "Marne" arrived from Foochow.

(b)

323

(b) The Assistant-in-charge of the Native Customs Mr. Ng Shiu-hung called upon the new Superintendent of Customs together with the Weiyuan of Native Customs. The Superintendent explained to them that he wished to carry out here those reforms which had been done in the Kuangtung province and he intended to collect the 2½ % tax. Mr Ng replied that all these questions should be referred by him to the Commissioner of Customs under whose direction they carry on their work. The Superintendent was very polite to them all the time.

2nd February. (a) The news received through wireless of "Tanikaze": 17th Army left Foochow for Wenchow via Ping-yang (平陽).

(b) The Japanese destroyer "Tanikaze" left for Foochow.

3rd February. The French Gunboat "Marne" left for Shanghai via Ningpo. The Gunboat took Post Office mails.

4th

5.

CUSTOM HOUSE,

........................, ...19...

4th Fenruary. The watar police gunboat Hsin Pao-shun returned to port.

5th Fenruary. A proclamation was posted by the Commander T'ang Ta-chao (唐大钊) of Chekiang Vanguard Troops of the People's Revolutionary Army (国民革命军浙江先遣军总司令) by which the population of Wenchow was informed of the passing of the Revolutionary Army throug this city within the next few days. That the Army is well disciplined and that the local soldiers can join the Army if they have the same policy.

6th February. (a) The water police gunboat "Haicheng" and "Yung-Ping" returned to port.

(b) The Wenchow garrison soldiers, about 200 in number, who returned to the city on the 8th January left Wenchow for Ch'uchow under the command of Lü Ho-yin (吕和音).

7th February. The S.S. Gochow arrived from Juian This vessel had been commandeered by the water police at Juian and brought 50 of them here.

8th

6.

CUSTOM HOUSE,

........................., ...19...... 325

8th February. (a) The S.S. Yung-chuan arrived from Fukien with about 40 cadet-soldiers on board and they are it seems to start a stronger pro-bolshevic propaganda in the city. The usual lectures have been read to the labouring classes in the hall of the Normal School on how to form unions, etc. and numerous leaflets and proclamations against imperialism have been posted everywhere.

(b) The water police and part of the Chekiang 1st Division left for Hai-men by the water police gunboats "Hai-Ping", "Hai-cheng", "Hsin Pao-shun", "Yung-ping" as well as by S.S. "Ping-yang", "Yung-chuan", "Nin-teig" and "Gochow".

(c) A proclamation issued by Ts'ao Wan-shun (曹 萬 順), the Commander of the 17th Division of the People's Army was posted here. It is stated in the proclamation that (1) the object of the expedition is to strike down the military oligarchy, (2) no conscription of coolies will be made by

7.

CUSTOM HOUSE,

..........................., ...19

by force but by willingness and (3) the Army is well disciplined and people are requested to help it by showing the way, giving information of the movement of enemies, etc.

(d) I made my official return call on the Superintendent of Customs. During this interview he told me that in accordance with my request he had made an arrangement with the military authorities not to search passengers and their luggage until the Customs officers had finished their work. I thanked him for this help.

9th February. (a) A notice was posted by Mr. Yeh Wei-chiu (叶维周), the chairman of the Wenchow Executive Committee (永嘉各界团体联合会执行委员会[illegible])which was formed by the local Kuomintang party requesting all the shops in the city to lend the authorities one month's rent for military expenses.

(b) A notification of the enrollment of coolies was posted by the Communication Department of the Wenchow Revolutionary

8.

~~CUSTOM HOUSE,~~

................................., ...19 327

tionary Army Welcoming Office (永嘉歡迎革命軍辦事處交通部) with the following details:
Required number of coolies: 1,500.
Age of coolie: 20-40.
Wages: $12 a month or 30 cents per 10 li.
Weight: under 60 catties.
Daily walk: 60 li a day.
Date of enrolling: from 7th instant, etc.

10th February. (a) Representatives of the 17th Division of the People's Army accompanied by members of the local Kuomintang party visited the Methodist, China Inland and Catholic Missions inspected their chapels and schools and posted notices on which was stated the number of soldiers they intended to put therein.

(b) Members of the gentry supported by soldiers began to collect the one month's rent from the shops in accordance with the notice issued by the Executive Committee on the 9th instant.

(c) The S.S. Kien-kong and Fook-sing arrived from Foochow. The first vessel had on board Mr. Yü Hsiang-wen (余憲文), the

9.

328

the Divisional General of the Chekiang Provincial 1st Division and the second one about 300 Fukien soldiers, belonging to the 17th Division of the People's Army.

ata concerning

If the Chinese Government does such thing to the Inspector General and the Foreign Ministers cannot help him it seems that the very foundations of our Service are shaking. Extremely sorry.

Yours truly,

E. Bernadsky.

CUSTOM HOUSE,

No. 389. Wenchow, 16th February 1927. 331

ation at
how

Dear Mr. Edwardes,

13th Fenruary. (a) S.S. Fook-sing left for Foochow. This vessel is said to have been released by the military authorities.

(b) S.S. Fuchuan arrived from Formosa with 300 tons of coal for the waster police. This vessel had been commandeered by the water police on the 21st January at White Rock on her way from Amoy to Wenchow

(c) The first batch of soldiers of the 17th Division of the People's Army arrived here via Ping-yang and Juian in number about 300 and part of them were put by the local Kuomintang party into the Methodist, China Inland and Catholic Missions schools.

(d) The Commander of the 17th

Division

F. EDWARDES, ESQUIRE,

Acting Inspector General of Customs,

P E K I N G .

2.

332

Division of the People's Army, General Ts'ao Wan-shun (曹萬順) called upon me at 4 p.m. and during our conversation he asked me to assure all foreign residents at Wenchow that they will be fully protected by him and that churches, schools and private residences which are under the control of foreigners will not be occupied by soldiers, if a list of these places shall be sent to him. This message was communicated by me to all the foreign residents at Wenchow, but the Methodist Mission and the China Inland Mission as far as I know are not going to send such a list to the Commander, because the local Christian population is welcoming the arrival of the soldiers and therefore they are not going to work against their will.

14th February. The soldiers who occupied the schools under foreign control left them by order of the Commander of the 17th Division of the People's Army.

15th February. (a) I returned my official call on

3.

333

on General Ts'ao Wan-shun. During our conversation he stated that they are fighting for nationalist ideals and not against foreigners.

(b) The S.S. Ping-yang arrived from Hai-men. There were about 30 water police on board.

16th February. (a) The S.S. Fu-chuan left for Hai-men with soldiers on board.

(b) According to the British Consul's advice all the English missionaries (16 in number) of the China Inland and Methodist Missions except the two doctors of the last Mission are leaving Wenchow for Shanghai by S. S. Tah-hsing: 5 men, 8 ladies and 3 children.

Yours truly,

E. Bernadsky

INSPECTORATE GENERAL OF CUSTOMS, 219

S/O

INDEXED

PEKING, 17th February 1927

Dear Mr. Bernadsky,

I have duly received your S/O letter No.385 of the 19th January:

"Tah-hsing" boarded and searched by police and soldiers: Commissioner complains to the Superintendent.

Have your representations been successful ?

Yours truly,

[signature]

...ndsky, Esquire,

...WENCHOW.

INSPECTORATE GENERAL OF CUSTOMS,

S/O PEKING, 17th February 1927

309

INDEXED

Dear Mr. Bernadsky,

I have duly received your S/O letter No. 386 of 26th January:

Commissioner enquires whether, if the Southerners occupy Wenchow, he may issue allowance to Superintendent appointed by them.

Yes, You may issue allowance to de facto Superintendent, provided he is duly appointed and accredited by the Southern authorities, and also provided he keeps his office open so that Customs routine work is not delayed.

Collection of surtax.

Do not oppose or offer any objection to the levy of these surtaxes by the Superintendent. On the other hand, do not associate yourself with them, but maintain a strictly neutral attitude. The Superintendent has full right to

rnadsky, Esquire,

WENCHOW.

210

to appoint a deputy to assess and collect these surtaxes, and, if he so wishes, to make use for this purpose of the Customs duty memos once such memos have been delivered by us to the merchants concerned. At Shanghai the Bank collects the surtaxes for the Superintendent.

Yours truly,

Inspectorate General of Customs, 114

S/O

Peking, 17th February 1927

Dear Mr. Bernadsky,

I have duly received your S/O letter No. 387 of 29th January:

Local situation.

Should any member of your staff be ordered by his national authorities to leave the Port, you are not to place any obstacles in his way.

Yours truly,

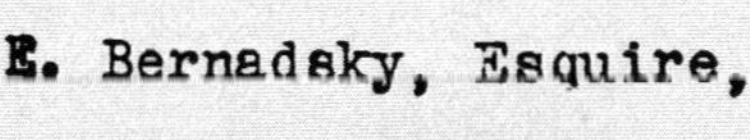

E. Bernadsky, Esquire,

WENCHOW.

INSPECTORATE GENERAL OF CUSTOMS. 292

S/O

PEKING, 18th February 1927

Dear Mr. Bernadsky,

I have duly received your S/O letter No.384 of the 13th January:

Matches containing phosphorus, seized but permitted to be re-exported: applicant fails to ship them and claims exemption from bond owing to damage done to cargo by climate.

No fresh instructions have been received from Ch'u since receipt of Ch'u despatch No. 1134 of 1925, instructing that the matches were to be re-exported to original place of shipment, transmitted to Wenchow in I.G. No. 1348/104761.

Yours truly,

[signature]

...adsky, Esquire,

WENCHOW.

CUSTOM HOUSE, 359

No. 390. Wenchow, 26th February 1927.

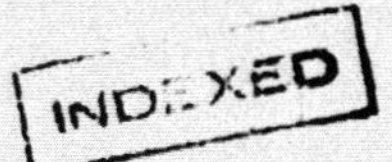

Dear Mr. Edwardes

...ution at ...chow.

16th February. (a) Mr. Chang Kuei-jung (張桂榮), the Secretary of the Superintendent of Customs (the former Acting temporary Superintendent of Customs) called upon me to say good-bye as he was going on leave to Shanghai by S.S. Tah-hsing. His reason for leaving was - as he said - the difficulty of working with the present military authorities. He mentioned also that it was not likely that the Native Customs collection outside the 50 li zone for the fund of Inspector General's National Loans Sinking Fund Account would be remitted to me by the Superintendent of Customs as all the military authorities here were carefully looking after them.

(b) The S.S. Yung-chuan left for Hai-men with about 400 Fukien soldiers on board.

H. F. EDWARDES, ESQUIRE,

...ting Inspector General of Customs,

PEKING.

340

board.

17th February. (a) The water police gunboat "Hsin Pao-shun" and S.S. "Kien-kong" and "Ping-yang" left for Hai-men with soldiers on board. The Superintendent of Customs Mr. Liu left for Hai-men by S. S. "Ping-yang". During the last few days there has been in the city a strong anti-Superintendent propaganda and even some caricature pictures of him were posted, therefore it is possible that he will not be able to keep his post for a long time.

(b) The S.S. "Wan-hsiang" arrived from Foochow under Customs clearance (rare case under the present circumstances) with 1,600 soldiers of the 17th People's Army, but according to the Captain's opinion there were not less than 2,500 soldiers on board.

18th February. The S.S. "Wan-hsiang" cleared by Customs and left for Ningpo with 1,600 soldiers of 17th Army on board. Ths ship at first will try to go near enough to Hai-men to be able to obtain there information

mation

3.

34

mation re the situation at Ningpo. The military authorities chartered the ship and paid $1,000 for this trip to Ningpo.

21st February. The Chinese training ship Tsi-mei No. 2 arrived from Amoy, having on board Mr. Ts'ai Yuan P'ei, newly appointed by the Southern Government as the Civil Governor for the Chekiang province according to the Captain's statement, and left for Ningpo on the same day.

22nd February. (a) The S.S. "Yu-hsing" commandeered by the military authorities arrived from Foochow with about 2,000 soldiers on board, belonging to the 17th Army.

(b) A crowd of coolies after passing a course of bolshevick lectures paraded the streets of the city dragging empty kerosene oil tins to make their procession more impressive and demanded that the price of rice should be lowered to 25 catties per dollar. All the shops were closed or semi-closed for fear of this crowd. Notices have

have been officially put up by the Yung-chia Magistrate, by which the labouring classes were informed that as the result of consultation with several unions the price of rice would be reduced to 20-21 catties to the dollar instead of 13-14 catties as at present. The rice-shops were accordingly pressed to sell the rice for this fixed price. The owners of the rice-shops sold out the rice in stock, but declared that they could not be expected to obtain and sell a fresh supply of rice at such a fixed price. The dissatisfied coolies therefore smashed furniture in some rice-shops.

(c) The Political Department of the 17th Army issued instructions to various districts to the effect that the District Assembly (縣議會), and the Committees for the control of affairs of the city (Ts'an-shih-hui 參事會) and villages (Tsu-chih Wei-yüan 自治委員) are to be abolished

and

342

and their funds, archives, furniture, etc. are to be handed over to the Kuomintang party of the district concerned.

23rd February. (a) The S.S. "Yu-hsing" left port for Ningpo with the same soldiers that she brought here.

(b) The photo-pictures showing the groups of dead bodies of children at Spanish Mission, Foochow, have been spread in the city by anti-foreign agitators, as a prove that foreign missions kill the Chinese children.

24th February. (a) The S.S. "Chusan" commandeered by the military authorities arrived here from the interior.

(b) Notices have been posted up by the Political Department of the 17th Army to the effect that the price of rice has been re-adjusted to 18 catties for a dollar instead of 20-21 catties, with a limit of sale to the value of $ 0.50 only to each person at a time. Persons buying

for

344

for military use upwards of $ 0.50 must produce a Certificate. The Notices mention the issue of the following instructions:

1. The authorities have instructed the neighbouring districts to adopt the fixed price of not less than 18 catties to the dollar.
2. Rice smuggled to out-ports if seized by officials is to be confiscated; if seized by labourers to be handed to the General Labourers Union, if seized by peasants to be handed to the Peasant Union, such rice to be confiscated and the proceeds used to cover expenditure of the respective union.
3. If any official takes part in smuggling he will be punished severely or discharged according to the nature of the case.
4. If rice-merchants or people store up paddy privately they will be fined.
5. Shops should open and do their business

at

7.

345

at once, otherwise they will be dealt with as disturbing local peace and order.

6. If any one loots he will be put to death.

7. Any request of people may be referred to Magistrate through representatives; if it cannot be settled by the Magistrate then appeal may be made to the Political Department of the 17th People's Army.

25th February. (a) The S.S. "Chusan" left port for Ningpo with 1,400 soldiers of the 17th Army on board.

(b) In the local newspaper Ou Hai Ku Poa (甌海公報) for 25th of February stated:

Circular letters have been issued to every guild by the Wenchow Community Society for the Preparation of Anti-British Propaganda (温州市民反英運動大會籌備會) stating that an Anti-British Society has been formed by an alliance between the Wenchow People Unions and Kuomintang party of the Yungchia District;

8.

346

District; that a meeting was held and that it was attended by various Unions with a result that on the 28th instant at 1 p.m. a great meeting for Anti-British propaganda will be held at the parade ground of the 10th Middle School and speeches will also be given to the public on the 27th at 1 p.m. at Ku-lou-hsia Hsin Ta-chieh (鼓楼下新大街); and that spectators and orators are requested to come at that time mentioned.

Unpaid pilotage

On the 21st instant the Captain of the training ship Tsi-mei No. 2 requested verbally, through the boarding Officer for a pilot to take the vessel out and the No. 3 pilot was instructed to go on board accordingly. The Harbour Master made out the usual Pilotage receipt and sent it through the Chinese Tidewaiter on board to collect the money. This vessel was anchored outside Harbour Limits and communication was difficult. When the Tidewaiter

9.

349

waiter returned, passing the pilot en-route, he trought a letter to the Harbour Master from the Captain, in which the Captain requested a discount from the full pilotage fee as the vessel was on government service This vessel had left port, with a pilot on board, before any answer could be sent to the Captain's letter. On the pilot's return to port he handed to the Harbour Master a letter enclosing $ 10.00 to cover pilotage, which means that the Captain of this vessel holds the receipt for $ 48.00 and has paid only $ 10.00. The Superintendent of Customs was informed of the case and was requested to obtain if possible from the Captain of the ship $38.00 - pilotage fee still owing.

Yours truly,

E. Bernadsky

CUSTOM HOUSE,

No. 391. Wenchow 5th March 1927

INDEXED

Dear Mr. Edwardes,

ue Collect
ate for

As the Bank of China has been closed since 20th of January 1927 the market quotations for Shanghai Taels during the month of February were obtained by me from the Money Market Guild (in accordance with I. G. despatch No. 734/65,362 of 9th June 1917) through the Bank of China's man who has still been working in the Customs Bank, and the average monthly rate obtained by this way was declared by me as the Revenue Collection Rate for the month of March. I did not consult the Superintendent of Customs or the Chamber of Commerce, because under the present political situation at Wenchow there are practically no responsible persons in charge of these establishments and if they were to try

F. EDWARDES, ESQUIRE,

ficiating Inspector General of Customs

P E K I N G.

2.

350

try to lower the rate of exchange to please the Wenchow merchants then my position would be very difficult at the time when the collection would have to be transferred to the Bank of China after its re-opening.

of Southern
ment re-
ed to be
ed.

On the 28th of February I received a letter from the local branch of the Kuomintang party requesting me to lower the five-colour flag at the Custom House and to hoist the Southern Government (國民政府) flag, the description of which was given in a separate enclosure to the letter.

A copy of the Kuomintang's letter was forwarded by me to the Superintendent and on the 2nd of March I received a reply from him. in which he stated that the Chekiang Province at present was under the Southern Government's rule and that therefore the flag of that Government was to be hoisted at the Custom House even as it had been hoisted at all other government establishments at Wenchow.

To avoid friction with the local

authorities

351

authorities and to deprive the Kuomintang party of any chance to create anti-Customs agitation I ordered the Tidesurveyor to lower the five-colour flag and to make and hoist the Southern flag.

acy of S.S. chow.

On the 1st of March S.S. Go-chow arrived here in distress. This Chinese ship left Juian with cargo and passengers on board for Shanghai on the 23rd of February. On the 25th of February she was obliged to stop at Nimrod Sound (牛鼻·島) to make some repairs to her leaky boiler. Soon after she anchored some scores of armed pirates boarded the ship and the result was that ship and passengers were robbed of $2,000 in cash and over $2,000 in clothing, although the cargo was not touched. After the repairs has been completed the ship was ordered by the pirates to proceed to Chu Su Island (西旗) outside Hai-men where they landed with their booty in small boats. The ship arrived at Wenchow for provisions and clothing for passengers. The Superintendent

was

4.

352

was officially informed of the case.

...tion at ...ow.

26th February. The S. S. Yung-chuan, Yung Ning, Yung-An and Ping-Yang arrived from Ningpo to take soldiers.

27th February. (a) The above all left for Ningpo with about 1,500 soldiers of the 17th Army on board.

(b) The Political Department of the 17th Army appointed Tai Yin-liang (戴蔭良) as the Chief of Police of the Wenchow district.

28th February. (a) The anti-British propaganda did not take place probably owing to the bad weather.

(b) The Political Department after having appointed Tai Yin-liang as the Chief of Police Office, which is now called Public Peace Bureau (公安局), has received a telegram from the Provincial Government appointing Chin Tsu-hsing (金祖星) as the Chief of the Public Peace Bureau.

1st March. (a) The former Chief of the Police Office

Office Ma Chen-chung (马振中) left Wenchow for Shanghai by S.S. Yi-li.

(b) An American - the last member of the China Inland Mission at Wenchow - left by the same ship for Shanghai in accordance with the instructions received by him from the Head of the Mission at Shanghai.

(c) The S.S. Foo-Shing en-route to Ningpo arrived from Foochow with about 800 soldiers and General Tu Ch'i-yün (杜起云) the Commander of the 2nd Division of the 17th Army on board and left for Ningpo on the next day.

4th March. At the meeting of various unions for anti-British propaganda held at the parade ground of the 10th Middle School the following resolutions passed:

(1) that wharf-coolies should not discharge any English goods arriving at jetty;

(2) that no shop-owners should privately import English goods and that for each

6.

354

each offence a fine be levied equal to 10 times the value of the goods imported in addition to confiscation of the goods;

(3) that no newspaper should insert advertisements of English goods and that they should announce in the paper "no English goods shall be advertised";

(4) that no raw or semi-raw materials shall be sold to English merchants, otherwise the goods shall be confiscated in addition to a fine of 10 times the value of the goods.

(5) No work to be done in conjunction with the English.

(6) All grades of Kuomintang party, all students, and all unions should start the ceremony of swearing not to buy English goods.

After the meeting was closed the anti-British procession consisted of about 1,500 students and coolies paraded the

streets

265

streets of the city and at 4.15 p. m. this procession passed the Custom House. Some of the rowdy demonstrators broke down the front gate of the compound and broke two panes of glass of the General Office windows. But as soon as the leaders of the procession noticed these actions they pushed out the energetic demonstrators from the Customs Compound and ordered the procession to pass the Customs without stopping. Soon after this the demonstrators met Mr. Ng Shiu hung, the Assistant in charge of the Native Customs in his sedan chair and roughly handled him, as could be seen from his memorandum, a copy of which is enclosed herewith. The Customs doctor stated that in a few days time Mr. Ng will be all right, as he is suffering more from shock than bodily injury. All the damage done by the mob could be easily be covered from Petty Cash Account. The Superintendent of Customs was

8.

36

was informed of the case and requested to afford a full protection to the Customs employees as well as to the Customs property.

Yours truly,

E. Bernadini

Wenchow S/O No. 391.

ENCLOSURE.

357

MEMORANDUM FROM CHINESE ASSISTANT IN CHARGE OF NATIVE CUSTOMS TO WENCHOW COMMISSIONER.

5th March 1927.

I have the honour to report the disgaceful incident occurred on my person yesterday afternoon. At 4.30 p.m. I went home in my sedan chair and on approaching the corner to the main street I noticed the mob coming along with banners and sticks. I at once ordered the chair coolies to put down the chair and let them pass first. The mob broke the chair into pieces and dragged me out. I managed to escape and go back to the Native Customs but only a few yards from the Custom House the mob caught me. They dragged me along the street shouting "British running dogs" and beat me on the head and arms with the flag handles. Several blows were struck on my back but luckily I had thick clothes on and did not feel much. They pushed me down to the ground three times and on arrival at the East Gate they lifted me up. My hat was snatched and shoes taken away. On reaching Kang Lok Fang (康樂坊) some coolies

with

2.

358

with big sticks came along and at the time I thought I would be severely beaten. Some students however stopped them from doing so. I took the opportunity to speak before them that I was serving the Chinese and not the foreign government and that the Customs was purely a Chinese organisation. I said that they should not treat a Chinese goevernment servant like this. Inasmuch, I continued, Kwangtung is a place where the Nationalist government first sets its saddle the Customs employees are however treated very well by the public for they understand that they help the Chinese government to get revenue. On hearing that I was a Cantonese the mob paused a little and afterwards decided to release me. I claimed a ricksha because I could not walk any more. They dragged a passer-by to pull a ricksha along and put me on it, all the ricksha coolies having run away. At first they wanted to send me to the Magistrate's yamen but ultimately they sent me home.

The above gives full details of the incident and in addition two of the chair coolies were

severely

3.

351

severely beaten. Apart from the great loss of face which I believe no steps can be taken to recover there is every danger that a similar incident may recur. I would earnestly request you to take every measure possible to ensure my safety in the future, otherwise to recommend a transfer for me to a safer port. I suffered this twice now during my career in the Service although in Kongmoon I managed to escape safely with no great loss of face as at present. It would be impossible for me to stay here long as after this incident no one will respect me.

I now feel fatigued throughout the body and must rest for a few days before I can resume my duties. I beg that in the meantime you will send someone to execute the Native Customs business.

(Sgd.) Ng Shiu hung,

3rd Assistant, B.

CUSTOM HOUSE, 361

). 392. Wenchow, 10th March 1927.

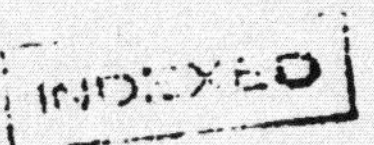

Dear Mr. Edwardes,

[illegible]on at [illegible].

4th March. (a) At the meeting of various unions for anti-British propaganda Mr. Chang Huan-shen (張炳坤), the member of the Provincial Assembly was mentioned as a person who had helped the Methodist Mission to buy land cheaply for their Hospital (Blyth) and School at Wenchow. It was decided to go to the house of this man and to smash there but not to loot everything possible. This resolution was carried out on the same evening.

(b) A white cloth with the inscription 收回海關 Shou Hui Hai Kuan is hung up across the street outside the Custom House. I asked the Superintendent of

[illegible]. EDWARDES, ESQUIRE,

O[illegible]ficiating Inspector General of Customs,

P E K I N G.

2.

of Customs to get it removed. He promised to do what he could.

(c) A notice is hung up at the China Merchants Steam Navigation Company's wharf warning coolies not to handle British goods.

(d) The Ningpo-Wenchow launches have at last been released by the military authorities and have now re-established their regular schedule.

5th March. (a) Some persons supposed to be in connection with the exportation of rice out of Wenchow were arrested by the members of the unions. The Military Authorities of the 17th Army were requested by the relatives of the arrested people to release them and they accordingly took them to the military barracks. The mob followed and demanded the execution of the prisoners. The Officer in charge of the Military explained to the mob that the case would have to be investigated and that even

then

then the offenders could not be so excessively punished. But the mob refused to accept this statement and began to throw stones at the quarters. The Officer then ordered the soldiers to fire on the mob and the result was: 1 killed and 2 wounded. The mob was dispersed for the time being but soon after it collected again and started to smash up some rice shops.

As the movement of the 17th Army had been accomplished General Ts'ao Wan-shun (曹万顺) left for Hangchow a few days ago and his leaving Wenchow was probably the main reason for all these anti-British propaganda and different demonstrations. He was the man who checked the movements of the various unions and the Kuomintang party.

6th March. (a) Leaflets were issued by the Self-supporting Chinese Christian Society of Wenchow to the effect that the anti-Christian party should know that as the Society is as much against Imperialism as the anti-Christian

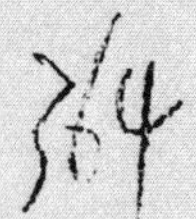

Christian party, so Self-supporting Chinese Christian Society accordingly must not be assaulted by the anti-Christian party.

(b) Notices have been posted for enlisting soldiers for the 2nd Division of the 1st Army, offering $13-15 monthly pay for soldiers and $17-23 for officers.

(c) Some hooligans broke the electric lamp and shade at the entrance gate to the Commissioner's Compound at about 11 p. m.

7th March. (a) The Officials newly appointed by the Military Authorities of Hangchow - the Superintendent of Customs, the Magistrate and the Chief of the Police Office - arrived here by the Ningpo steamer "Ping-yang".

(b) In connection with destruction of the rice shops some of the agitators have been arrested by the military authorities, and evidently there has been some upheaval in the Kuomintang party, because about 100 active members of this party

left

5.

245

left Wenchow for Ningpo by S.S Yung-chuan on the 8th instant.

8th March. The newly appointed Superintendent of Customs called upon me. During our conversation he expressed his opinion that all the demonstrations against the Customs which had taken place during the last few days was the product of a misunderstanding on the part of the local Kuomintang party and some unions and would be stopped.

9th March. (a) I returned my official call on the Superintendent of Customs. Mr. Hsü told me that he had already explained to the Kuomintang party that the Customs was a Chinese and not a Foreign Government establishment and that the employees of the Customs Chinese and Foreigners as well as the Customs property are to be properly protected. According to this opinion it is quite advisable for all foreign missionaries to return to Wenchow now.

(b) The S.S. "Foo-ching" arrived

from

6.

311

from Ningpo with 400 of Marshal Sun's disarmed soldiers, who were captured by the Southerners somewhere near Ningpo.

(c) The white cloth poster 收回海關 Shou Hui Hai Kuan that was hanging up opposite the Custom House as well as some other posters of a Bolshevick character have been taken down by the Kuomintang party.

10th March. In the local paper Ou Hai Ku Poa (甌海公報) there has appeared an apology on the part of the organisation which had lead the anti-British demonstration on the 4th instant to Mr. Ng Shiu hung, the Assistant in charge of the Native Customs for the disgrace brought on him by some demonstrators. A copy of this apology and its English translation are enclosed herewith.

Yours truly,

E. Bernadsky.

WENCHOW S/O NO. 392.

ENCLOSURE.

367

录瓯海公报 三月十日

温州市民反英大会启事

敬启者日前同人等开反英大会游行示威路过东门外地方适瓯海常关帮办吴君汰泉乘轿而来一时因言语误会致将其轿撕破加以侮辱查海关本系中国国家机关之一所有办事员役咸系中国国家之官吏并非外人所雇用且吴君亦属爱国热忱一份子此次实属误会恐各界未明真相特此登报声明

Wenchow S/O No. 392.

ENCLOSURE. No. 2

A TRANSLATION OF AN INSERTION IN THE LOCAL NEWSPAPER OU HAI KU POA (瓯海公報) of the 10th March 1927.

Notice is hereby given by the Anti-British Demonstration of Wenchow, that we the other day made an Anti-British procession and when we passed outside the East Gate we happened to meet with Mr. Ng Shiu hung, the Assistant in charge of the Wenchow Native Customs coming towards us in his chair. Owing to some misunderstanding on the part of the demonstrators his chair chair was smashed and he was dishonoured. The Customs is a department of the Chinese Government and all the employees therein are officials of the Chinese Government and not of any foreign Government. Furthermore Mr. Ng is an enthusiatic patriot. This accident is entirely due to misunderstanding. Fearing that the public do not know the exact facts we have thought it necessary to have this notice published in the Newspaper.

CUSTOM HOUSE,

). 393. Wenchow, 21st March 1927. 370

INDEXED

Dear Mr. Edwardes,

; from Commis- for fin- help.

In view of the suspension of the Bank of China at Wenchow the Hangchow Postal Commissioner asked me last February whether I would be willing to assist the Post Office by supplying funds to the Wenchow Postmaster at par in return for Shanghai cheques drawn on the Hongkong and Shanghai Banking Corporation. I replied that under the conditions at present prevailing at Wenchow we were not certain of being able to collect sufficient to cover our own current expenditures and that therefore I could not grant the help he asks for. But that if in the future circumstances would allow me to help the local office, I should always be glad to

supply

F. EDWARDES, ESQUIRE,

:ficiating Inspector General of Customs,

P E K I N G.

2.

371

supply funds to the Wenchow Postmaster in return for Shanghai Tael cheques on the Hongkong and Shanghai Banking Corporation, Shanghai as per Wenchow Customs monthly rate of exchange. On the 15th of March I received a reply in which the Postal Commissioner expressed his thanks for the promised assistance. At present we have in the Customs safe $20,000.00 and if the Postal Commissioner could supply me with the cheque for Shanghai Taels 8 - 9 thousand I should be glad to furnish him with the required amount in cash, as it is not very safe to make such transfers to Shanghai through the local native banks and at the same time there are no foreign firms here through which these remittances can be made. There is a rumour that the Bank of China will soon be opened, otherwise at the end of the month I am going to send part of this money to Shanghai by ship.

During 1926 and the March quarter of 1927 the two clerks in the General Office were

unable

3.

372

unable to keep up with their work without assistance from the second clerk in the Secretary's Office. I thought that such a state of affairs would not last, but that the work would decrease after the revision of the Returns had been completed. But experience has shown that it is really necessary to send in an application for the appointment of an extra clerk. It is clear enough now that the General Office work cannot be carried on by only two clerks even with the occasional assistance from the Secretary's Office. Though the present General Office and Secretary's Office staffs begin their work at about 9 a. m. and leave at 6-7 p. m., yet there are signs that the current work cannot be finished by them in time. If I send the second clerk from the Secretary's Office to speed up the Returns work which requires the longest time, then the Secretary cannot keep his secretariat and accounts work up to date. The preparation of the Returns requires considerably longer time than before

and

4.

312

and the appointment of a clerk for that work is much to be desired. A junior clerk would adequately meet the case.

Many thanks for my promotion.

...tion at ...

11th March. (a) The Superintendent of Customs officially informed me by a letter that he had requested the Kuomintang party and the police to take precautionary measures for the protection of the Customs employees both Chinese and foreign - as being Government officials - in addition to the actual Customs buildings.

(b) The S.S. Pingyang, the Ningpo-Wenchow steamer was again commandeered by the Military and sent to Foochow with 360 new recruits of the Southern Army on board.

(c) The S.S. Tah-hsing commandeered by the local authorities, was finally released after payment of $100 to the police, $100 to the Magistrate and $300 to the Military.

12th March. A joint notification concerning

rice

374

rice was issued by the Headquarter of the 17th Army, the Magistrate, and the Police Office:

1. that the lowest price fixed for the time being is 15½ catties for a dollar, based on the price in the rice producing districts, and that the price of paddy is pro rata;
2. that for vessel's use not over 10 piculs are allowed for a big sea-going sailing vessel, 8 piculs for a middle size vessel, 6 piculs for the small one, and 2 piculs for Ch'uchow inland boat;
3. that for the rich must sell all rice not required for immediate use;
4. that smuggling to out ports is absolutely prohibited;
5. that if the public discover any breach of the above rules by rice shops, rich people, or boatmen, they may inform the military, the police, or the Magistrate; that if investigation proves the accusation

375

sation a fine of 20-30 times the value of the case will be levied; and for smuggling or more serious cases a heavier fine will be inflicted. But the community are absolutely prohibited from searching or smashing property: such actions will also be severely dealt with as disturbances to the local peace and order. The general labourers union and police have been asked to attend to this and at the same time the Society for Maintenance of People's Food (民食維持會) are gathering large stocks from Pingyang and Juian to provide against a shortage.

15th March. (a) The departure of S.S. Yi-li was prevented by the local Authorities for 2 days, but after the payment of the usual squeeze the ship was allowed to proceed to Shanghai.

(b) The S.S. Yung-chuan arrived from Ningpo with 140 soldiers of the Southern Army on board and left for

Ningpo

316

Ningpo on the next day with ordinary cargo.

(c) The S.S. Pingyang returned from Foochow and left for Ningpo on the next day with newly recruited soldiers for the 1st Division of the 17th Army.

17th March. The S.S. Goohow having cargo on board wished to clear for Amoy on this date but was suddenly commandeered by the Military and was ordered to leave port at once for Foochow to take there some members of the Political Department of the 17th Army. As she was not cleared by the Customs the Clearance Record with explanatory note was handed over to the Agent of the Company to be sent to the port of destination.

19th March. (a) The S.S. Yung-chuan arrived from Haimen. The vessel brought 100 southern soldiers and landed them at the Lungwan Fort (Salomis Point).

(b) During the last 10 days several men either half mad or pretending to be have appeared in the streets and they

377

they have often followed me on my way to or from the Customs and used insulting words. Similar incidents have sometimes occurred to Mr. W. Neville, 2nd Class Tidewaiter on his way to or from the Native Customs. The Superintendent of Customs was requested to communicate with the police on this subject.

20th March. (a) The S.S. Fook-hsing arrived from Foochow with 100 southern soldiers on board. These soldiers remained on board waiting for orders.

(b) A notice was issued by the Kuomintang party to the effect that in regard to the relations between the Kuomintang and the Magistrate the following resolutions have been passed at the 25th meeting of the Chekiang Provincial Executive Committee:

1. that the Magistrate shall follow the opinion of the Kuomintang party about local administration;
2. that the Kuomintang party acts as a supervisor

378

supervisor of the Magistrate;

3. that the Kuomintang party may present to the Magistrate for his consideration proposal for the reforming of local administration;

4. that the Kuomintang party through the Provincial Kuomintang may demand an investigation by the Provincial Government if the Magistrate has neglected his duty, is guilty of irregular practices, or has disregarded the laws; and

5. that the Kuomintang shall not interfere with the administration of justice.

The above resolutions have already been circulated by the Provincial Kuomintang party to every district Kuomintang party.

Now since the official opening of the Wenchow District Kuomintang there have been people who did not clearly understand the organisation of the party and its functions and therefore nearly every day many applications and petitions for all kinds

319

kinds of cases have reached this party. These people must understand that this party is the representative of public opinion and also an organisation for supervising the existing local authorities and that the local authorities are still responsible for all local affairs, and that the functions of the Kuomintang do not extend beyond supervision. If the authorities do not administer the laws correctly or make an excessive use of their power, the case may be reported to the Kuomintang party by any responsible union or by above three members of the party and then the case will be dealt with there. Everything relating to the labourers of the Labourers Union, and the peasants of the Agricultural Union shall be dealt with by the Wenchow General Labour Union and the Wenchow General Agricultural Union or by the respective Union concerned. There are two such organisations in the Kuomintang party, but their

object

11

380

object is to assist in examining conditions and organising unions and nothing more. In the question of the people's food the Magistrate is entirely responsible and to assist him there is already an organisation, the Society for the Maintenance of the People's Food. The Kuomintang party can only give voice to public opinion and supervise administration, beyond that they will not go. Taking the advantage of the public's ignorance of the limits of the party's functions agitators may succeed in damaging the position of the party in community. As a matter of fact this party has been benefiting the public for several years so that the traitors' agitation will surely be in vain. We consider that the public should be aware of these facts.

Yours truly,

E. Bernadsky

CUSTOM HOUSE,

Wenchow 23rd March 1927 3/2

Dear de Luca,

The Wenchow Annual Returns will be sent to you at the end of this month. I am really very sorry for such a delay. The pressure of work and the shortness of the staff are the chief reasons for this. I have lately applied to the Inspector General for the appointment of an extra clerk to this office. I am afraid that our Returns for the March Quarter will be prepared also with some delay, if the new appointee arrives here late.

Yours truly,

E. Bernadsky

Luca, Esquire,

Statistical Secretary,

Inspectorate General of Customs,

SHANGHAI.

INSPECTORATE GENERAL OF CUSTOMS.

S/O Confidential PEKING, 26th March 1927

INDEXED

Dear Mr. Bernadsky,

Washington Surtaxes: non-participation of Customs in collection of: method by which collectors may distinguish between luxuries and non-luxuries from Duty Memos.

The Washington Surtax of half of the usual Import Duty is now being assessed and collected in most of the Treaty Ports by the Superintendent's deputies, functioning in the Customs Bank, and using for the calculation of the Surtax the figures given on the Customs duty memos. As duty memos are essentially Superintendent's documents, this method of Surtax collection has the great (and for us necessary) merit of keeping the Customs in a position of detachment; but for the deputies assessing the Surtax it has the defect of not supplying the information necessary for them to distinguish whether any one duty memo covers a luxury or non-luxury. At present the demand for such information is not so instant as to be embarrassing, but, as the collecting of the Surtax becomes more and more of an accepted procedure

418

procedure, it is inevitable that strong pressure will be brought to bear upon us to supply the information which will enable the Surtax collectors to tell quickly and infallibly whether a duty memo covers a luxury or not. To be prepared for this, and at the same time to maintain our present attitude of non-participation, I have to request you to issue instructions to the member or members of your Staff who are responsible for the assessing of duty on Import Applications to insert on each application (or, if an application covers more than one article, against each article specified) the Tariff number and, if necessary, sub-letter as it appears in the Revised Import Tariff. This number should stand out clearly and prominently, and to this end it would perhaps be as well to have a stamp made, thus | T. No. | . The insertion of this Tariff number on each application should facilitate very considerably the task of preparing correct trade returns, and it is from this point of view that this new practice is to be considered should any enquiry be made. On the other hand, the lushih, who it should not be forgotten is the Superintendent's nominee, when making out

/the

41

the respective duty memos can insert this Tariff number alongside the duty involved, thereby providing an additional safety check between the duty memo and this application. It will thus become a comparatively simple matter for the Superintendent's deputy at the Bank, who has already been provided by the authorities with a list of luxuries enumerated under their Tariff numbers, not only to tell what the article is but also to assess the correct luxury or non-luxury tax. In the few cases where the Tariff number does not convey any indication as to the exact nature of the goods, as for instance Nos. 417 and 582, it will be an easy matter for the Surtax collector to throw on the merchant the onus of proving that his goods are not liable to the luxury tax. So long as we confine ourselves to specifying Tariff numbers, leaving to the Surtax collectors all decisions as to whether the articles concerned are luxuries or not, no serious objection can be raised to our action. It is highly advisable that this procedure be introduced at once, so that it may become well established before the question of the luxury tax becomes acute. When the Superintendent does approach you for

assistance

122

assistance in this matter you should take the opportunity of explaining this procedure personally to him pointing out at the same time that its existence obviates the necessity of creating any special boarding and examining staff for the levy of these Surtaxes. It would also tend to ease matters considerably if the Superintendent, when announcing to the public that from such and such a date he intends collecting the luxury Surtax, informs merchants that when paying the Surtax they will be required to declare the nature of their goods.

When issuing orders, which should be done in the usual way by the Commissioner's Order Book, for the introduction of this procedure of inserting Tariff numbers on Import Applications and Duty Memos, you are to take particular care to avoid all reference to the Washington Surtaxes and to make clear that this new practice will greatly facilitate accurate compilation of Customs trade returns.

Yours truly,

INSPECTORATE GENERAL OF CUSTOMS, 54

S/O

PEKING, 28th March 1927

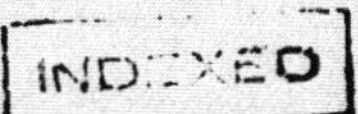
INDEXED

Dear Mr. Bernadsky,

I have duly received your S/O letter No. 390 of 26th February:

Extra 50 li N.C. duties.

You can protest to the Superintendent if these extra 50 li N.C. duties are not remitted to the National Loans Sinking Fund A/c, but I do not expect that such protests will be of any avail.

Conditions at Wenchow.

Many thanks for your long and detailed S/O giving so much interesting information about conditions and events at your Port. I am glad, however, to see that the Service is not being attacked or badly inconvenienced at Wenchow.

Yours truly,

Bernadsky, Esquire,

WENCHOW.

386

No. 394   Wenchow   31st March 27

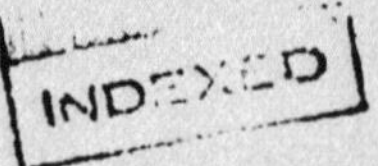

Dear Mr Edwardes,

uation Wenchow.

20th March. In the local newspaper "Ou Hai Ku Poa" (瓯海公报) of the 22nd of March 1927 there appeared the following note. About 50 members of the Wenchow Government Establishments:- The Superintendent's Office, the Yung chia Court of Justice, and the Yang Kuong Chü - held a meeting in the house of one of the members to organise a Union of Members of Various Government Establishments at Wenchow. At the meeting four members were elected to draft the Regulations of the Union, and it was decided that

when

H. F. EDWARDES, ESQUIRE

Officiating Inspector General of Customs

P E K I N G.

when the Regulations had been drawn up and passed, a formal meeting of the Union would be held.

22nd March. The S.S Tah-hsing left for Shanghai via Ningpo. There were on board for the last port some members of the Political Department of the Kuomintang and also the soldiers, who had escorted prisoners to Foochow and had then been brought here by S. S. Fook-hsing.

23rd March. Some students were watching the unloading of S. S. Yi-li to see if any British goods were landed. Nothing was found.

24th March. (a) The Manager of the Bank of China returned by S. S. Ping-yang with about $60,000. Also about 70 active members of the Kuomintang party came from Ningpo by this vessel.

(b) The S. S. Nan-hai left for Ningpo with about 100 Southern soldiers and the Magistrate of the Wen-chow District; the Superintendent of Customs, Mr Hsu Lo-yao left for Tai-chow - his native place - by the same ship.

25th March.

3.78

25th March. (a) Though the Bank of China was not opened officially, the Manager agreed to take over the Customs collection, which had been kept in our safe. I tried also to remit as big an amount as possible to Shanghai, but the Manager could not do so before his Accountant's office started functioning.

(b) In the local newspaper "Ou Hai Ku Poa" (甌海公報) there was stated "The Wenchow Magistrate has received instructions from the Head-Quarters of the Commander-in-Chief of the Eastern Division of the People's Revolutionary Army to the effect that as the Provincial Political and Financial Committees had been formed, all the officials appointed by the Military Authorities must from now on obey the orders of these two Committees.

26th March. (a) A notification was issued by Hung Chu-chang (馮柱璋), the Aide-de-Camp of the Engineering Corps of

the

4. 389

the 17th Army to the effect that his corps has been despatched here from Ningpo for the maintenance of peace and order in Wenchow; that he has ordered his officers to take patrols out every day; and that ruffians disturbing the peace will be arrested and brought to his quarters for punishment.

(b) Six members (American:- 1 man, 2 ladies, and 3 children) of the Wenchow Adventist Mission left for Shanghai by S. S. Yi-li for the annual conference of their Mission as they stated.

27th March. The following telegram has been received by me: "Following from British Consul Ningpo for British residents at Wenchow. In view of possible reaction from events at Nanking you should take into consideration the question of the necessity for evacuation. You alone can judge if situation demands this action, and I must leave it to your discretion to act accordingly. Situation here quiet, but uncertain owing to labour trouble. Consul." The foreign residents at Wenchow were informed

5. 391

informed by me of the contents of this telegram.

28th March. There appeared in the local newspaper "Ou Hai Ku Poa" of the 27th the following Note. "The formal opening of the Union of Members of Various Government Establishments took place in the house of one of it's members. There were present 121 members, a deputy of the Wenchow Kuomintang party, and Vice-Chairman of the Lawyers Union. After speeches had been made by the Chairman for the time being and other members, several committees were elected by voting.

29th March. (a) In my conversation with Mr Chang Kuei-jung, who is in temporary charge of the Superintendent's office now, I mentioned my intention to request him officially to remit me the Native Customs collection outside the 50 Li radius zone for the Inspector General's National Loans Sinking Fund Account. He answered that under the present circumstances he could not reply to this letter as the Superintendent was instructed by the Military and Financial authorities to detain this money. Not until the question of their

disposal

6391

disposal had been settled by the Provincial Government would he be able to give an official reply.

(b) The following telegram was sent by the local British community to their Consul at NingpO.

" Custos NingPo
With reference to consul telegram Mazch 27 what has happened at Nanking and Shanghai. No outside communication. Keep us informed. Britbish Community. "

30th March. (a) All the ricsha coolies declared a strike to try to obtain better terms with the ricsha companies.

(b) The S.S. Yung-ning left for Ningpo with about 120 soldiers of the Southern Army. The last member of the Adventist Mission - American - left also for Shanghai via Ningpo by this ship.

(c) Some information about the situation at Nanking and Shanghai was received by the French Catholic Mission.

(d) The following telegram was received by the British community from the British Consul at Ningpo.

" Consul to British Community

At

7.

At Nanking British and American troops opened fire on Southern troops to save foreign refugees, and to enable them to evacuate. In Shanghai situation terrible owing to communist action trying to stir up mob violence. It is possible that drastic action is contemplated against Southern government, when evacuation of Shanghai would become necessary. Consul. "

The foreign community was informed by me of the contents of the telegram.

31st March. (a) Mr Susuki the representative of the Japanese Community here called upon me and stated that the Japanese here were sure that in case of emergency their Government would give them the necessary protection. He does not think that the situation is serious, because the Shanghai firms send their regular business telegrams here and do not mention any approaching danger.

Though this may be true, still the situation of the foreign residents in Wenchow is very unpleasant, as we have received

8. 392

received many ominous rumours, and there is a general lack of information and communication with the outside world.

(b) In the "Ou Hai Ku Poa" it was stated that at a meeting of the Kuomintang party held on the 28th it was decided to form a committee to reclaim land occupied by foreigners at Wenchow.

(c) The office of the Labour Union was opened in the C. I. Mission Church here.

(d) Some members of the Labour Union informed the Chinese, who are looking after the Missionary houses, which are at present unoccupied, that they want these for quarters for their own use. Doctor Stedeford, who is at present in charge of the Missionary property in Wenchow, asked me to help him, that is to write on his behalf to the Commissioner for Foreign Affairs, which I agreed to do.

Pilotage Service Wenchow.

I should be much obliged if you will let me know if we are to continue the existing practice of issuing 3/5th of the pilotage fees as reward to the Customs boatmen

9.1914

boatmen for taking vessels in and out of port, or whether this practice may be changed into 3/10ths of the fees, as was recommended by my despatch No. 4,015 of January 5th 1927.

Yours truly,

E. Bernadsky

INSPECTORATE GENERAL OF CUSTOMS,

S/O PEKING, 4th April 1927

Dear Mr. Bernadsky,

I have duly received your S/O letter No. 391 of 5th March:

<u>Nationalist flag.</u>

Your action is approved. The Nationalist flag is now being flown at practically all the Custom Houses situated in Nationalist territory.

Yours truly,

E. Bernadsky, Esquire,

WENCHOW.

INSPECTORATE GENERAL OF CUSTOMS,

S/O

PEKING, 4th April 1927

INDEXED

Dear Mr. Bernadsky,

I have duly received your S/O letter No. 392 of 10th March:

Situation at Wenchow.

I am very glad to hear that you and the Customs generally have come out so well through the recent agitation. From your account the new Superintendent seems to be a reasonable man, and you ought to have no difficulty in getting on well with him, and in maintaining the Customs position. Please convey my sympathy to Mr. Ng Shiu-hung for the senseless attack that was made on him by the processionists, and say that his action in what must have been an alarming and most trying situation reflects great credit on him. I am very glad to hear that the offenders have duly apologised.

Yours truly,

adsky, Esquire,

WENCHOW.

395

Wenchow 6th April 27

No. 395.

INDEXED

Dear Mr Edwardes,

uation Wenchow.

31st March. The following telegram was received by the British Community from the British Consul at Ningpo.

" Consul to British Community. Situation becomes more difficult. I advise withdrawal of women and children at first available opportunity. Consul."

1st April. (a) Dr Kervrann of the French Catholic Mission called on me just before he left on S.S. Sorachi Maru for Japan to ask me in accordance with the advice of Mr Suzuki, the representative of the Japanese community to visa his passport for Japan. I agreed to do so, but I told him that I was afraid that there

would

H. F. EDWARDES, ESQUIRE

Officiating Inspector General of Customs

P E K I N G.

would be objections on the part of the French authorities to such a visa. But Dr Kervraun assured me that he would explain the situation to the French Consul and that there certainly would be no objection to an effort to help a French subject in a case of emergency. At present there is no communication with Shanghai, and he therefore decided to take a passage on the first charcoal steamer, which was leaving the port. The situation here had become intolerable for him, he said. The Chinese students instigated by the Chinese doctor, whom he had replaced at the French Mission Hospital, had issued pamphlets and posters against him nearly every day during the last two months, and lately had even begun to throw stones at him on his way to and from the hospital. The students instigated by the same doctor also issued many pamphlets against the Rev. C. Aroud, the head of the French Catholic Mission in Wenchow.

(b) The following telegram has been

sent

3.

sent to the British Consul at Ningpo by the Customs British :-

" To Consul. Women and children not yet evacuated. No ship. Situation strained. Anti-British demonstration April 2, trouble expected. Customs British. "

(c) The Chinese Staff of both the Maritime and Native Customs sent a letter to the General Labour Union to the effect that the Customs Staff Union had been formed.

(d) It became known that the Kuomintang party and the General Labour Union were organising a big Lantern Procession to celebrate the victories of the Southern troops and that the extremists were going to make use of this procession to make a demonstration against foreigners and particularly against British subjects. I tried to communicate privately with the Superintendent on the subject, but could not find him.

<u>2nd April.</u> (a) As the rumours of the demonstration brought in by foreigners and Chinese were not of a reassuring character

401

acter, the Customs Staff - foreign and Chinese - asked me if I could guarantee their safety. I again tried to communicate with the Superintendent, but with no result. Then the Staff asked my permission to be absent from the office that afternoon for their own as well as for the Customs safety. I agreed. The Britishers and myself and family gathered together on the Conquest Island at about 2. pm and remained there up to 3. am of the 3rd of April. During that time we received several messages, by which we were informed that the procession passed without incidents and was over at about 11. pm. But that at the meeting held before the procession there was a lot of anti-foreign agitation and that an appeal was made to all Chinese patriots to make the life of foreigners in Wenchow as hard as possible: and that there were also shouts about reclaiming the Customs. But that after all the extremists failed this time to stir up the mob to violence.

(b) Two telegrams were received by me

5.

me that evening : -

1. " Please send pilot for British ship. Wilding "

2. " Two British destroyers should arrive White Rock afternoon April 3rd and will await arrival of transport evacuating Wen-chow. Transport should be arranged locally for journey down river as destroyer cannot come nearer. Consul. "

As it was not clear enough whether the evacuation of Wenchow meant complete evacuation or only that of the women and children, I instructed Mr Cross the Harbour Master to get in touch with the commander of the destroyers and to find out from him what his instructions were. The rest of the foreign community were notified of the contents of the telegrams.

(c) The S.S. Yung-chuan arrived from Haimen with about 400 soldiers of the Southern Army on board.

3rd April. (a) All the efforts of the Harbour Master to reach the destroyer during

6.

during the day were unsuccessful, but he managed to send down a note requesting them to let us know the instructions received by the commander of the destroyer about the evacuation.

(b) A lot of new posters appeared in the streets urging the people :-

1. to stop financial dealings with the British.
2. to avenge the slaughter of Chinese by the British Government in Singapore.
3. to regain control of the Customs etc.

(c) Mr Yu, a very active member of the Kuomintang party and that minister of the Methodist Mission, who last year formed an independent Church, has been elected one of the heads of the anti-British section of the Kuomintang party. In a speech he stated that in addition to the numerous crimes previously committed by the British 1000 Chinese patriots had lately been slaughtered by British and American gun-boats at Nanking and that after this every

7.

every effort must be made to stop all trade in British goods.

(d) The girls' school of the Methodist Mission has been occupied by the Labour Union.

4th April. (a) A strong rumour has been spread about that Sia Liang, the Chinese Tidewaiter, has been conducting the anti-foreign agitation in the Kuomintang party about the Customs employees, I accordingly sent a telegram recommending his transfer.

(b) Pickets were placed round the examination shed to see that no British cargo was handled and these pickets followed the examiner to the East gate, where he went to examine cargo. He was not interfered with; in fact the pickets consisted of small brokers and shopmen and were treating the matter as a joke.

(c) The following telegrams have been received : -

1. British Residents. I advise (evacuate) of all British residents. Consul.
2. British Community. please inquire

whether

8?.

475

whether Roman Catholic Fathers and Sisters wish to be evacuated. If so Veteran will try to include them in party. Consul. "

The contents of these telegrams were communicated to the foreign community here.

(d) A note was received by the Harbour Master from the Commander of the destroyer "Veteran" in which he informed the the British community that British and French subjects and all other foreigners are to be evacuated from Wenchow unless they wished to remain there, and that for this purpose he had communicated with the captain of the S.O.C. ship "Meinan" on her way to Shanghai and that the latter would proceed to Wenchow to embark refugees on the 5th of April; and that those, who wished to go all the way to Shanghai on the Meinan could do so. The foreign community was informed of this note. The question of evacuation was discussed by the British community and it was decided that all women and children must leave port.

The

9. 426

The question of the evacuation of the men was left open until further information about the general situation should be obtained. At the same time the Customs Foreign staff - all British subjects - declared that they would not leave me alone and that if I decided to stay here they would remain also. I asked them to be guided by the point of view of their own safety and by their consul's advice, but they did not change their attitude.

5th April. (a) The S.S Meinan" arrived. The captain of the ship being told that some Catholic missionaries were expected shortly from the interior agreed to wait till the next morning.

(b) The following telegram was received from the Consul at Ningpo.

" What are British subjects doing? Veteran cannot remain much longer at White Rock. Handley Derry.

6th April. (a) The Meinan left for Shanghai with the following refugees :-

Mrs Bernadsky, six children, governess and nurse.

Mrs Cross, wife of our Acting Tidesurveyor.

Mrs Finch

10/427

Mrs Finch, wife of our Assistant Examiner, and 3 Fathers of the Catholic Mission. Mr Cross, the Acting Tidesurveyor with my permission also left for White Rock to obtain from the Commander of the destroyer more particulars about the general situation, and to explain to him that the British and other residents at Wenchow could not evacuate as quickly as had been wanted, because they had been unable to get to the ship. I took this opportunity to send the following wireless telegram to you.

> " Is the situation so critical that the Customs foreign staff should evacuate by destroyer waiting at White Rock. Communications are very uncertain, and if the crisis becomes known to Chinese beforehand, we shall be isolated.
>
> Foreign staff stand by me voluntarily. Bernadsky. "

(b) Mr Suzuki, the Japanese representative here called upon me to say good-bye, as he was going to Japan via Shanghai

11.

Shanghai. He had, he said, received to-day a telegram from the Naval authorities at Formosa enquiring if they wanted protection. The Japanese community considered that the presence of a warship at Wenchow was undesirable, but that a merchantman with wireless would meet the case; however he doubted that such a ship would be sent here.

Yours truly

E. Bernadsky.

421

INDEXED

No. 396.   Wenchow   12th April   27

Dear Mr Edwardes,

Situation in Wenchow.

6th April. Mr G.E. Cross reported to me that Mr Suzuki interviewed him and requested on behalf of the Japanese community that all the British members of the Customs would remain at the port and stated that in a case of emergency the Japanese destroyer would protect them.

7th April. (a) In the local newspaper "Ou Hai Ku Poa" there was stated :-

" The Union of the employees of the Piece Goods shops held a meeting yesterday and passed a resolution to boycott piece goods of British manufacture and to send from time to time search parties to the steamer wharves. "

(b) Mr G.E. Cross, Acting Tidesurveyor

H. F. EDWARDES, ESQUIRE

Officiating Inspector General of Customs

P E K I N G.

2. 622

Tidesurveyor, reported that had returned from the White Rock at 11.pm the night before. He had explained to the commander of the destroyer "Veteran" our difficulty in being guided by the local situation in the matter of evacuation. Though there is strong anti-foreign agitation here, up to now it has not been very successful, but if a clash were to occur between foreign and Southern troops at Shanghai or any other place, the situation may change rapidly and then our isolated position will be distinctly uncomfortable. The commander promised to put this explanation before the military authorities at Shanghai. In view of some difficulties in transmitting my telegram to you, the wording of which was given in my S/O No. 395, the commander proposed to convey by wireless the contents of my telegram with a short description of the local situation to the Shanghai Commissioner of Customs in the hope that the latter would

transmit

transmit it to you if necessary. Mr Cross agreed to the proposal, but I am sorry to say, he has failed to bring me a copy of this telegram prepared by the commander of H.M.S. Veteran on my behalf.

9th April. (a) In the local paper "u Hai Ku Poa" appeared a notice announcing that the China Inland Mission Church (内地會) has been kept by the Chinese members and that the foreign missionaries have been there in the position of advisers only and that this Church will now be called the Chinese Christian Mission Church (中華基督教會) and that the inauguration will take place on the afternoon of April 10th.

(b) The S.S. Pingyang left for Ningpo with 150 soldiers of the Southern army on board.

10th April. The Union of the women workmen paraded the streets of the city as an announcement of the formation of their Union.

11th April. A summary of the local situation and

4.

and the application for means of communication have been sent to you by telegram as follows : -

" Custos Peking.
Local situation from time to time strained. British consul strongly advises all British subjects to leave but all foreign staff stand by me voluntarily. Communication uncertain and infrequent and only by means of Chinese owned steam vessels. Only Chinese pilots know channel of river and in case of crisis they may refuse to serve foreign ships sent to evacuate and we shall be isolated. Can Customs cruiser with wireless if possible come to learn channel and stand by in case of necessity of evacuation meanwhile surveying river. If cruiser cannot come please consider means to meet situation. Bernadsky. "

<u>12th April</u>. (a) Two telegrams with a request for a pilot have been received for

a

5.

425

Japanese destroyer and a French gunboat, both expected to be in port tomorrow.

(b) The inauguaration of the Wenchow Post Office Staff Union in the General Labourers Union has taken place.

f. Mr. Lau Kieng Hing, 1st Clerk C of this office asked me to recommend to you his son Liu Chi Tuan (劉祁端) for appointment as Clerk in the Customs Service. I told him that so far as I understood all clerks at present received their appointment after graduating from the Customs College and that therefore outsiders had hardly any chance, but that in any case if he wanted to try his luck he must bring his son to be examined. I examined Liu Chi Tuan today and found him to be quite suitable for our Service. Particulars as follows: Age 20, single. Born in Shanghai. Graduated from the Wenchow Methodist College in 1926. He speaks, reads and writes English pretty fluently; knowledge of Chinese dialects: Foochow, Wenchow and Mandarin. Health good. If you consider that this man can be taken into

our

6.

126

our Service then I take this opportunity to ask you to appoint this candidate to the Wenchow office, if there is any inconvenience in making a transfer from any other ports. The pressure of work here is too heavy at present and I shall be much obliged if my application for clerk, as stated in S/O No. 392 will be treated as urgent.

Lo; Leave.
IG Circ.3677.

The only member in the Wenchow Customs, whose leave is overdue, is myself, but I am sorry I cannot apply for it because of some financial difficulties, which up to now have not yet been solved.

Bank of China
resumes business.

The Bank of China resumed business on the 1st April and in view of uncertainty of the local situation I remitted to Shanghai all the money we had in hand, i.e. Revenue A/c Hk.Tls.23,400.00 and Service A/c Hk.Tls.7,000.00. In normal times we keep here in the Bank Hk.Tls. 9,000.00, an amount which covers two months expenditures, but at present

421

present it is probably advisable to keep in Shanghai as much money as can be spared.

Yours truly,

E. Bernadsky

INDEXED

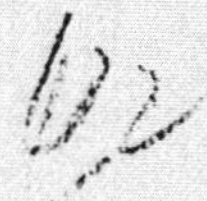

COPY OF TELEGRAM RECEIVED FROM I.G. DATED 12TH APRIL, 1927.

Following telegram received from Wenchow
"Local situation from time to time strained British Consul strongly advises all British Subjects to leave but all Foreign Staff stand by me voluntarily. Communication uncertain and infrequent and only by means of Chinese owned steam vessels Only Chinese pilots know channel of river and in case of crisis they may refuse to serve foreign ship sent to evacuate and we shall be isolated. Can Customs cruiser with wireless if possible come to learn channel and stand by in case of necessity of evacuation meanwhile surveying river If cruiser cannot come please consider means to meet situation Bernadsky"
Consult British Consul General and if he advocates evacuation arrange in conjunction with Coast Inspector for Revenue Cruiser to evacuate. Inform Wenchow of arrangements made.

Edwardes.

INSPECTORATE GENERAL OF CUSTOMS,

381

PEKING, 18th April, 1927

INDEXED

Dear Mr. Bernadsky,

I have duly received your S/O letter No. 393 of the 21st March:

Postal Commissioner requests financial help: Revenue remittance.

In unsettled times like the present it is not advisable to keep such large sums in actual cash in your safe. Keep only so much as may be actually required, and remit the balance to Shanghai. The arrangement you mention with the Post Office is probably as good as any other for such remittance.

Yours truly,

na[illegible]ky, Esquire,

[illegible]NCHOW.

CUSTOM HOUSE,

/O. No. 397. INDEXED Wenchow 19th April 1927.

Dear Mr. Edwardes ,

Handing over charge.

In accordance with your instructions I am today handing over charge to Mr. Ng Shiu hung , 3rd Assistant, B., after obtaining concurrence from the Superintendent. I take this opportunity to say a few words about the Staff . In spite of nervousness caused by the uncertainty of the situation during last 4 months the Staff - Chinese and Foreign - worked as hard as they could . The Chinese Staff formed their Union only for self protection . As far as I could understand they have kept me informed of the work of their Union and I could not find anything against our regulations . The behaviour of the Foreign Staff and the Customs Medical Officer during last few weeks deserve your special

commendation

F. EDWARDES , ESQUIRE ,

Officiating Inspector General of Customs ,

P E K I N G.

436 2.

commendation. They did not follow the British Consul's order to evacuate but remained on duty and preferred to share with me all possible difficulties until I could leave port together with them.

Situation in Wenchow.

12th April. (a) In accordance with the instructions received from the Provincial Authorities a notification was issued by the local military to the effect that Chinese and Foreigners must not to be molested by anybody and that peace and order are to be enforced. Those who break these instructions would be severely punished.

(b) In spite of this proclamation the United Methodist College has been occupied by students. The college was under the Superintendent's seal, but the students withdrew the seal and entered the school. The case was reported to the Commissioner for Foreign Affairs and to the Magistrate. An official of the Magistrate's office certified the case and remarked that the students had no right to do this.

13th April. (a) The Japanese destroyer "Kawakaze" arrived

3.

121

arrived from Amoy .

(b) Two telegrams have been received : one from you of the 12th instant and the second from the British Consul at Ningpo as follows: "Please inform British subjects I again urge withdrawal to place of safety . If they remain British Government must disclaim responsibility . Please inform me what they decide to do. Consul".

14th April.(a) The French gunboat "Marne" arrived from Shanghai . The Commander of the gunboat called upon me and stated that he would take any foreigners to Shanghai and that the ship would be leaving at 4 p.m. He also stated that the British Admiral had instructed him to inform the foreign community that this would probably be the last opportunity to get away by a foreign vessel . In view of this statement and the British Consul's telegram of yesterday I strongly advised the foreign staff to leave by the French gunboat . But they together with Doctor Stedford after finding out that the Japanese destroyer would give full protection to all foreigners in case of troubl

decided

4.

decided to remain here until I could hand over charge. The gunboat "Marne" left for Shanghai at 5 p.m. with all the Catholic missionaries - fathers and sisters - on board.

(b) A telegram was sent by the British Community to their Consul as follows: "To Consul, Japanese destroyer standing by, Customs and Doctor making five British remain till Commissioner of Customs receives expected instructions to hand over charge then all go first opportunity".

15th April. (a) The Superintendent of Customs Mr. Hsü returned by S.S. "Pingyang". Also Mr. Tai Jen (戴仁), newly appointed by the Provincial Government as the Yungcha Magistrate, arrived by the same ship.

(b) Four leaders of the extremists were arrested by the local military, and a notice was issued by the same authorities promising a reward of $30 to whoever would produce Mr. Yu, a minister of the Methodist Mission who lately was elected to be one of leaders of the anti-British agitation. I was told that all these people were paid members of the communist party, each getting

$28

5.

459

$28 per month .

(c) Your telegram of the 8th instant sent through the Shanghai Commissioner was just received this evening .

16th April. (a) Some placards appeared in the city: "Down with those who oppose Dr. Sun's principles"; Down with those who make disturbances in the city".

(b) All British subjects received letters from the British Consul at Ningpo stating that the British Minister had advised in the strongest terms that all British subjects should evacuate . This letter states also that the mere fact that the local situation may be peaceful and that the local authorities may have promised protection is no reason for remaining in a position from which evacuation is difficult and , under certain circumstances, almost impossible .

(c) The China Merchant ship "Hae-an" arrived from Shanghai . It is the first ship sent by this Company since 10th December 1926.

18th April . The Revenue steamer "Chuentiao" arrived from Shanghai to evacuate the Customs Staff if necessary . In view of the British

Consul's

6.

Consul's instructions they all together with the Customs Medical Officer Dr. Stedford are leaving by this ship on the 20th instant. After that the only foreigners in Wenchow will be Japanese.

Yours truly,

E. Bernadsky.

CUSTOM HOUSE,

) NO. 398. Wenchow 20th April 19 27.

INDEXED

662

Dear Mr. Edwardes,

umption of
rge.

In accordance with your instructions I took over charge from Mr. Bernadsky yesterday. While thanking you heartily for your appointment of myself to such an honourable position I beg leave to say that in such a hard time it is no easy matter to overcome all difficulties, but I will do my best to keep work running on smoothly and to protect Customs interests as far as the local situation permits of.

. on
rintendent.

Mr. Bernadsky went with me to call on the Superintendent Mr. Hsü yesterday afternoon. The latter at first advised Mr. Bernadsky not to leave port and assured him of safety at Wenchow. On being informed by Mr. Bernadsky that he had no option but to leave with the last foreigner in

the

. F. EDWARDES, ESQUIRE,

Officiating Inspector General of Customs,

P E K I N G.

143

the Customs, the Superintendent insisted on that he would appoint a deputy to the Customs while Mr. Bernadsky was away to help me in smoothing matters with the public. Mr. Bernadsky told him that this was quite unnecessary because I was authorised by you to take full responsibility of the Customs business here, and that if there be any expected trouble I should always be glad to ask for his assistance and to consult with him any difficult questions that might arise from time to time. The Superintendent however, still claimed that a Weiyüan was necessary because he was in apprehension that after the departure of all the Customs foreign members merchants might raise opposition and that the appointment of a deputy here was not to interfere with Customs business, but to help me in smoothing the public in order that I could carry on business without undue interruption. To this Mr. Bernadsky replied that he would expect of no opposition from the merchants; that I was already an

3.

144

an experienced man in the Customs; and that the appointment of a weiyüan here would not only infringe our established procedure but would create misunderstanding from the public. Mr. Bernadsky added that in case of necessity or trouble I would be glad to apply for his assistance to clear the outside atmosphere, but that at the present juncture it was quite unnecessary to send his man here. When the conversation came to this point Mr. Hsü agreed and merely asked Mr. Bernadsky to return as soon as he possibly could.

He returned call on us in the same afternoon and his attitude was quite different from what he maintained in his office. He promised to help me in all difficulties and did not mention about the sending of a deputy again. His real attitude may reveal itself in a few days and in case he raises this question again I shall do my best to put it down failing so I shall wire to you for instructions.

...tion of ...n Staff.

All the Foreign members of the Staff including

4.

45

including the Customs Doctor left by R. S. "Chuentiao" at 9 o'clock this morning.

ff. The Chinese Indoor Staff has already been short by one clerk owing to trade expansion of this port (vide S/O Nos. 393 and 396) and with the departure of Mr. Cholmondeley and my appointment to the present position the number of shortages now comes to three, 2 in the Maritime Customs and 1 in the Native Customs. As to the Outdoor Staff, 3 Senior Tidewaiters are required to make up the deficiency caused by the evacuation of the Foreign Outdoor members, 2 for the Maritime Customs and one for the Native Customs. One of them should know how to carry on Tidesurveyor's and Harbour Master's duties. At present the Native Customs is only in charge of the Senior Examiner Mr. Lin Yin-li (林银梨) under the supervision of Mr. Lin Chan Ngau (林占鳌), 3rd Clerk B, who visits the Native Customs office every day and takes charge of the Accounts there.

This

D.

446

This arrangement is not quite satisfactory but, with the limited Staff at my disposal at present, I cannot make better arrangement than this. Therefore I shall be much obliged if you will send here three Chinese Clerks and 3 Senior Chinese Tidewaiters by telegraphic transfers to meet our urgent needs.

G.'s
legram.

Your telegram sent through the Shanghai Commissioner instructing me not to grant any local leave to Chinese employees entailing absence from port was received by me last night. The instructions will be acted upon.

uation in
chow

19th April. A proclamation was issued by the local military yesterday stating that all foreigners residing in China must not be molested and that they are entitled to the same protection as the Chinese emigrants enjoy in foreign countries. The notification ends that violation of these instructions by anyone will entail severe punishment.

20th April. In spite of the proclamation issued yesterday the so-called Anti-British Association

sends

6.

sends a circular letter to all the labour Unions telling them to send representatives to attend a meeting to be held tomorrow to discuss measures for suppressing the importation of English goods to Wenchow and for stopping economic dealings with the English subjects.

Yours truly,

Ng Shin Tsung.

CUSTOM HOUSE,

No. 399.

INDEXED

Wenchow, 23rd April 1927

Dear Mr. Edwardes,

[..]tude of [..]chants.

After the evacuation of the Foreign Staff we have been dealing with the merchants alright and work has been going on smoothly.

[..]rintendent [..]mpts to [..]rfere with [..]oms business.

The Superintendent's Kochang Mr. Chang Kuei-jung (張桂榮) made an informal call on me yesterday morning and stated that the Superintendent was afraid that without the supervision of the Foreign Outdoor Officers the Chinese Outdoor Staff may not be reliable and suggested that 2 Supervisors (稽查) might be sent by his office to co-operate with our Staff in examination and searching work. If I agreed he would issue badges to be stamped by the Superintendent and myself for the Supervisors to wear. I replied that this was quite unnecessary because our Outdoor Staff Officers have been very honest and energetic in their duties and very reasonable to merchants. Of

course

H. F. EDWARDES, ESQUIRE,

Officiating Inspector General of Customs,

P E K I N G.

2

course these conversations were informal and the Superintendent only wanted to know through Mr. Chang what my attitude was.

The transmission of the Ts'ai-cheng Pu's instructions for the remittance of $100,000 to meet military expenses (vide my telgram of 22nd April and Wenchow despatch No. 4034) to this office is another instance that he wants to lay his hands to the Customs. He must be fully aware that no Revenue moneys of the Maritime and Native Customs under the Commissioner's control can be appropriated for any other purpose than meeting foreign loan obligations and his action in this respect shows that he is finding every opportunity to interfere with our business. The Ts'ai-cheng Pu's instructions are evidently meant for his own offices only.

Your telegram in reply was received at 4 p.m. this day. I am going to send him another letter and besides quoting your instructions I am taking the opportunity to claim from him the Native Customs collection outside

the

3.

451

the 50-li radius zone (vide page 11 of Mr. Bernadsky's Handing-over-charge Memorandum to me enclosed in Wenchow despatch No. 4033/I. G.).

He is now trying to find fault on us and only a small leak may lead him to make his ground for interference. However I must stand firm no matter what suggestions he may offer. I have warned the Outdoor Officers to be very careful and discreet in the execution of their duties so as not to leave any ground for outside complaint, at the same time inducing the merchants to observe our regulations as far as possible.

[..]tion in [..]chow.

21st April: (a) News to hand that the S/L. "Yun Ta" (運大) plying between Wenchow and places at the mouth of the river was pirated at Chiang Hsia (江廈) on the morning of the 14th instant. Some few hundred dollars including cash and passengers' belongings were stolen and the vessel was released at Shih Tang (石塘) on the 16th.

(b) A proclamation was issued by the military

152

military forbidding rough handling of people and molesting business shops by processionists.

(c) S.S. "Pingyang" arrived from Niggpo with news that all the Labour Unions there were smashed.

22nd April: (a) On receipt of a letter from Dr. Stedeford by the Commissioner of Foreign Affairs requesting retrocession of all foreign property at present occupied by Students and Labour Unions the Wenchow Magistrate to whom the letter was transmitted summoned the Unions to a meeting today to discuss the question.

(b) Pingyang (平陽), the place bordering Fukien and Chekiang, was invaded on the morning of the 21st instant by 300 soldiers said to be the rampnants of the late Fukian Tuchün Chou Yin-jen (周蔭人) from Taishun (泰順) and fighting took place between the troops stationed there, numbering only 50, and the invaders. The former were overpowered and disarmed. All officials and many residents there fled for safety. It was reported that about 300 soldiers were already sent from

Wenchow

5.

453

Wenchow to clear the invaders there.

(c) Placards with the expressions "Down with Imperialism", "Down with corrupt officials", etc., etc., again appeared in the streets.

(d) The Customs Union has so far not yet been inaugurated. The real object of forming this Union was for self protection and the protection of the Customs. As the present situation indicates that this Union may not be necessarily formed it is decided to put the matter aside for the time being.

Representatives were sent by the Customs Union to attend the meeting of the anti-British Association. Two Customs members were invited to sit on the Committee but the request was cordially declined.

(e) The S.S. "Yungchuan" which should be due here today has not yet arrived. The vessel is said to be commandeered at Haimen for conveyance of troops to Ningpo.

(f) Martial law is being proclaimed here owing to the Pingyang incident mentioned in (b). City gates are closed at 8 p.m.

Yours truly,

Ng Shi-[illegible]

CUSTOM HOUSE,

No. 400. Wenchow, 25th April 1927.

INDEXED

Dear Mr. Edwardes,

rintendent npts to rfere with oms business.

In continuation of my S/O No. 399, the Superintendent dropped me a letter this morning in reply to mine of the 22nd instant saying that I made a wrong statement regarding remittance of all revenue moneys to Shanghai by Mr. Bernadsky because the March Report on Collection and Remittance sent him still shows a balance of Hk.Tls.16,580.765 Maritime, and Hk.Tls. 7,866.533 Native Revenue unremitted. He asked me to keep these sums in hand as well as the daily collections hereafter pending instructions from the Minister of Finance.

The sums referred to were already remitted to Shanghai by Mr. Bernadsky after the Bank of China resumed business. At the time of receipt of the above letter my letter conveying your telegraphic instructions and claiming

F. EDWARDES, ESQUIRE,

Officiating Inspector General of Customs,

P E K I N G.

2.

456

claiming for the Native Customs collection for the three months of this year was not yet sent out and I deemed it advisable to forward this letter on to him without replying to his absurd letter.

I am afraid that this man may still scheme other ways to cause us more trouble. If he does I shall wire to you from time to time for instructions.

In the meantime all revenue and Service Accounts moneys available for remittance have been duly remitted to Shanghai and it is my intention to leave as little money as possible in the local bank.

Yours truly,

Ng Shin Lung

515

INSPECTORATE GENERAL OF CUSTOMS,

PEKING, 26th April, 1927

Dear Mr. Bernadsky,

I have duly received your S/O letter No. 394 of the 31st March:

Pilotage Service at Wenchow: question of rewards to Customs Boatmen.

This question has been dealt with by despatch.

Yours truly,

sky, Esquire,

NCHOW.

INSPECTORATE GENERAL OF CUSTOMS,

PEKING, 26th April, 1927.

INDEXED

Dear Mr. Bernadsky,

I have duly received your S/O letter No. 395 of the 6th April:

Dr. Kervrann's request to have his pass-port vised for Japan.

Your reference to the visa for Japan on Dr. Kervrann's pass-port is not clearly understood here. Did you actually make such a visa? If so, by what authority did you do so? What precisely was the nature of the visa?

Behaviour of Customs Staff in trying Situation.

It is very reassuring to see the way in which you and your staff have faced the situation, which was certainly a far from pleasant one. The community owe you a

considerable

[illegible]sky, Esquire,

[illegible]CHOW.

4/7

considerable debt of gratitude for the assistance you have rendered, and I am glad to think that in a crisis of this sort leadership fell to the men of the Customs Service, and was worthily borne.

Yours truly,

CUSTOM HOUSE,

No. 401. Wenchow 28th April 1927.

INDEXED

44

Dear Mr. Edwardes,

[Cla]im for [Cus]toms Revenue [b]y Superintendent.

Your telegram of the 27th April in reply to mine of the 26th was received at 9.20 p.m. last night. I am glad to learn that the Southern Authorities at Shanghai and Hankow are being requested to instruct the Superintendent not to interfere with our revenue. The code words in your telegram between "interfering with revenue" and "Hold in both Service and revenue Accounts..." were however mutilated and could not be decoded. I have asked the Telegraph Administration here to repeat them. I am writing to the Superintendent conveying the sense mentioned in your telegram, though I may expect to receive a peculiar reply from him if he has not received instructions from the proper channels. All his letters to me and my replies were forwarded to

you

[T]H. F. EDWARDES, ESQUIRE,

[Of]ficiating Inspector General of Customs,

P E K I N G.

2.

465

you in Wenchow despatches Nos. 4034 and 4035. It seems to me that this Superintendent does not know the traditions of the Customs and diplomatic matters at all and his only aim is to put his hands to anything from which money can be extracted. He is a military man, very hot-tempered also.

[Prot]ection of [Cust]oms and Staff [in c]ase of danger.

A Japanese destroyer is always standing by here and after the evacuation of the Foreign Staff the Manager of the Mitsui Bussan Kaisha here Mr. Suzuki very kindly offered to give me assistance should anything occur in the spot. Though situation now appears to be very quiet we are however in a very uncertain position, agitation regarding retrocession of the Customs again reviving, and with the Superintendent working against us we must be prepared to face difficulties. I am very doubtful if I may avail of the protection of the gunboat in case of danger as the Commander kindly offers to take myself and my family on board in time of emergency. But the protection of the Customs

and

3.

066

and the Staff must be taken into consideration in case the officials here may work together with the agitators and on this point I wish to have your views as to whether this gunboat may be of any use to us.

ttance of
ice and
me Account
ys.

All available sums have been duly remitted to Shanghai and only what is absolutely necessary is kept in the local Bank of China. Before receiving your telegram in this connection I have already made up my decision on this point (vide S/O. No. 400).

tion in
ow.

The outlook of this City is very quiet but agitators are working underground. Since the arrest of the Communists placards ceased to appear in the streets for sometime but re-appear again now with wordings almost as before. All the labour unions are reorganised but strictly speaking this reorganisation is only nominal.

The S.Ss."Haean" and "Yili" arrived on the 25th. The latter left here yesterday afternoon and the former this morning.

Export

4.

47

Export cargoes were plenty.

The S. S. "Yung Chuan" arrived from Ningpo yesterday with soldiers and left this morning.

Yours truly,

Ng Shin-hung.

CUSTOM HOUSE,

No. 402

Wenchow, 2nd May 1927.

INDEXED

Dear Mr. Edwardes,

[Clai]m for Customs [rev]enue by [Su]perintendent.

The Superintendent has so far not raised this question again since I wrote him in the sense conveyed in your telegram of the 27th April. Probably the Southern Authorities have kept him quiet as a result of your request. I have got the mutilated code words repeated on the 30th April and the text has been quite plain now.

[Po]tato Cuttings: [Re]quest for [exe]mption from [Nat]ive Customs [d]uty of, by [Su]perintendent.

On the 14th April the Superintendent wrote to Mr. Bernadsky requesting him to exempt from Native Customs duty 5,000 catties of Potato Cuttings to be shipped by junks from Hsi Ch'i (西 溪), a place in the up river, to Yung Ch'iang (永 强), a place near our Ningtsun Station, in two consignments for relief of the clansmen in the latter place by the gentry there owing to bad crops in that vicinity.

Fearing

[F.] H. F. EDWARDES, ESQUIRE,

Officiating Inspector General of Customs,

P E K I N G .

2.

470

Fearing that a precedent might be established for future request of this kind Mr. Bernadsky asked the Superintendent to get a Huchao from the Provincial Authorities. The Superintendent however wrote again on the 21st April to say that as these Potato Cuttings were immediately required for releif purposes they might be passed first and a Huchao produced afterwards. In view of this promise and of the amount of duty being only an insignificant sum, Kp.Tls. 2.50, I have instructed the Native Customs Office to pass this stuff free. The correspondence will appear in the Return of Non-urgent Correspondence for April.

[illegible]age [illegible].ce.

I duly received your despatch No.1446/112,060 regarding scale of remuneration to be issued to the Boatmen-pilots and an order in Chinese conveying the instructions in this despatch has been duly issued for the information of the Boatmen concerned.

ta[illegible].

Since the evacuation of the foreign Staff the General Office work has been managed by two Clerks only, the senior Clerk having

also

3.

471

also to do the Foreign Assistant's work. With so many applications to handle coupled with issue of Transit Passes these two Clerks have been working early and late everyday to clear the daily work and practically no time is left for preparing the various returns. The Secretary's Clerk has to attend to Native Customs work in the morning and help the Secretary and General Office in the afternoon. There has already been a Clerk short (vide S/O Nos. 393 and 396) and the Annual Trade Returns were only despatched on the 16th April with all the Staff including myself and the Secretary working from early morning to 8 p.m. for more than a week. The Quarterly Trade Returns for March Quarter are still left untouched. Also the steamers have been running regularly now and cargoes are plenty. A little delay in examination would create great excitement while our Outdoor Staff is severely depleted. I therefore wired to you on the 30th April that the Staff applied for in my S/O. No. 398 are urgently required. I regret this state of affairs should have occurred but it is really

the

417

the shortage of Staff that work cannot be brought up to date. With the arrival of the required hands I am sure that all would be going on well provided the situation be calm.

[...]ation in [...]how.

The Labour Unions are resuming their activities. Various extortionate claims are being presented to owners of shops, amongst which, the most unreasonable ones are those to the Medicine Guild. These claims are:

(a) The lowest salary of any employee should be $14 a month.

(b) In case of sickness employers are responsible for all medical expenses.

(c) Employers to give $500 to the family of any employee in case of death.

(d) The Medicine Guild should divide the reserves, now amounting to $50,000 or $60,000 between the Guild and the employees in the proportion of 60% to employees and 40% kept by the Guild.

The employers are not acceding to any one of these claims and are contemplating to suspend business. Various other merchant Guilds are

likely

5.

443

likely to follow on the same lines. The so-called "Right Wing" Kuomintang are doing exactly what the radicals were doing i.e. to uplift labourers and press down capitalists.

A big procession consisting of all sorts of labourers paraded the streets yesterday in honour of the Labours Day. At night there was a lantern procession.

The Japanese destroyer Nishimura arrived this morning to relieve the Kawakaze which leaves today.

The S.S. Kwanhchi arrived this morning as is also the S. S. Yung Ning.

Yours truly,

Ng Shui Leung

P.S. Since writing the above the Superintendent writes again, with regard to his claim for Customs revenue, to say that as this Customs is under the jurisdiction of the Finance Minister of the Nationalist Government all orders either in telegram or by despatch from Peking cannot be recognised by him.

The

6.

471

The letter continues to say that the matter has been referred to the Finance Minister whose instructions I have to obey. I think therefore that your request to the Southern Authorities may not have been settled yet.

INSPECTORATE GENERAL OF CUSTOMS, 489

S/O PEKING, 5th May 1927.

INDEXED

Dear Mr. Ng Shiu hung,

I have of late been receiving so large a number of applications from Commissioners for the invaliding of House coolies, Gardeners, Gatekeepers, etc., that I am led to the belief that the invaliding clause of the Pensions Scheme is being availed of largely for the purpose of getting rid of employees of these ranks whose work for some reason or other is unsatisfactory.

I wish to point out that this procedure, which throws on Pensions Account a strain for which it was not intended, and with which it is not adequate to cope, is also contrary to the Service rule that employees who perform their duties in an unsatisfactory manner should be discharged with pay to date. To recommend such servants for benefits which they have not earned, and no not deserve, is not in order.

While on the subject of employees of this type, whose employment is not absolutely essential to the main objects for which the Service exists, and of whom there are

490

are a great many in the Service, I shall be glad if Commissioners will, further, carefully consider how many of these employees on their staff could be dispensed with without replacement. It is a growing burden on our finances to meet the continuous increases of pay being granted to men of these ranks, and I am of the opinion that if the case of each man were looked into closely, from the point of view of discharge or retention, no small economy could be effected in this direction. Since men of this class are demanding more pay, we should, on our side, require a correspondingly increased return in labour; and the interest of the whole Service demands that any possible economy in this or any other direction must be taken advantage of at the present time. In future, therefore, in every case of a withdrawal you are personally to consider before appointing a successor whether instead of replacement a readjustment of the Staff will not meet your requirements.

Yours truly,

CUSTOM HOUSE,

476

No. 403.

INDEXED

Wenchow, 6th May 1927.

Dear Mr. Edwardes,

[Su]perintendent's [Cla]im for [Cus]toms Revenue.

In reply to the Superintendent's letter mentioned in the P.S. of my S/O. No. 402, I emphasised the point that Customs revenue being pledged for the service of foreign loans and indemities could not be diverted to other uses and requested him further that in order to uphold the country's faith the three months' Native Customs collections outside the 50-li radius may be sent me for my remittance to your National Loans Sinking Fund Account. To my great delight the tone of his letter in reply - received yesterday afternoon - was entirely changed, not only soft but melodious too. There was no mention made about our revenue but with regard to his Native Customs collections claimed by me he said the money was in the custody of the Bank of China and

that

[A]. F. EDWARDES, ESQUIRE.

Officiating Inspector General of Customs.

P E K I N G.

2.

417

that as to whom these collections shall be remitted he was waiting for insbructions. This is a sign that he has received instructions from the Southern Authorities. I hope the trouble may now come to an end. Very probably in the final run he may release these funds to us.

ttances to Revenue Service unts.

Your telegram of 3rd May sent through the Shanghai Commissioner reached me at 12 midnight on the same day. The Revenue was then more than sufficient to cover our official allowance which was accordingly drawn on the following day. After deduction of the amount to cover our Staff Salaries for the month and a small sum to meet other expenses all the surplus revenue and service moneys were duly remitted to your respective accounts at Shanghai as instructed (vide my telegram of the 4th May, 1927). It has already been my original intention to remit as frequently as possible before receipt of your repeated telegraphic instructions to this end (vide my S/O. No. 400). The other instructions contained in

3.

478

in your telegram will be strictly adhered to.

ning of
um

25 catties of native raw opium were seized on board the S.S. FUCHUEN from Amoy on the 17th April on information. Acting on Mr. Bernadsky's advice to burn this opium at an earlier date than the end of the quarter, I wrote to the Superintendent on the 28th April to this effect and the burning took place on the following morning in the presence of the Superintendent's WeiYuan.

Staff.

I was rejoiced to receive your telegram of the 4th sent through Shanghai informing me of your sending 2 Chinese Clerks and 3 Chinese Tidewaiters to this port. I am sure that with their arrival our work can be easily brought up to date Many thanks for your kindness in acceding to my request.

Uniforms for
Watchers,
Boatmen, etc.

The time is due for the renewal of the Summer uniforms for these lower grade employees. In view of your telegram of the 3rd instant I hesitate to sign the demand submitted to me by the Senior Outdoor Officer. I instructed him to find out whether these men's

49

men's uniforms can still be worn for the summer and his enquires show that although the uniforms are not quite presentable they can still be worn for the time being. I think the watchers and boatmen can have their new suits but the supply of uniforms to the Commissioner's chair-bearers, T'ingch'ai, etc. can be withheld for the time being. I wish to have your instructions on this point.

ge Allowance.

As the Accountant desires to know what amount of charge allowance is issuable to me in order to settle his paysheet I beg leave to submit this question to you.

ation in
now.

The Kuomintang forced the Medicine shops to yield to all the claims submitted by their employees. A majority of the owners under threat were about to signify their agreement when suddenly some with courage offered their strong opposition resulting in none of the claims being accepted. Then all the employees walked out and business suspended to the great annoyance of the patients. This condition lasted for two days. As a result of protests made

5

483

made by sick people the Public Peace Bureau (公安局), formerly the Police Department (警察局), issued a notice prohibiting strike. Business was therefore resumed yesterday but the claims are still under discussion. The owners have wired to General Chang Kai-shek for his giving a justifiable solution on the case.

The Wenchow Magistrate has again been changed. The present incumbent is Mr. Hu T'ing-jen (胡鼎仁) who assumed office on the 2nd instant.

The four Communist leaders here arrested sometime ago were sent to Hangchow via Ningpo per the S.S. YUNG NING on the 2nd instant. It is said that severe punishment will be meted out to these radicals.

A special feature in the City during these few days is the discarding of hair by the gentle sex. A majority of the girl students have already had their hair off.

Yours truly,

Ng Shi-hung.

S/O

CUSTOM HOUSE,

41

SHANGHAI, 7th May, 1927.

INDEXED

Dear Mr. Edwardes,

Dr. Kervrann's request to have his pass-port vised for Japan:

(Your S/O Letter of the 26th April, 1927).

I explained to Dr. Kervrann that the requisite visa to allow him to go to Shanghai via Japan must be made by Consular Authorities. He replied that he quite understood that, but as he could not obtain it in time from the Consul and in view of the urgency of the case, he was applying to me as a senior member of the foreign community who occupied an official position, in the hope that I could solve the difficulty by giving him the visa for transit through Japan, without which the captain of the ship could not take him on board. As at that time the situation at Wenchow was really strained, and as there was no communication with open ports, I decided to grant him the required visa if he was prepared to take full responsibility if the French or Japanese Authorities objected

to

A. H. F. Edwardes, Esquire,

Peking.

012

to the stamping of the Customs seal on his passport. I thought that it was better to risk a breach of regulations than to keep this man in danger and therefore granted his request.

A few days ago I met Dr. Kervrann in Shanghai. He thanked me for the visa and informed me that everything had passed without incident and that he was not troubled by anybody on his way either in Japan or Shanghai.

Yours truly,

E. Bernatsky

426

INSPECTORATE GENERAL OF CUSTOMS,

S/O

PEKING, 9th May 1927

INDEXED

Dear Mr. Ng,

I have duly received your S/O letter No.396 of the 12th April:

Mr. Lau Kieng Hing requests appointment of his son Liu Chi Tuan as Clerk.

There are no vacancies for either Service or Local Clerks at present and no prospect of any for a considerable time. The usual channel is as you say through the Customs College.

Bank of China resumed business: Remittances.

Care must be taken during present disturbed conditions to retain only very small balances locally. If you remit all Service Account surplus balances to Shanghai and require to transfer a part back to Wenchow, you should

experience

Ng Chiu hung,

WENCHOW.

experience no difficulty in disposing locally of a Shanghai Tael cheque. All revenue collection, after the month's local commitments have been met, should be remitted promptly to I.G. Revenue Accounts at Shanghai. In the event of a shortage in Revenue collection in a subsequent month, you should be guided by the instructions of Circular No.3697.

Yours truly,

948

INSPECTORATE GENERAL OF CUSTOMS,

PEKING, 9th May, 1927

INDEXED

Dear Mr. Ng,

I have duly received your S/O letter No. 398 of the 20th April:

Assumption of Charge.

I am very glad to see that you are taking up your work in the right spirit. If all the members of the Service keep loyal to it and the objects for which it stands, then we can face the future withour fear.

Yours truly,

Ng Shiu hung,
WENCHOW.

INSPECTORATE GENERAL OF CUSTOMS, 459

PEKING, 11th May, 1927

Dear Mr. Ng,

I have duly received your S/O letter No. 399 of the 23rd April:

Superintendent's interference.

You are in a delicate and difficult situation; but you can always ward off any attempts of the Superintendent to get control, by telling him that no changes of any kind in present procedure can be made unless you have first obtained the approval of the Inspector General. This will throw the onus of the refusal on me.

Out-door Officers: Discretion ordered.

Quite right.

Yours truly,

[signature]

[illegible]g Shiu hung,
[illegible] WENCHOW.

CUSTOM HOUSE, 402

No. 404.

Wenchow 13th May 1927.

N.C. collections
I.G.'s
National Loans
Sinking Fund
Account.

Dear Mr. Edwardes,

The Superintendent has this day remitted to me the N.C. collections outside the 50-li radius for the months of January to March this year as claimed for by me amounting to $2,854.90 in all which sum I am remitting to your National Loans Sinking Fund Account today. It is gratifying to say that my claim has at last proved successful.

Revenue
Collection

The M.C. Collection for April has been very satisfactory amounting to Hk.Tls. 13,427.329 showing an excess of Hk.Tls. 3,133.416 over the figures for the same month last year. The collection for N.C. totals Hk.Tls. 5,652.495 showing a decrease of Hk.Tls. 852.993 as compared with the corresponding month in 1926. In view of the abnormal conditions prevailing everywhere one

EDWARDES, ESQUIRE,

etc. etc. etc.,

PEKING.

2.

one would be more than gratified that this N.C. figure might have been obtained. The M.C. trade still shows signs of progress and plenty of export cargoes are being shipped every trip by the 3 steamers viz. the Haean, Kwangchi and Yili which are now maintaining a regular Wenchow-Shanghai service without interruption. So far merchants have been satisfied with us and work has been going on smoothly thanks to the hearty co-operation of all the Staffs both Indoor and Outdoor.

h erected
R ky Point.

With reference to page 3 of Mr. Bernadsky's handing-over-charge Memo. to me enclosed in Wenchow Despatch No. 4033/I.G., also subject No. 3 in the Return of Non-urgent Correspondence for April, I have given the full particulars of this light to the Coast Inspector and asked his views as to whether a proclamation should be issued jointly by the Superintendent and myself regarding its establishment. His reply received on the 12th May advises me not to associate with the Superintendent regarding any notification pertaining to the light which is

3.

184

is a private one. He further suggests that the Superintendent may be informed that the Customs only issues notifications in respect to aids to navigation which are under their control and for which they are responsible. I therefore wrote to the Superintendent on the same day giving him this idea accordingly.

Mr. Henry Yao, 3rd Class (Chinese) Tidewaiter B, arrived by the "Kwangchi" on the 12th instant. The others have not turned up yet.

...nion in ...chw.

Both the local Kuomintang Executive Committee and the General Labour Union have undergone their re-organizations since the 6th instant when a new batch of members arrived from Hangchow to take over these managements. A notice was then put up by the Kuomintang to the effect that the previous Committee members consisted chiefly of Red elements who were responsible for the disorderly state of the city; that they were ordered by the Hangchow Committee to make a thorough re-organization of the local Executive branch; and

that

4.

125

that the former Committee were formally declared as being dissolved. The General Labour Union also issued 11 commandments for the strict observance of its members as follows.

1. Orders given and resolutions passed by the General Labour Union should be strictly observed.
2. Members should attend to meetings as appointed and pay fees as fixed.
3. Neither strike nor resumption of work is allowed unless by order of the General Labour Union.
4. No Union can be formed without permission from the General Labour Union.
5. Assault on civilians and inter-Union conflict are prohibited.
6. Smashing of shops or factories is prohibited.
7. Arrest and detention of people at will prohibited.
8. Pickets of each Union are directly under control of the General Labour Union without whose authority no Union can commission their own pickets for any business whatsoever.

whatsoever.

9. Owners of shops or factories are not to be worried with unreasonable demands nor can they be threatened at will.

10. Deceiving of members' fees is prohibited.

11. Any acts tending to ruin the reputation of the General Labour Union are prohibited.

Members in contravention of any one of these rules are subject to heavy disciplinary measures.

A procession consisting of about 2,000 persons paraded the streets on the 9th instant in memory of the 'National Disgrace Day'. The demonstration passed off quietly.

In spite of the notice put up by the Public Peace Bureau forbidding strike the local seamen are however contemplating a general walk-out but they are closely watched by the Bureau.

As a result of a telegram sent by the Medicine Guild to General Chang Kai-shek complaining of unreasonable demands being sent them by their employees the local Kuomintang Executive Committee received a telegram yesterday from

6.

from Hangchow instructing them to investigate into the circumstances leading to this complaint.

Yours truly,

INDEXED

INSPECTORATE GENERAL OF CUSTOMS, 457

PEKING, 14th May, 1927

Dear Mr. Ng,

I have duly received your S/O letter No. 400 of the 25th April:

Revenue and Service moneys.

I am glad to see you have appreciated the necessity for keeping your local balances as low as possible. Remit every cash of Surplus as it becomes available.

Yours truly,

Ng Shiu hung,
WENCHOW.

INSPECTORATE GENERAL OF CUSTOMS.

S/O

PEKING, 14th May, 1927

Dear Mr. Ng,

I have duly received your S/O letter No. 401 of the 28th April:

My telegram of the 27th April.

The missing words are "continue to remit as frequently as possible".

Agitation against Customs reviving.

I rely upon you to do all in your power to keep the Office running as best you can in the difficult circumstances you are faced with. Extra Staff is being sent you.

Yours truly,

Mr. Ng Shiu hung,
WENCHOW.

INSPECTORATE GENERAL OF CUSTOMS,

075

S/O

PEKING, 21st May, 1927

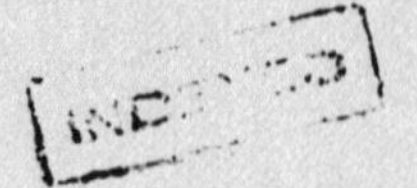

Dear Mr. Ng,

I have duly received your S/O letter No. 402 of the 2nd May:

Superintendent claims Customs Revenue.

Some Superintendents are, of course, more difficult to deal with than others, but the policy to follow is to keep relations on as friendly a basis as possible, to discuss with him fully either orally or in writing whatever Customs or Customs revenue matters he may bring up for discussion, but never to hand over to him the collection or control of the revenue, except when he actually resorts to the use of force. In the meantime everything possible will be done at this end to support you.

Yours truly,

[signature]

Mr. Ng Shiu hung,
WENCHOW.

CUSTOM HOUSE,

49

No. 405. Wenchow, 21st May 1927.

INDEXED

Dear Mr. Edwardes,

...e servants: ... instructs ... question ...ischarge or ...ntion to be ...d into.

I duly received your S/O. of the 5th May instructing me to consider carefully how many of the House Coolies, Gardeners, Gate-keepers, etc could be dispensed with without replacement. The question will be carefully looked into.

...es containing ...w phosphorus. ...Despatch No. ...104,761).

As this case has been outstanding for a long time (vide Wenchow S/O. Nos. 380 and 384 and your S/O. of 24th December 1926 and 18th February 1927) I wish to have your instructions as to how it is to be dealt with.

...oms Medical ...er.

Since the evacuation of the Foreign Staff on the 20th April this port has been without a Customs doctor. Dr. Stedeford on departure from here did not hand over the post to anybody. Luckily the Staff have been

L. F. EDWARDES, ESQUIRE,
Etc. etc. etc.
PEKING.

2.

1492

been all keeping on well during this period but as summer is now on the outbreak of cholera or other epidemic disease is at any time apprehended, particularly as the port of Shanghai is now crowded with so many people. Dr. Stedeford's assistant, Dr. Ch'ên Mei-hao (陳梅豪) of the Blyth Hospital is well known to be an able hand here and possesses an excellent diploma issued to him by Dr. Stedeford. He wishes to take on this post during Dr. Stedeford's absence. He is the only man in Wenchow that we can take on if Dr. Stedeford be not back soon. May I forward his application officially for this vacancy ?

f. The two clerks from Shanghai, Messrs. Shih Shih Han (施賓漢) and Hsei Hui (謝烽) arrived here on the 16th and Mr. Wong Tai-kwan (王秋奉), 3rd Class (Chinese) Tidewaiter A from Chinkiang came by the S.S. "Kwangchi" yesterday. The Staff is now nearly up to the requirements and all work is being taken on actively. I have put Mr. Ling Chan Ngau (林占鰲), 3rd Clerk B, in charge of the

3.

493

the Native Customs as he has got acquainted with the work there and proved that he can manage the business in a smooth way.

ation in
ıcw.

The local conditions have been improved somewhat though there are still lots of Communists in the City. They are however strictly watched.

On the 15th the pickets of the various Labour Unions were suddenly beseiged by the military and police who, after taking away all their uniforms and sticks, forced them to disperse. This raid carries a good effect on the business shops for, on the following day, a lot of the employees declared themselves to sever their connections with the different Unions through the local newspaper.

The Japanese destroyer standing by here left for good on the 14th and consequently there is no longer a foreign gunboat in this port.

Two French Fathers returned to this port on the 15th.

The Tea season is now in and lots of

4.

479

of tea go out per the C. M. S. N. steamers "HAEAN" and "KWANGCHI".

Last night the local military made a sudden raid on the Ou Hai Middle School (瓯海公学) now occupying the building of the United Methodist Mission College and arrested two students, from whom some documents relating to communistic propaganda were discovered.

Yours truly,

Ng Shin-huang

INSPECTORATE GENERAL OF CUSTOMS,

421

S/O

PEKING, 24th May, 1927

Dear Mr. Ng,

I have duly received your S/O letter No. 403 of the 6th May:

Change in attitude of Superintendent.

It is gratifying to hear that the necessity for the normal functioning has been recognised. I hope you will now be able to remit regularly without interruption.

Remittances to I.G. Revenue and Service Accounts.

It is more than ever necessary for you during the trying times we are passing through, to retain locally sufficient funds only to cover immediate needs.

Renewal of Uniforms.

Reduce your running expenses to a minimum, but where uniforms are due for re-newal and are also unserviceable you may arrange for re-newal for those for whom a uniform is essential.

Yours truly,

[signature]

Mr. Ng Shiu hung,
WENCHOW.

491

CUSTOM HOUSE,

No. 406. Wenchow, 26th May 1927.

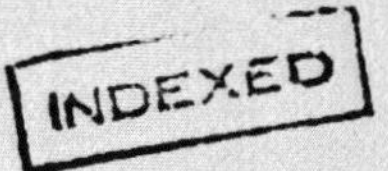

Dear Mr. Edwardes,

...intment and ...otion.

Many thanks for the appointment and promotion given me as conveyed in your despatches Nos. 1452/112,609 and 1453/112,640. Facing these hard times I have been doing my utmost to keep the office running on smooth lines with the hearty co-operation of the whole Staff and am happy to say that up to now nothing untoward has occurred and that both the Maritime Customs and Native Customs revenues are on the increase.

...e Report ...: mistakes ...ranslation.

I am really very sorry that such silly mistakes as were pointed out by the Chinese Secretary in his Memorandum of the 16th May should have been made by me. I cannot explain how they were made but only express my regret for these uncalled for blunders.

Situation

F. EDWARDES, ESQUIRE,

etc. etc. etc.,

P E K I N G.

2

497

Situation in Wenchow.

More than 500 soldiers belonging to the former Fukien Tuchün Chou Yin-jen (周荫人) are now occupying Pingyang (平阳). They are said to be on sound financial footing and best equipped with arms. Some of the local soldiers sent there to intercept them were wounded and some even turned to their side because the local men's pay has been several months in arrears. Reinforcements from Shanghai are said to have been applied for. In the meanwhile the City is under martial law, City Gates being closed at 8 p. m. and nobody allowed to be out after 10 p. m. In spite of this unpleasant news calmness still reigns the port.

Six French Sisters returned on the 22nd May per the S. S. "HAEAN".

Three students of the Ou Hai Middle School arrested on 20th May for possession of Communistic documents were shot on the 24th instant in the Compound of the Shih Chung (十中) School.

The S. S. "HAEAN" left on the 25th

May

3.

May with 200 newly-recruited soldiers for Shanghai.

The China Merchants Steam Navigation Company has fixed a schedule of sailings for their two steamers. Under this new arrangement there are two arrivals and two departures weekly, arrivals on Sundays and Thursdays and depatures on Wednesdays and Saturdays.

Yours truly,

CUSTOM HOUSE, 500

s/o

SHANGHAI, 27th May, 1927.

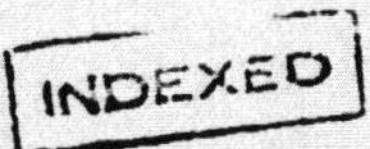

Dear Mr. Edwardes,

Proposal to recommend appointment of a temporary Medical Officer at Wenchow:

Mr. Ng Shiu-hung, the Chinese Assistant-in-charge of the Wenchow Customs, has just asked me to find out if Dr. Stedeford - the Customs Medical Officer who had been evacuated together with all of us - was coming back to Wenchow and if not, then he (Mr. Ng) was going to recommend the temporary appointment of a Chinese doctor to the Customs Staff. Dr. Stedeford stated that if the Customs Foreign Staff was going back he was also ready to return with them at any moment.

Application for leave:

A few days ago I sent my application for three months leave of absence and I should be much obliged if you could grant it to me. Certainly I am quite prepared to proceed at any moment to Wenchow or any other place if you wish to send me there, but if the Service requirements and the political situation permit, I am going to take my family to Harbin and keep them there for the time being.

Yours truly,

E. Bernard Ng.

H. F. Edwardes, Esquire,

P e k i n g.

No. 407.

INDEXED

CUSTOM HOUSE,
Wenchow 31st May 27.

Dear Mr. Edwardes,

...stration
...th May.

A very big programme was arranged for the day and even ricksha coolies were forced to suspend work for participation in the procession. Very exciting articles directing anti-British agitation were published in the two local newspapers. Handbills were sent to the Customs, inviting Customs employees to join the proceedings. The atmosphere being an unpleasant one, all the Staff applied to me for permission to give them half day's leave for staying away. In view of the situation I had no option but to grant them their leave and the Customs were therefore closed for the half day. Luckily the demonstration was dispersed by heavy rain and nothing untoward occurred.

...s of
...s employees
...al Court to
... witnesses
...um smuggling
...se

With reference to the seizure of native raw opium on the S. S. "FUCHUAN" mentioned in page 3 of my S/O. No. 403, the case

...F. EDWARDES, ESQUIRE,

ETC. ETC. ETC.

PEKING.

2.

507

case has led to some complications between the local Court and the Customs. The circumstances are as follows:-

On the 17th April acting on information a searching party boarded the S. S. "FUCHUAN" on her arrival from Amoy and discovered 25 packages of native raw opium weighing 25 catties. These were seized but the smuggler disappeared. It happened that a passenger on board had chatted with our watchers Lin T'ing-fang (林廷芳) and Kuan Pin-fu (管宾孚) among the searching party before the seizure was effected. According to these watchers this passenger was their personal friend. The compradore of the vessel, undoubtedly being involved in the smuggling of this drug, detained this passenger's luggage on the ground that he acted as informant to the Customs. He was so suspected because he had a conversation with the two watchers at the time.

Now this passenger brings the case to the local Court, accusing the compradore of seizing his luggage and mentioning the names of the two Customs employees as witnesses of

3.

508

of his being not an informant. The Court, without giving notice to me, sent two summons to these two men yesterday morning, demanding their presence in Court at 1 p. m. When the matter came to my knowledge I refused to let them go because the Court did not follow the proper formalities. It should notify the Superintendent first and must give ample allowance of time for the Customs employees to appear if they be allowed to do so.

At 2.30 p.m. however the Court addressed a letter to the "Wenchow Customs", requesting that these two men be instructed to present themselves at the Court at 1 p.m. This letter was sent to my house and, owing to the closing of the Customs at that time, I had no means to find the Staff and these two men. I however gave my card to the messenger of the Court and said that I would give a reply later on in the day. On finding our Writer I was going to reply that the case being not concerned with the Customs, the two employees could not act as witnesses, when the Court

4.

509

Court issued warrants for their arrests. It was then nearly dark and as nothing could be done at that time I allowed them to go to avoid complications, because the present claimed-to-be civilized men do not care much about proper formalities but had the law in their own hands.

This morning I put the case to the Superintendent, pointing out the improper procedure adopted by the Court and requesting him to notify the procurator that, in future, if any Customs employees be required by him, he must go through the proper channels.

It appears to me that the Court acted quite wrongly in the matter. Summons as witnesses must be sent to individuals several days beforehand but in this case only a few hours notice was given. Also I don't think it right that witnesses can be arrested if they were not permitted to go by their Chief. And the Court did not respect our administration and everything looks like child's play. I hope the Superintendent will put the matter straight as I have given him exalted words in the letter

Situation

5.

40

...tation in ...chow.

Regarding the Pingyang trouble mentioned in my last S/O. the S. S. "YUNGCHUAN" brought in 400 soldiers from Ningpo on the night of the 27th instant and left with them to Pingyang the following morning. The Fukien rowdies are said to have retreated to a mountain bordering Chekiang and Fukien where the reinforcements could have no way to pursue them. The trouble is that on the withdrawal of these reinforcements they will come out again. Martial law is still in force in the City but 12 midnight is now the limit for people going out.

The S. S. "YUNTA" (運大) plying between Wenchow and places at the month of the river was pirated and captured by pirates on the 24th instant. The amount of losses is said to be between $30,000 and $40,000. The whereabouts of this vessel are now unknown. The Superintendent has been approached to request the military authorities to trace the vessel and capture the pirates.

Yours truly,

Ng Shi-hung

CUSTOM HOUSE,

S/O No. 408.　　　　Wenchow　　1st　June　27　　51 42

INDEXED

Dear Mr. Edwardes,

Closing of Custom House for half day on 30th May to avoid complications with agitators.

With reference to my last S/O. reporting this matter I was surprised to read from the local newspaper 新瓯潮 this morning a notice said to be issued by the Wenchow Customs for the commemoration of this day. The cutting is herewith sent for your perusal. I am going to ask the paper to correct it.

In this connection I beg to assure you that the whole Wenchow Staff are loyal to the Service and have not the slightest idea of associating themselves with these senseless people in creating any of these ignorant acts. Their application for half day's leave was with the sole aim of avoiding complications and they did not participate in the procession yesterday. The notice was entirely manufactured by the reporter of this paper.

Yours truly,

Ng Shin Luang

A. H. F. EDWARDES, ESQUIRE,

Etc., Etc., Etc.,

PEKING.

513

CUTTING FROM LOCAL NEWSPAPER "SIN NGAU CHAO CO."

(新甌潮) DATED 1ST JUNE 1927.

甌海關、以前日係五卅紀念日、憤外人之慘殺工人、由該關同人公議封關、以誌不忘慘案紀念日、玆錄其佈告如下、今日爲五卅紀念、本關同人公議停止辦公半天以表哀忱、仰各商周知、特此佈告，云云

S/O No. 409.

INDEXED

CUSTOM HOUSE,
Wenchow 3rd June 27.

Dear Mr. Edwardes,

Closing of Custom House for half day on 30th May.

In continuation of my S/O. No. 408 I am glad to say that I have succeeded in asking the local newspaper 新甌潮, to have the notice corrected according to the exact wording. From the cutting herewith appended you will see that the Staff only announced that on the anniversary of the 30th May they unanimously passed a resolution to apply for half day's leave.

Remittances to Shanghai.

This time I remitted all the Account A moneys drawn from the Foreign Revenue to Shanghai for credit to the Wenchow Customs Official Account, so not a cash has been left in the local bank. In case of payment of salaries and other needs I decide to dispose of Shanghai Tael cheques to the Brokers, etc. and at the end of a month the available balance in this Account may be transferred to your Service Account direct. I hope this procedure

H. F. EDWARDES, ESQUIRE,
Etc., etc., etc.,
PEKING.

2.

41

procedure may meet with your approval.

As regards revenue moneys I am continuing to remit as frequently as possible whenever there are available sums in hand.

Situation in Wenchow.

The reinforcements from Ningpo sent to attack the Fukien disbanded troops in Pingyang were badly defeated and more than 200 were disarmed by the latter because of their pursuit after these guerillas in the mountain bordering Fukien and Chekiang. Many wounded were carried back yesterday.

The 10th Middle School was searched by armed police on the 30th May for Communists but the students escaped beforehand and none were arrested.

The policy of the Kuomintang now looks rather strange, On the one hand they denounce Communists but on the other ~~hand~~ they encourage anti-foreign agitation for, in these few days, placards with catch phrases "Down with British and Japanese Imperialism", "Down with all foreign Monarchism", etc. appear in all streets. The situation

does

3.

517

does not look quite clear yet.

The Superintendent left for Shanghai per the S. S. "Haean" yesterday.

Yours truly,

Ng Shin Kwang

4.

CUTTING FROM LOCAL NEWSPAPER "SIN NGAU CHAO CO." (新甌潮) DATED 3RD JUNE 1927.

▲更正　前日本報新聞欄內登載海關佈告一則中有若干字繆誤特此更正茲錄其原文如下以便改正「今日爲五卅紀念本關全人公議全體請假半天仰即知照此佈」

INSPECTORATE GENERAL OF CUSTOMS. 418

S/O PEKING, 6th June 1927

Dear Mr. Ng,

I have duly received your S/O letter No.404 of the 13th May:

Revenue Collection.

I am greatly pleased to hear of your increased revenue collection. Our revenue generally has fallen off so much that we shall need every possible cent in order to meet our obligations.

Yours truly,

Ng Shiu hung,

WENCHOW.

CUSTOM HOUSE,

S/O No. 410.

Wenchow 10th June 1927.

Dear Mr. Edwardes ,

venue Collection or May.

Both the Maritime and Native Customs collections for May have been very satisfactory , the figures being Hk.Tls. 13,455.346 and 7,080.515 respectively . The former exceed the last year's by Hk.Tls. 2,740.476 and the latter by Hk.Tls.714.431. Although it is due entirely to the brisk trade conditions which contribute to the swelling of the revenue the credit owed to the Staff in carrying out their duties efficiently towards protecting the revenue interests of the Service should however not be lost sight of.

uperintendent's ollections for .G.'s National oans Sinking und Account.

On the 8th instant I received from the Superintendent's office the collection for April amounting to $1,280.811 which sum I was immediately remitting to your

A. E. F. EDWARDES , ESQUIRE ,

Etc., etc., etc.,

P E K I N G .

2.

your National Loans Sinking Fund Account at Shanghai on the same day . It is gratifying to say that the Superintendent has now seen fit to comply with my wish as to remit his collections to me monthly .

Irregularities of local law court in summoning Customs employees as witnesses.

With reference to my S/O. No. 407 , the Superintendent has represented my complaint to the Court and requested the Law authoriiies to adopt proper formalities in future should Customs employees be required by them as witnesess.

Staff.

The strength of the Staff is now up to our requirements by the arrival of Mr. Yuen Zur Ling , 3rd Class (Chinese) Tidewaiter, A. on the 6th instant.

It has now shown that Mr. Lin Chan Ngau , 3rd Clerk, B., whom I have put in charge of the Native Customs , fits quite well the position. He appears to me to be a man full of common sense and quick wit and quite capable of handling the business there in a nice and smooth way . Mr. Lin also knows the M.C. General Office work quite thoroughly and Secretary's and

Accountant's

3.

Accountant's job too. He proves in every way to be a useful employee in the Service.

Mr. Sia Liang , 3rd Class (Chinese) Tidewaiter, A., who has been taking on the Tidesurveyor's and Harbour Master's job in addition to Tidewaiter's and Examiner's work since the evacuation of the Foreign Staff has given every satisfaction in the execution of his duties. Although he was at one time suspected of having directed agitation against the Foreign Staff here - I cannot say whether he really entertained that idea or not - I have however found him to be a very intelligent and hard-working officer and very subordinate too. At the time when our Staff was severely depleted he showed much ability in getting through all the difficult parts of the Outdoor work leaving no ground of complaints from merchants for delay, etc. May an allowance be given him for taking on these extra important responsibilities ?

Another man whom I wish to bring to your notice is N.C. Watcher Tung Hua (董華). He is the type of man quite distinct from that of the ordinary Watchers.

He

4.

He has been continually very well reported on by the former Tidesurveyors and Foreign Officers detached to the Native Customs and during my time in the N.C. I have found him to be really a very useful and capable man. As a test of his real ability Mr. Bernadsky appointed him a Head Watcher since January 1926 , whose duty it is to supervise all the other Watchers at the Head Office and stations. Again he has proved to be quite efficient in this job which was highly admired by Mr. Cross , the then Tidesurveyor here. It was Mr. Bernadsky's intention to submit a recommendation to you for the issue of a small monthly allowance to him as a reward for his useful services. Before his departure from port Mr. Bernadsky told me to take up this question officially if I so wished. I feel it glad to do so provided you have no objection in my so doing . Mr. Bernadsky and I were of the same opinion that in order to distinguish the Head Watcher from the ordinary Watchers an allowance of Hk.Tls.2.00 a month may be

issued

5

issued provided the man holding the position continues to give satisfaction in fulfilling this duty. Should however the man fail to discharge his duty satisfactorily later on another man may be selected to take up the job no matter what his seniority will be. This will give an encouragement to this class of men for a competition of their abilities and the Service will be benefitted by the result obtained in that the work being carried out in a more proper and efficient manner.

Situation in Wenchow.

On the 30th May the S.L. "Li Tai" plying between Wenchow and places at the mouth of the river was pirated by the same band that pirated and captured the S.L. "Yunta" as noted in my S/O. No. 407. The captured vessel was used this time to attack the "Li Tai". After looting money and valuables to the value of $30,000 or $40,000 both vessels were released. Nearly all the cash taken represented debts collected by the Wenchow shops from the villages on account of the Dragon Boat Festival.

More reinforcements were coming from

Ningpo

3.

525

Ch'ên-chi (林承基) was acting as an agent for the Japanese firm Suzuki & Co. (鈴木) to export charcoal from here to Japan. I told them that I had no knowledge of this man and that charcoal was exported direct by Japanese firms here and not through any agent. Fearing that they would involve the Customs into trouble, I told them that personally I quite sympathise with their patriotic movement but that they must realise that the Customs is working for the international interests and is standing neutral in all political movements and that it would be beyond my power to stop goods of any nationalities from coming in or native produce going out, unless China actually declares war against such nations. Therefore, I continued, that they will not burden the Customs with any sort of this business. They were satisfied with my words and went off happily.

General Labour Union request Customs co-operation in enrolling members for the Seamen's Union.

The General Labour Union addressed a letter to the Native Customs this morning, requesting that seamen on board junks be asked to join the Seamen's Union, and that, in case of failure to do so on the part of the

individual

4.

426

individual or on the high-handed action of junk owners, such junks be detained. This is a very silly letter and were the times normal it can be thrown into the waste paper basket. But, as the labourers are in power, to ignore them means to take in more trouble. Therefore I am sending a copy of this letter to the Superintendent, requesting him to reply that Customs only undertakes to collect duty and to prevent smuggling and that it is beyond its power to do anything outside the scope of this work. As I want to avoid direct correspondence with these people, I am, therefore, putting my answer through the Superintendent.

Situation in Wenchow.

Chuchow (處州) has been occupied by Chou Yin-jen's disbanded soldiers from Pingyang numbering now about a thousand and heavy re-inforcements are being sent from Ningpo and Shanghai to attack them. Yesterday the S. S. "Yung Chüan" conveyed 300 soldiers from Ningpo and the "Haean" 500 from Shanghai en-route to that place.

The S. S. "Yung Chüan" was pirated near Taichow by about 150 pirates on her recent trip inward.

5.

521

inward. Luckily the soldiers were on board and a sharp fighting took place, resulting in the sinking of 2 pirate boats, killing 40 pirates and capturing 4. The soldiers were 1 killed and 1 wounded. One of the "Yung Chuan's' crew was also hurt. The local authorities decide to mutilate the bodies of the 4 captured pirates alive to-day.

Yours truly,

Ng Shiu-keung

. 411.

INDEXED

CUSTOM HOUSE

Wenchow 13th June 27.

Dear Mr. Edwardes,

n
Parcels.

The question as mentioned in S/O. No. 346 now crops up again and this time it has been brought to me by the Postmaster here.

The Postmaster showed me a letter from the Hangchow Postal Commissioner, embodying copy of a letter from the Director of the Yang Kwang Chü (洋廣局) here to the Hangchow Financial Committee, suggesting that Likin on postal parcels might be collected by his men in the Post Office instead of through the Customs and that, if his suggestions be approved, an additional thousand dollars could be reaped annually. The Hangchow Financial Committee have instructed the Hangchow Postal Commissioner to adopt this new practice but he now asks the Postmaster here to consult with me first. I told him that, if the matter be put to me by the Superintendent, I will

. EDWARDES, ESQUIRE,

&c., Etc., Etc.,

PEKING.

2.

159

will refer the question to you officially as change of office practice cannot be made without your authority.

I believe the Likin Authorities here must want to see their aim achieved, so I write to enquire as to what attitude I should adopt when the question comes to me through the Superintendent.

Yours truly,

Ng Shin-kuan

INDEXED

S/O

INSPECTORATE GENERAL OF CUSTOMS,

41

PEKING, 17th June 1927

Dear Mr. Ng,

I have duly received your S/O letter No.407 of the 31st May:

Demonstration on 30th May.

Your action in closing the Custom House on the 30th May is approved. I am glad to hear that no untoward incident occurred.

Summons of Customs employees by Local Court and their subsequent arrest.

It would seem that the Court acted very arbitrarily in this matter. You did right in placing the case immediately before the Superintendent, and I hope that his intervention will have due effect.

Yours truly,

Ng Shiu hung,

WENCHOW.

INSPECTORATE GENERAL OF CUSTOMS, 44

S/O INDEXED PEKING, 17th June 1927

Dear Mr. Ng,

I have duly received your S/O letter No.408 of the 1st June:

Notice in Local Newspaper supposed to be issued by Wenchow Customs Staff. Paper to be asked to correct it.

It is wiser to ignore such obvious propaganda.

Yours truly,

[signature]

Ng Shiu hung,

WENCHOW.

INSPECTORATE GENERAL OF CUSTOMS, 549

S/O INDEXED PEKING, 17th June 1927

Dear Mr. Ng,

I have duly received your S/O letter No.409 of the 3rd June:

Statement supposed to have been issued by Staff corrected in local newspaper.

You are to be congratulated on having got this newspaper correction made.

Remittances to Shanghai.

I quite approve of what you have done in this connection. It is necessary to reduce our risks as much as possible.

Yours truly,

[signature]

Ng Shiu hung,

WENCHOW.

412.

INDEXED

CUSTOM HOUSE,
Wenchow 17th June 27.

Dear Mr. Edwardes,

lying

On the 13th instant lorcha "Chin Hsing Fa" applied for permission to ply between Wenchow and Ningpo viâ inland according to the rules laid down in I. G. Despatch No. 1410/109,203. This lorcha has been fitted with an oil motor and, as ruled in I.G. Circular No. 2767, No. 431, a sailing lorcha fitted with an oil motor cannot be treated to be a steam vessel, I take it to mean that she still maintains her status as a lorcha and I have granted her the permission accordingly. I may add that nearly all the lorchas now plying between Wenchow and Shanghai have been fitted with oil motors.

This is the first time that a lorcha takes the privilege granted in I. G. Despatch No. 1410/109,203. I have instructed the Native Customs office to keep a special record on the movements of this class of vessel so that

F. EDWARDES, ESQUIRE,
Etc., Etc.,
PEKING.

562

that a report on its working may be submitted to you in due course.

y Several of the fish shops in the North Gate have become insolvent and closed their doors. At first I feared that our fish revenue might suffer for our Native Customs rule is to collect fish duties from fish shops every ten days. Luckily these shops had no direct dealings with the Customs and we therefore suffer none. As a safeguard for the future I instructed Mr. Ling Chan Ngau, Clerk in charge of the Native Customs, to discuss with the leading fish merchants and request them to sign a mutual guarantee. The negotiations went on very satisfactorily. The merchants' idea is that, if the closing of any shops involves the loss of fish duties due to the Customs, this loss should be made good by the Fish Guild. This guarantee may be signed in a few days' time.

The Pingyang situation is now better but the reinforcements have no plan to sweep out all these disbanded lots. Although short of ammunition they are still financially sound and are hiding themselves in the mountain bordering

Fukien

3.

513

Fukien and Chekiang. Once the reinforcements go they will come out again.

An anti-Japanese demonstfation took place on the 15th instant coinciding with the Commemoration Day on the anniversary of the sufferings of Sun Yat-sen in Canton. All the students and labour unions took part.

As a consequence of an Act passed by the Chekiang Financial Committee for the inauguration of a Government Monopoly for the sale of Cigars and Cigarettes the local shops dealing with this trade are suspending their business as a protest against its operation. It is feared that their protest would be of no avail for the Chekiang Government is very resolute in carrying out this Act. It will cause many shops to shut and drive many men out of their livelihood. The Act provides that no shops can sell cigars and cigarettes for any of the Tobacco Companies but must get their supplies from the Government Monopoly. The local branches of the Tobacco Companies have to be closed once the Act comes into force.

Yours truly,

Ng Shi-hung

INSPECTORATE GENERAL OF CUSTOMS, 499

S/O

PEKING, 20th June 1927

Dear Mr. Ng,

I have duly received your S/O letter No.406 of the 26th May: Appointment and Promotion.

You have done very well since you took over charge, and I was very glad to recognise your good work.

Yours truly,

hiu hung,
ENCHOW.

S/O

INSPECTORATE GENERAL OF CUSTOMS, 301

PEKING, 20th June, 1927

INDEXED

Dear Mr. Bernadsky,

I have duly received your S/O letter of the 27th May:

Proposal to recommend appointment of a temporary Medical Officer at Wenchow.

No instructions have been sent concerning a successor as there is no one at Wenchow entitled to medical attendance. When Dr. Stedeford returns to Wenchow he can apply for re-appointment, until which time we had perhaps better leave the question of a Customs Doctor in abeyance.

Yours truly,

[signature]

M. Bernadsky, Esquire,

SHANGHAI.

576

Inspectorate General of Customs,

Peking, 20th June 1927.

Dear Mr. Ng,

During the past four or five months many queries have come forward from Ports in districts controlled by Nationalist Authorities as to what flag should be flown on Customs property. Seeing that the Service is essentially a non-political institution, existing solely to carry on its special work irrespective of what particular political tendency may distinguish the Government of the time, the answer to these queries has invariably been to give permission to fly the flag of the party in power when the Commissioner concerned is requested by that party to do so.

This has naturally raised the further question whether any distinctive emblem should be displayed on our floating property, the necessity for which is keenly felt in districts where the military have shown no scruple in commandeering launches at sight, but have, nevertheless, in some cases shown willingness to respect our rights when it was made clear that the vessel in question was genuinely Customs property and required for Customs work. The answer to this latter question is not the designing and exhibiting of a new Customs emblem - which, apart from the expense involved, might have to be discarded later on, and which would probably not be recognised by all parties, - but to continue using, whenever and wherever practicable, the Customs Jack which has been associated with the Service for the past sixty years.

The

hung,

OW.

597

The Customs Jack alone has not, however, proved sufficient, and I have, therefore, to request you to note that under present conditions Customs vessels are to fly the flag of the party in power, and in order that they may be readily distinguished from other Chinese ships they are, in addition to the ensign which has to be flown, to exhibit the Customs Jack from the "Jack Staff" forward, both when at anchor and under way. If necessary, an inscription may also be painted on the side in Chinese to the effect that the vessel is the property of the Chinese Maritime Customs.

When once more a Chinese national flag - national in the sense of being recognised as the flag of the whole country - comes into being, there will be no difficulty in embodying the Customs emblem on it, either as a square set in the upper inner corner, or as a circular disc in the fly.

Yours truly,

INDEXED

CUSTOM HOUSE,
Wenchow 23rd June 1927.

413.

Dear Mr. Edwardes,

[...]thorities [...]to seek [...]oms help [...]ovement [...]tion.

The Director of the Yang Kuang Chü (洋廣局) here has recently submitted a series of suggestions to the Hangchow Financial Committee for the improvement of his Likin collection, amongst which, the intended collection of likin on postal parcels by his own men in the Post Office as reported in my S/O. No. 411 is one. The other suggestions that have concern with the Customs are:-

(1) that all bills of lading covering import cargo should be sent him by the Customs, and

(2) that Likin Officers should be empowered to board steamers and lorchas for examination of cargo just as Customs Officers do.

The Hangchow Financial Committee have approved of all his suggestions and instructed the Superintendent

F. EDWARDES, ESQUIRE,
etc., etc., etc.,
PEKING.

2.

Superintendent to take up the matter with me. In the absence of the Superintendent who has gone to Nanking to attend the Financial Conference, Mr. Chang Kuei-jung (張桂榮), the Ko-chang in temporary charge of the office, came to see me on the 21st instant and asked my views in the matter. With regard to (1) I told him politely that the request can hardly be complied with as, once the merchants have gone through the proper Customs formalities, we have no right to detain their bills of lading. The Customs administration, I continued, is entirely separate from the Likin Collectorate and that, if they want the bills of lading, they can rightly ask for them from the merchants themselves after they have satisfied our side. As to (2) Mr. Chang concurred with me that this could not be done and said he was going to refute it emphatically. He told me that he would transmit the despatch to us and that on receipt of my reply he would answer the Hangchow Financial Committee in the way we talked of.

It was found out afterwards that the Director of

3.

567

of the Yang Kuang Chü went to see Mr. Chang and asked whether the instructions of the Hangchow Financial Committee could be carried out by us. Mr. Chang gave him a negative reply and at the same time explained to him plainly our Customs position. On hearing of this he asked Mr. Chang not to transmit the despatch to us but said he would propose other scheme instead, canceling those he had submitted to, and already approved of, by, Hangchow.

The question of collecting likin on postal parcels in the Post Office has not been put forward yet.

of
s as
s by
rt.

With reference to my S/O. Nos. 407 and 410, the Court again summons the two watchers as witnesses, their presence being required on Friday, the 24th instant. This time the Court gives three days notice to them but the summons were sent them direct. Neither has there been an official letter to the Superintendent nor to me to that effect. I have given permission to these watchers to go but I saw the Superintendent's Ko-chang yesterday, telling him that the Court took no regard of the

Superintendent's

4.

568

Superintendent's representations. Mr. Chang promised to write to them again but he did not think the Court would listen to anything on account of the authorities there being all young and inexperienced men, particularly as it is an independent organization.

I understand that the watchers are merely required to say that the complainant is not an informant in the opium case.

Really the informant's name is even not known by us. There has been no one claiming for, so far, the issue of seizure rewards in this case.

r boat with 7 lives.

At 9 o'clock yesterday morning a Nanch'i (楠溪) passenger boat, being unable to manage the strong tide, dashed to the bow of Junk "Yin Lung Shun" (尹隆顺) and capsized. The junk was prompt on the rescue of lives but 7 persons were drowned. The fault was wholly due to the passenger boat itself. The junk anchored in the right place which did not obstruct navigation. The Nanch'i Guild however insisted that it was due to the junk mooring in a wrong place that this accident occurred.

[
59

occurred. I have instructed the Senior Outdoor Officer to hold a formal enquiry into the case. The Nanch'i Guild has lodged a petition with the local Court.

The Wenchow Magistrate has again been changed. The new incumbent, Mr. YÜ Chao-hsiung (虞兆熊), assumed office yesterday.

The designation of the Police Department has again been changed from 公安局 to 警察局.

The Japanese destroyer "Tanikazi" came on a short visit on the 19th from Foochow and left for Amoy the next day.

Police launch "Haiping" (海平) arrived this morning after a sharp fighting with pirates at sea, resulting in the killing of 10 pirates and capturing the same number on board. Four junks have been taken back. The number of the pirates is said to be about 70.

Yours truly,

Ng Shin-kuang

(91)

CUSTOM HOUSE,

414. INDEXED Wenchow 29th June 27.

Dear Mr. Edwardes,

Collections of Loans Fund A/c. — The collection for May has been to hand today. It amounts to $2,323.016 which sum is being immediately remitted to your account per this day's mail.

Passenger ... seized: ... of Guild ... detention pending ... of Law Court. — With reference to page 4 of my S/O. No. 413 the chairman of the Nanch'i Guild, Mr. Yeh Shou-tung (葉壽桐), went to see Mr. Ling Chan Ngau, Clerk in charge of the Native Customs and insisted that the junk "Yin Lung Shun" (尹隆順) be detained until the case be settled by the law court. This man has been noted for his notoriety in Wenchow and was formerly a member of the District Assembly here.

As our enquiry shows that the junk anchored in the right place according to our Native Customs Regulations when the accident occurred, we really have no right to detain the junk. Yeh however claimed that in the

Ching

...WARDES, ESQUIRE,

..., etc., etc.,

...EKING.

572

Ching Dynasty the Local Authorities had issued a notification prohibiting junks from anchoring at that spot. We had nothing on record about this contention. In view, however, of the accident involving the loss of 5 (not 7) lives and of the case having been referred to the law court I put the matter to the Superintendent and asked his views whether the junk should be detained. His reply is to the effect that, as the case involves the loss of lives and as the matter is now in the hands of the law court, we should detain the junk's papers for the time being. I have deemed it advisable to refer this case to the Superintendent so as to make him responsible for the detention or otherwise of this junk to avoid arguments by all the parties concerned in this time of uncertainty. I hope my action may meet with your approval.

With reference to page 2 of my S/O. No. 412 the Fish Guild has signed a guarantee for all the fish shops to the effect that in case of the closing of any of the fish shops the Fish Guild will be responsible for making good any fish duties owed the Customs by the

insolvent

3.

insolvent shops. Our fish revenue is therefore adequately safeguarded.

Min

The Chinese gunboat Chao Wu (超武) arrived on the 24th June with the remains of the late Mr. Hsia Ch'ao (夏超), formerly Civil Governor of Chekiang. A big gathering of the local authorities and gentry paid their last respect to this deceased gentleman at the China Merchants Steam Navigation Company's office specially borrowed for the purpose and after the sacrificial ceremonies were over the coffin was removed to a small boat sailing at once to Tsingtien (青田), the deceased's native place.

The local Cigarette dealers are still opposing to the Act for the institution of a monopoly to sell cigars and cigarettes. Posters have been freely stuck in all the streets denouncing the Chekiang Government's policy as against the 3 People's Principles. According to their declaration this act would deprive altogether 20,000 persons from their livelihood in the Wenchow and Chuchow Districts. It is understood that representatives have been sent to Nanking to urge for the cancellation of

this

4.

574

this Act and the result is as yet unknown. Meanwhile all shops are suspending their business. In spite of this the local Government Monopoly announces that the Act will be operative from the 1st July.

Yours truly,

Ng Shin-Cheng

INSPECTORATE GENERAL OF CUSTOMS,

S/O

PEKING, 4th July 1927

INDEXED

Dear Mr. Ng,

I have duly received your S/O letter No.405 of the 21st May:

Matches containing Yellow Phosphorus.

The Ch'u has instructed that these matches must be re-exported to original place of shipment and it is for the Superintendant to move if he considers that these instructions should be altered.

Customs Medical Officer.

Dr. Stedeford must be held as having resigned from the date he left Wenchow. The question of a successor should be left in abeyance for the present.

Yours truly,

[signature]

[?]iu hung,

[WEN]CHOW.

10

INDEXED

INSPECTORATE GENERAL OF CUSTOMS,

PEKING, 4th July 1927

Dear Mr. Ng,

I have duly received your S/O letter No. 411 of the 15th June:

Likin on Postal Parcels.

You may hand over the collection of likin on postal parcels to the "Yang Kwang Chü" if the Superintendent requests you to do so in writing. When you do so, report officially for approval.

Yours truly,

578

CUSTOM HOUSE,

415. Wenchow 5th July 27.

INDEXED

Dear Mr. Edwardes,

I duly received your S/O. of the 20th June on Saturday regarding the kind of emblem to be displayed on our floating property. The instructions will be carried out. The Nationalist flag together with a Customs Jack hoisted on our gig, houseboat, and sampan will be quite sufficient for our purpose in this port.

These have been regularly inspected by the Senior Outdoor Officer and well protected. So far none of them have ever been occupied.

The month's collections for both the Maritime and Native Customs have, I am glad to say, again reached very satisfactory figures, amounting to Hk.Tls. 12,495.621 and Hk.Tls. 7,450.195 respectively. Comparing with the figures for the same month of last year an excess of Hk.Tls. 3,932.407 for the Maritime

Customs

[.] DWARDES, ESQUIRE,

Etc., Etc.,

PEKING.

2.

579

Customs and Hk.Tls. 961.991 for the Native Customs has been obtained. Altogether the Maritime Customs June Quarter's collections show the satisfactory increase of Hk.Tls. 9,806.299 and the Native Customs Hk.Tls. 823.429 over the figures for the corresponding quarter of last year. The unfailing efforts of the whole Staff towards protecting the Revenue interests of the Service have brought this gratifying result which I am very glad to bring to your notice.

Owing to bad crops the price of rice has been raised to unprecedented high figures in the district, in some places, Yuhuan (玉環) for instance, $1 can only get 5 or 6 catties. Big quantities of foreign rice have been imported by steamers during the recent trips with a view to relieving the situation. The Superintendent has requested me to pass 1,000 bags of rice for Yuhuan to ease the situation there and promised to send me a Provincial Government's Huchao later. I have instructed the Native Customs to pass them and keep a special record of the quantities shipped everyday. They are being shipped by the launches "Yun Ta" and

"Li

3.

580

"Li Tai" under the Native Customs Passenger Station's control.

The Court has at last been awakened to the fact that to ask for information through the Superintendent is better than to summon our watchers as witnesses too frequently for, on the 30th June, they addressed a letter to the Superintendent (copy will appear in the Non-urgent Correspondence for June) inquiring whether the opium was seized in the passengers' deck or from the Compradore's room. Although the Superintendent's letter to me was dated the 30th June it was not sent to me until late in the afternoon of the 1st July and I accordingly replied on the 2nd July that it was, according to the seizing officers' statement, seized in the passengers' deck but taken to the compradore's room for safe-keeping at the time when the officers had to search other parts of the ship but that a Watcher was specially put on watch there.

The complication between the compradore of the S.S. "Fuchuan" and the passenger has been due to old spite and this matter has only been taken as a basis for creating trouble, I am

4.

(81)

am informed. However the Superintendent's intervention in the irregularities already done by the Court regarding the summons and arrest of our employees has brought some better result.

The boycott on Japanese goods is now on full swing. Shops are warned not to take in any new goods in future and coolies are forbidden to carry Japanese goods from steamers. Charcoal merchants are warned not to sell any charcoal to the Japanese Companies and pickets are being sent to hills to watch if any woods are cut for sale to the Japanese. The Mitsui Bussan Kaisha have already suspended business since the outbreak of the financial crisis in Japan and all its Staff are sitting idle, the agent, Mr. Suzuki, having gone to Japan.

The Cigarette merchants being unable to resist the Monopoly Act have all opened their doors, the plea being to sell all the old cigarettes in stock and not take in new ones.

The S. S. "Yili" is going into dock in Shanghai and it would take her 70 days to resume the run.

Yours truly,

Ng Shi-heung

INSPECTORATE GENERAL OF CUSTOMS, 46

S/O PEKING, 6th July, 1927

Dear Mr. Ng,

I have duly received your S/O letter No. 410 of the 10th June:

Revenue Collection.

I am gratified to note these satisfactorily increased figures.

Remittance of Superintendent's Collection.

Yes; your representations have been very successful in this respect.

Mr. Sia Liang.

The question as to whether Mr. Sia should draw an allowance as senior Outdoor Officer will be decided later on.

N. C. Watcher Tung Hua.

There is no objection to your reporting all the circumstances officially,

but

Mr. Ng Shiu hung,

WENCHOW.

57

but an allowance such as you propose is exceptional, and no promise of its being granted can be held out.

Yours truly,

INSPECTORATE GENERAL OF CUSTOMS, 546

S/O

PEKING, 6th July, 1927

INDEXED

Dear Mr. Ng,

I have duly received your S/O letter No. 412 of the 17th June:

Bankruptcy of fish shops: Merchants to sign a mutual guarantee.

The idea of a mutual guarantee on the part of the fish merchants in order to protect revenue due is an excellent one.

Yours truly,

Mr. Ng Shiu hung,

WENCHOW.

583

CUSTOM HOUSE,

416. Wenchow 7th July 27.

INDEXED

19

Revenue: ...ted ...ring ...nking ...t.

Dear Mr. Edwardes,

Mr. Chang Kuei-jung (張桂榮), the Ko-chang in temporary charge of the Superintendent's office, whom I entertained to a dinner last night privately informed me that he received a circular despatch from the Finance Ministry of the Nationalist Government at Nanking instructing that all revenue collected by the Custom Houses under the jurisdiction of the Nationalist Government must be remitted *in toto* monthly to the Nanking Government acting on the resolution passed in the Financial Conference recently convened at Nanking. As he is not aware of the minutes of this Conference at which the Superintendent attended and as the expression 'Customs revenue' is rather vague he therefore does not transmit these instructions to me until the return of the Superintendent. He further told me that the Ministry also instructs

F. EDWARDES, ESQUIRE,

Etc., Etc.,

P E K I N G.

2.

582

instructs that from the month of June the remittance of the Native Customs collections outside the 50-li zone to the Commissioner is to cease and that these sums are to be directly remitted to the Nanking Government henceforth.

I believe this Circular must have been passed to all the ports in the sphere of the Nationalist Government and the Officers in charge must all have been approached by their Superintendents to that effect. I would request your instructions in the matter by telegraph.

Yours truly,

Ng Shi-heung

INSPECTORATE GENERAL OF CUSTOMS, 5?2

S/O INDEXED PEKING, 8th July, 1927.

Dear Mr. Ng,

I have duly received your S/O letter No. 413 of the 23rd June:

Likin Authorities seek Customs Help for Improvement of Collection.

Your replies to Mr. Chang regarding the proposals of the Yang Kuang Chü are quite in order.

Yours truly,

M. Ng Shiu hung,

WENCHOW.

CUSTOM HOUSE,

17. INDEXED (59)

Wenchow 11th July 1927.

Dear Mr. Edwardes,

Revenue: ...sed ...eding Nanking ...en.

As the Superintendent has not yet returned nothing further about this question has been heard by me. However I doubt very much about this step to be taken by the Nationalist Government, as, without the sanction of the Powers and yourself, I don't see how this can be done except that they actually resort to the use of force. I have written semi-officially to the Shanghai and Ningpo Commissioners, requesting them to inform me whether this information is true and whether they have been approached by their Superintendents on the subject.

...c ...te foreign ...ee ...ha ...tch No. ...5).

I feel it hard to offer any official opinion on the subject so I am sending you a Nil comment on this despatch. The situation here cannot be called bad but anti-foreign feeling especially anti-Japanese and anti-British is

F. EDWARDES, ESQUIRE,

Etc., Etc., Etc.,

P E K I N G.

592

is running very high. The Japanese are termed to be the tool of British Imperialism. Today those in the employ of the Japanese firms have been warned to be out. A big demonstration is being held this afternoon.

Many regulations have been formulated by the anti-Japanese Association amongst which the following are the important ones:-

(1) Merchants found to take in new stock of Japanese goods after to-day's meeting will be fined 10 times the value of the goods in addition to their entire confiscation.

(2) People found to be dealing with Japanese will be caged in a wooden case for exhibition to the public.

(3) Chinese employees of Japanese firms should walk out after to-day's meeting.

(4) No raw materials of any sort should be sold to the Japanese.

On the 7th instant 4 representatives of the anti-Japanese Association came to see me, handing me an official letter in which they asked me to ascertain whether a man named Lin

Ch'ên-

3.

immediately wired to you to this effect.

This morning the Ko-chang wrote me a very nasty letter telling me to remove all the books from the library for the Superintendent's men to come here. He claimed that the Customs is Chinese Government property and that the Superintendent is at liberty to use any room as he likes. In conclusion he gave me the hint that if I object the Superintendent will compulsorily occupy it. Having no backbone I cannot do anything but to wire to you for instructions. I may add that if you do not take any steps at your end to prevent this man's aggression on us he will soon trespass our authority and make us impossible to work here.

Abolition Likin and Autonomy.

From the Shanghai papers a notification announcing abolition of likin and tariff autonomy from 1st September next already appeared. According to this all goods must then be subject to the Nationalist Tariff. We will have no position once this comes into effect. I believe the Shanghai Commissioner must have written you the particulars. I beg to ask your instruction by

4.

594

by telegraph as to how our position will be should this illegal action of the Nationalists be not interfered with by the Powers.

stitch According to I.G. Circulars Nos. 3433 and 3454, it is clear that Native Customs duties are leviable on this kind of goods as the Circulars do not bear any Native Customs numbers. However sometime ago the 綺文女工社 here imported 39 dozen of cross-stitch napkins from Yotsing (樂清) and refused to pay duty on the plea that cross-stitch work is free from both Maritime Customs and Native Customs import and export duties. A dozen of these napkins have been detained by the Native Customs to cover the amount of duty that should be paid pending settlement of the question. I beg to ask your instructions as to whether Native Customs duties are chargeable.

tie in
ow. The anti-Japanese boycott is being carried on very rigorously, many goods having been confiscated by the anti-Japanese Association The owner of a reputable firm here has been put in the cage for one day for having attempted to export rape-seed to Japan via

Shanghai

5.

375

Shanghai. Our revenue has been seriously affected due to this effect because rape-seed and wood oil which are our main revenue producers are not allowed by the Anti-Japanese Association to go out from Wenchow.

The employees of the Japanese firms have not walked out and they have so far not been molested.

Yours truly,

Ng Shi-hung

CUSTOM HOUSE, 549

S/O. No. 418. Wenchow 15th July 1927.

INDEXED

Dear Mr. Edwardes,

Likin on Postal Parcels.

I duly received your S/O. of the 4th July, wholly wet with water, instructing me to hand over the collection to the Yang Kwang Chü if the Superintendent requests me to do so in writing. I will report officially when this is done. But I doubt whether the question will be taken up again as the Nationalist Government is now talking of abolition of Likin and increase of duty.

Customs Medical Officer.

You instructed that the question of appointment of a Customs doctor should be left in abeyance for the present. In case of enforcement of quarantine regulations we shall be without a medical officer. Cases of cholera already appeared in Shanghai and when this disease comes to an epidemic stage we have inevitably to declare Shanghai infected. On this point

A. H. F. EDWARDES, ESQUIRE,

Etc., Etc., Etc.,

P E K I N G.

2.

180

point I beg to apply for your instructions. Since my taking over charge a watcher has been sick for two days, otherwise all have been keeping well.

unk detained in connection with capsizing of a Passenger boat.

With reference to my S/O. No. 414, after investigation by the law court it has been found that the fault did not lie on the junk "Yin Lung Shun" (尹隆順) and the Superintendent has requested me to release the papers of the junk. The Nanch'i people, the most wicket lot in the Wenchow district, simply attempted to squeeze something out from the junk owners.

Situation in Wenchow.

A big anti-Japanese demonstration comprising of nearly 10,000 people paraded the streets on the afternoon of the 11th instant. The mob threw stones into certain Japanese shops on passing through. When passing the Custom House the mob shouted "Down with the Customs", "Down with the Compradores", etc. Luckily nothing untoward occurred.

The Chinese servants of the Japanese firms were warned to be out, but they took no notice. These servants are taking a very

strong

31

strong attitude and, in case they be forced to strike, they will probably join together and start a fight. There are two to three hundred people in the employ of the Japanese in the City including godown Coolies. If the authorities do not plan a way to stop the foreseen trouble the situation will be very serious.

The Head of the Police Department, Yeh Lin-shêng (葉林森), was suddenly arrested two days ago though on what purpose it is still unknown. This man has been responsible for restoring some order here and his reputation is not bad. His sudden arrest is a mystery to all.

On the 12th July ten soldiers stationed in the Wenchow City went across the river and committed a robbery in a village opposite here. They took about $500 away. The leader was, however, caught yesterday morning.

The four captured pirates from the S.S. "Yung Chüan" have not yet been dealt with.

In the Ou Hai Kung Pao (甌海公報) of today's date appears the news that the Customs is also in strong favour of the anti-

Japanese

4.

532

Japanese movement, and that any goods reported for shipment to Japan are being rejected, This is an obvious propaganda which I deem it advisable to ignore. Furthermore no Japanese steamers have come here for more than two months and therefore we never know what goods are destined for Japan as the destinations of all exports here are Shanghai and Amoy.

Yours truly,

Ng Shin Leung

575

INSPECTORATE GENERAL OF CUSTOMS,

S/O

INDEXED

PEKING, 15th July 1927

Dear Mr. Ng,

I have duly received your S/O letter No.414 of the 29th June:

Capsizing of Nanch'i Passenger Boat: Detention of Junk.

You acted quite rightly in making the Superintendent responsible for the detention of the junk.

Yours truly,

[signature]

...hi hung,

...WENCHOW.

INSPECTORATE GENERAL OF CUSTOMS, 532

S/O  PEKING, 19th July 1927

Dear Mr. Ng,

I have duly received your S/O letter No.415 of the 5th July:

Increase in Revenue Collection.

Well done !

Yours truly,

hiuhung,
WENHOW.

CUSTOM HOUSE,

S/O. No. 419. INDEXED Wenchow 20th July 1927.

Dear Mr. Edwardes,

Customs revenue: revival of attempt to interfere with by Superintendent.

The Superintendent returned on the 16th instant after having attended the Financial Conference in Nanking. Early on Monday morning, the 18th instant, he dropped me the letter about remittance of Customs revenue to Nanking. When I heard of his Ko-chang's intimation (vide my S/O. No. 416) I immediately wrote semi-officially to Messrs. Maze and Wilding, requestin information from their sources as I was afraid that the instructions of the Nanking Government were general. However Mr. Maze replied on the 13th July - letter received on the 17th - that he heard of no such intention from the Nanking Government, and, immediately after the despatch of my telegram to you, Mr. Wilding's letter dated the 15th July came to hand saying that he did not receive such a request from his Superintendent. It is therefore certain that the Superintendent here attempts to

A. H. F. EDWARDES, ESQUIRE,

Etc., Etc., Etc.,

PEKING.

2.

540

to trick me again.

I received your telegram in reply last night.

With regard to remittances of revenue to Shanghai I have been doing so very frequently and as regards Service Accounts moneys there is no A/c. A money kept in the local Bank save little amounts for Accounts C and D as, immediately after drawing the monthly allowance from the revenue, the whole sum is remitted to Shanghai for credit to the "Wenchow Tael A/c." and payments are made here by disposing of Shanghai Tael cheques (vide my S/O. No. 409 and your S/O. of the 17th June in reply).

I duly wrote to Mr. Maze telling him that you authorised me to request his assistance if the Superintendent continues to interfere with my remittances and requesting that if he receive a telegram from me at any time to this effect he will do what he can to assist me in warding against the Superintendent's interference.

I am again explaining the purpose of our

3.

509

our revenue to the Superintendent, as instructed, and I am still grasping the opportunity to claim the extra 50-li collections though I don't think this time he can comply with my request. Mr. Wilding told me he had not received these for sometime past and that protests were of no avail.

Yours truly,

Ng Shin-keung

INSPECTORATE GENERAL OF CUSTOMS, 528

S/O INDEXED PEKING, 26th July 1927

Dear Mr. Ng,

I have duly received your S/O letter No. 417 of 11th July:

Boycott of Japanese goods: reply to representatives of anti-Japanese Association.

Your answer was quite correct. The Service is essentially a non-political institution, and we must avoid being drawn into questions of this sort.

General Labour Union request Customs cooperation in enrolling members for Seamen's Union.

You acted wisely in sending your reply through the Superintendent, but I wonder if he passed it on!

Yours truly,

Mr. Ng Shiu Hung,

WENCHOW.

65

420.

CUSTOM HOUSE,

Wenchow 26th July 27.

INDEXED

Revenue:
d
ence
endent.

Dear Mr. Edwardes,

Nothing further has been heard from the Superintendent after my reply to him in the sense as instructed by your telegram of the 19th instant. Very probably he has transmitted my reply to the Nanking Government and if the latter has no intention to commandeer the revenue pledged for foreign loans and indemnities the question may drop altogether. However this Superintendent is more troublesome than many others for he was formerly the Chief of Staff of the late Chekiang Civil Governor Hsia Chao (夏超) and is now an adviser to General Chou Feng-Ch'i (周凤岐). His letters to me have always been in an instructive sense.

ist
nt's
to
ffective
August.

Early yesterday morning the Superintendent sent me a letter together with notices from the Finance Minister and a pamphlet

EDWARDES, ESQUIRE,
., Etc., Etc.,
PEKING.

2.

554

pamphlet containing articles termed as luxuries, requesting me to attend a meeting to be held today at his office at 8 a.m. to discuss how to collect the 2½ % tax on exports, 5 % on luxuries, 2½ % on transit and 50 % on tonnage dues. I replied that I have already received instructions not to involve myself in the collection of what has not been sanctioned by the Treaty Powers and that therefore I was sorry I could not attend. I also returned him the notices, etc.

In the afternoon he sent his Ko-chang to see me and asked me to give a room in the Maritime Customs for his Staff to collect the surtaxes. The Ko-chang stated that four men will be sent here and that no matter whether we shall give him a room or not these men must come. I then proposed that they may work in the Banker's office. He said that the room was too small but I pointed out that if a square desk be placed there 4 or 5 men could sit without congestion. He seemed to agree and left. After his departure I

immediately

6

Ningpo and Haimun for despatch to Pingyang to control the situation there. 400 came on the 5th and 200 arrived on the 6th, the last batch bringing a field gun with them. The Fukien disbanded lot are said to be already short of ammunition now and unable to resist long.

All the foreign property in this port is now free from occupation by students or labour unions. The notorious students of the Ou Hai Middle School who occupied the United Methodist Mission College and refused to move out in spite of repeated orders to do so by the Commissioner of Foreign Affairs were forced to quit the premises at the end of May by the military who arrested and shot one student on proof having been found to have been a communist.

On account of the news that the British and Japanese troops will concentrate at Tientsin and Shangtung and occupy certain railways thus checking the advance of the southern troops anti-foreign agitation is growing intense.

Yours truly,

Ng Shi-leang

597

CUSTOM HOUSE,

21. INDEXED Wenchow 29th July 27.

Dear Mr. Edwardes,

Since despatch of my urgent telegram to you on the matter and my reply to Ko-chang Chang that according to your instructions their men can only work in the Banker's office, no further development has occurred in these two days although it is uncertain what further aggressive measures they are still going to take. In the meantime I hope you have already taken some action in the matter.

According to yesterday's Shanghai papers the Nationalist Government only allows the Customs to collect 5 % import duties while export, coast, coast-trade, transit, and Native Customs duties will all be cancelled. If this decision be put into effect it will cause the Wenchow Customs to shut up altogether. Already the Native Customs merchants are holding up their goods and very probably little can be collected in August. Many other Customs

such

...WARDES, ESQUIRE,

... Etc., Etc.,

...EKING.

2.

578

such as Ningpo, Hangchow, Santuao, Foochow, etc. have to be automatically closed down due to this wonderful policy. I and all the Staff are anxious to know what our position will be when this act will be in operation without intervention. I shall be much obliged if you will send your instructions by telegraph

m r
i ustoms
ti n to
en

While one and all of the Wenchow Chinese Staff are aiming at the non-disruption of the Service and carrying out their duties whole-heartedly we are astonished to read a telegram from the Shanghai Chinese Customs Association to the Nanking Government, giving voice to the taking back of the Customs and Tariff Autonomy. The most objectionable words are that they are going to abide by the Superintendent's instructions. This has an adverse effect especially on me for I have been continually fighting against the Superintendent's encroachment on our rights. In case the Shanghai Commissioner has not forwarded you the paper I beg now to append the cutting for your perusal. We all object to the utmost the contents of this telegram.

In

3.

591

In case an evacuation is necessary I shall be much obliged if you will send me to a foreign port such as Dairen, Kowloon, Lappa, etc. as I have suffered enough from the Nationalists and a port with foreign protection may set my mind at ease. During my charge for over three months my health has already suffered much due to the strain of the situation and while exerting my duty I have offended this naughty Superintendant very much. Therefore I hope you will kindly give me some relief.

Yours truly,

Ng Shin Leung

4.

CUTTING OF SHANGHAI SHEN PAO (申報)

OF 23RD JULY 1927.

海關華員擁護關稅自主

海關華員聯合會昨致政府電云、南京國民政府財政部古總長錢次長鈞鑒、報載中央政治會議議決自九月一日起、實行裁撤粵桂閩浙蘇皖六省厘金、同日宣告關稅自主、所有裁撤國內通過稅條例國定關稅暫行條例、業由國民政府公布在案等因、伏讀之下、仰見我國民政府愛護關稅主權、注重國民經濟之至意、凡在國民、無不同聲感戴、竊查吾國自江寧條約締結以來、課稅自由之主權、全部斷送、自厘金創行以來、土貨流通之機會、酷受阻礙、國民外感列強經濟之侵略、內被猾吏秕政之摧殘、產業日衰、生計日蹙、及今不圖、破產立待、幸政府當局毅然決然、宣布關稅自主、廢除厘金惡制、民困既蘇、國庫自裕、當今凡百設施、無有更重要於此者、同人等供職海關、感受痛苦最深、爰於今春聯合全體華員、努力於關稅解放之研究、以恢復關稅自主權、收回海關管理權及實施貫澈民生主義、關稅政策爲目標、近復組織稅權討論會、討論恢復稅權之切實辦法、方冀建設政府、藉供采納、而政府適斷然宣布關稅自主、同人等渴望此舉、如大旱之望雲霓、既經政府宣告在前、益當振刷精神、竭誠奉行於後、倘有藉口條約、甘心破壞行政權完整之原則、希圖私用任何組織以反抗者、同人等當一致奮鬥、爲國民經濟後盾、決不使全國國民淪於經濟被榨取之奴隸階級也、至於厲行國定稅則之切實辦法、除隨時秉承江海關監督奉行外、擬再選派代表晉謁台端、面領訓誨、俾策進行、是否有當、希賜裁奪爲幸、上海海關華員聯合會叩、

CUSTOM HOUSE,
Wenchow 1st August 27.

Dear Mr. Edwardes,

s office
i by
tendent's
collection
axes.

I am glad to say that the men sent by the Superintendent for collection of surtaxes have at last contended to occupy our banker's office instead of the Library which the Superintendent threatened to take the other day. I am telling the Staff to be friendly to them and if they want to know something better explain to them provided the information given is not forbidden by our Service. It is my desire to carry on as smoothly as possible within the month and as regards how we should do in September I am anxiously awaiting your instructions. From the appended cutting of the Shanghai Shen Pao of the 28th July you will see from (2) that the intra and extra 50-li Native Customs duties are to be abolished and from (3) that the Maritime Customs are to abolish (a) Transit dues, (b) Coast-trade

duties

F. EDWARDES, ESQUIRE,
Etc., Etc., Etc.,
PEKING.

608

duties, (c) export duties from one Treaty port to another, etc. The notification concludes that if any one who on whatever pretext shall collect such dues and duties as stipulated in (2) and (3) on 1st September shall, after summary jurisdiction, be sentenced to imprisonment for various terms in addition to a fine not exceeding $10,000. This really means that if we collect dues and duties on the strength of Treaties on the 1st September we shall be liable to such penalty.

Customs
nd duties:
tion of, by
ntendent.

On the 30th July the Superintendent's Ko-chang went to the Native Customs and told the Clerk-in-charge that the Superintendent received telegraphic instructions from the Ts'ai-cheng Pu to collect Native Customs dues and duties as well on 1st August. He asked for two rooms for his Staff and the Native Customs Weiyüan, who has always been a bad chap and whose retention in the Native Customs does more harm than good to us, lost no time to show the Ko-chang the rooms without the permission of the Clerk-in-charge. The Ko-chang then told Mr. Ling that he shall take the

two

two selected rooms, seizure room and the one opposite the Watcher's room. On being asked whether he has obtained the Commissioner's promise the Ko-chang said that it was not necessary. As this appears to me to be a high-handed policy which might have been pre-arranged in the Financial Conference, protest would be of no avail and I therefore sent an urgent telegram to you to this effect. As they are going to collect the same dues and duties as we do both in Wenchow City and at the out-stations, and as they occupy the same buildings much agitation might be expected from the merchants. However I told Ling to carry on with his wit and do all he can to push things smoothly for the month. This morning the Superintendent sent six men (3 Indoor and 3 outdoor) to the Native Customs Head Office and 3 men to the North Gate Station. Men will be sent to Puchow, Chuangyüanchiao and Ningtsun too. These men will all occupy our station houses. There are then two Native Custom Houses functioning in the same buildings and collecting the same duties and dues. I

wonder

4.

610

wonder if this state of affairs occurs in other ports. It is absolutely beyond my power to check the Superintendent's action.

From the time of my assuming charge I have been always trying to maintain friendly relations with the Superintendent and that was shown by my entertaining his Ko-chang Chang Kuei-jung, who really is the man responsible for all these deeds, to a dinner as reported in my S/O. No. 416. As things have now come to this stage to protest means to invoke more ill-feeling unless there must be some strong backing behind. In the meantime I intend to take no notice of these irregular doings, which are likely to develope further as time goes on.

Yours truly,

Ng Shin-liung

P.S. I just learn that our Native Customs Weiyüan Wu Chi-tse (吴繼澤) has been appointed by the Superintendent as Chief Supervisor (總稽查) in addition to his Weiyüan's duties. He therefore takes charge of the extra Native Customs duties now collected. NJ

5.

CUTTING OF SHANGHAI SHEN PAO（申報）
OF THE 28TH JULY 1927.

◉財部通令裁撤國內通過稅

▲九月一日起實行 ▲落地稅一併裁撤

國民政府財政部、爲裁撤國內通過稅、特於二十五日、通令所屬各機關、於九月一日實行、幷附發條列一份、茲錄條例如下、（令文已見二十五日本報）「裁撤國內通過稅條例」、第一條、國民政府爲減除民困、整理稅制起見、所有國內通過稅、無論中央收入、或地方收入、悉行裁撤、第二條、內地應行裁撤各項通過稅如左、㈠厘金、㈡商埠五十里內外常關稅、及其他內地常關稅、但陸地邊境常關所徵國境進出口稅、不在此列、第三條、海關應行裁撤各項通過稅如左、㈠子口稅、㈡復進口稅、㈢由此口到彼口之出口稅、第四條、落地稅應與通過稅一併裁撤、第五條、陸路邊境、常關徵收國境進出口稅者、改稱陸關、其徵收稅按照國定進口關稅暫行條例及現行出口稅則辦理、第六條、沿海常關徵收國境進出口稅者、由財政部分別歸併海關、或令海關改設子卡、第七條、自本條例施行日起、如有假藉名義、仍有徵收第二條第三條及第四條所指各稅者、查出審訊屬實後、除將所收稅金追繳交返本人外、幷處以一等至三等有期徒刑、仍得科以一萬元以下之罰金、第八條、軍人犯前條之罪者、由該管軍事機關審訊處罰之、第九條、本條例於民國十六年九月一日施行、

621

S/O. 423 ~~414~~.

INDEXED

CUSTOM HOUSE,
Wenchow 5th August 27.

Superintendent's interference outdoor officers' duties.

Dear Mr. Edwardes,

The men sent by the Superintendent for collection of surtaxes at the Maritime Customs are empowered by the Superintendent to board steamers and interfere with our outdoor officers work. Yesterday when the "Kwangchi" arrived our officers already collected duties on certain articles taken by passengers but the Superintendent's men seized some iron beds, etc. and reported to the Superintendent that our officers released them without charging duty. There were also 50 packages fruits which should pay duty at the General Office after release and note by our officers and these men also accused our officers as freeing them. The Superintendent wrote me a nasty letter this afternoon saying that he has right of supervision of our work and asking me to explain why the stuffs were free from duty. I have given full explanations to him. He is

F. EDWARDES, ESQUIRE,
Etc., Etc., Etc.,
PEKING.

623 2.

is now claiming supreme power over us.

In the Native Customs the Weiyüan and the whole Superintendent's collecting staff are boarding steamers and junks and re-examining any cargo which has been examined by our officers. One man also sleeps in the Native Customs at night.

He has now trespassed all our rights but it is absolutely beyond my power to check him. The Shanghai Commissioner has been informed of this and though the Nanking Government may promise him anything it is doubtful whether instructions would be sent out to him. In my opinion the Nanking Government will only be too glad to see him grasping our power gradually.

stitch With reference to my S/O. No. 420, page 4 the merchant Huang Chi-wen (黄起文), the most troublesome chap in Wenchow and a relative of the present Superintendent, accused our Examiner of the Passenger Station as detaining his napkins on account of his failure to get a squeeze from him. He also petitioned to the Superintendent that a squeeze of $2

was

622

3.

was paid last year to the same Station. The Superintendent has asked me to investigate the case. It is really the trick of the Superintendent to spoil our reputation in order that he may have the chance of sending men to supervise our work.

Referring to his alleged payment of $ 2 squeeze to the Passenger Station last year this was really the duty due. I specially took this man to see Mr. Bernadsky at that time and shew him the Circular instructions that Native Customs duty was not exempted.

This time when the napkins were seized he was asked to pay a deposit of duty pending settlement of the case by you. The man however openly cursed the Clerk-in-charge, and denounced our policy.

It shows that the Superintendent is a very simple headed man knowing nothing at all but a trouble-maker.

o and Bureaux.

The Ts'ai-cheng Pu has instructed that the deputies of these Bureaux be stationed at the Bank in the Customs to collect cigarette, wine, alcohol, fire-cracker and aerated water surtaxes.

4.

624

surtaxes. The Customs will soon be filled up with these tax collectors. I am at a loss of whaf to do.

Yours truly,

[signature]

542

INSPECTORATE GENERAL OF CUSTOMS,

S/O

PEKING, 8th August, 1927

INDEXED

Dear Mr. Ng,

I have duly received your S/O letter No. 419 of the 20th July;

Revival of attempt by Superintendent to interfere with Customs Revenue.

It looks as if the Superintendent had misinterpreted his instructions deliberately. Stick to your guns and resist interference. If force is used, protest in writing.

Yours truly,

Mr. Ng Shiu hung,

WENCHOW.

596

INSPECTORATE GENERAL OF CUSTOMS,

/0 PEKING, 9th August, 1927

Dear Mr. Ng,

I have duly received your S/O letter No. 420 of the 26th July:

Superintendent threatens to seize Customs Library.

I have instructed the Shanghai Commissioner to intervene on your behalf, and I hope his representations will succeed.

Abolition of Likin and Tariff Autonomy.

I cannot give you any instructions for the present. Carry on as usual until further notice.

Cross-stitch work: is N.C. duty leviable?

Native Customs duty is leviable.

Yours truly,

Mr. Ng Shiu hung,
WENCHOW.

CUSTOM HOUSE,

424
~~415.~~

INDEXED

Wenchow 9th August 1927.

629

Dear Mr. Edwardes,

ated big
ation.

A demonstration on a very big scale is being arranged, urging the retrocession of the Customs to the Chinese. The situation can be imagined to be very serious then. I will close the Customs on that day to avoid trouble.

Autonomy.

All of us are perplexed over the question and over our future. We also entertain the apprehension that the Service may be disrupted therby. However I think the Powers may not abandon their rights so easily, but it now looks as if the Powers are allowing this scheme to come into force without intervention.

tion of
s premises
erintendent's

The Superintendent's men continue to occupy the two rooms in the Native Customs Head Office and North Gate Station to collect surtaxes. Men have also been sent to Puchow,

Chuangyuanchiao

F. EDWARDES, ESQUIRE,

Etc., Etc., Etc.,

PEKING.

2.

130

Chuangyüanchiao and Ningtsun too. They are still searching steamers and junks.

Customs
)-li
ions.

In accordance with the instructions contained in your despatch No. 1460/113,497, I have written to the Superintendent requesting him to continue to remit these collections to me.

Our Native Customs No. 2 T'ingch'ai Ch'ên Shêng died of cholera yesterday. In accordance with the instructions of your telegram of the 3rd May I am not replacing him for the time being.

ion in
y.

It is rumoured that the Communists have reached Chin Hua (金華), Martial law is being proclaimed here

General Chou Feng-ch'i (周鳳岐) is said to have the desire of proclaiming Chekiang independent. Situation is very complicated now.

It is estimated that the abolition of likin will throw more than 10,000 people in Chekiang alone out of employment.

Yours truly,

Ng Shi-tung

P. S.

INSPECTORATE GENERAL OF CUSTOMS, 601

S/O

PEKING, 11th August 1927

INDEXED

Dear Mr. Ng,

I have duly received your S/O letter No. 421 of 29th July:

Threatened compulsory occupation of Customs Library by Superintendent.

Keep in touch with the Shanghai Commissioner, whom I have instructed to intervene on your behalf.

Tariff Autonomy.

I cannot give instructions for the present. Meanwhile, carry on as usual.

Telegram from Shanghai Customs Association to Nanking Government.

All through China's troubles, the Service operates for China's good. Be assured that in remaining loyal to it, you and your staff have done your duty towards your country.

Yours truly,

Shu-hung,

WENCHOW.

INSPECTORATE GENERAL OF CUSTOMS, 112

/0 PEKING, 15th August, 1927.

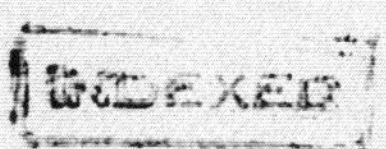

Dear Mr. Ng,

I have duly received your S/O letter No. 422(?) of the 1st August:

Nanking Government and Tariff Autonomy: Commissioner requests instructions.

I am sorry I cannot give you instructions for the present, but must wait for the situation to develop further.

Yours truly,

Mr. Ng Shiu hung,

WENCHOW.

632

CUSTOM HOUSE,

425. Wenchow 15th August 1927

Dear Mr. Edwardes,

lon. The Japanese boycott has adversely affected our Maritime Customs revenue for July which was however less than last year's by Hk.Tls. 64.577 only. The export of rape seed and wood oil has been held up by the Anti-Japanese Association and this action alone has deprived from us much receipts. The Native Customs revenue for July however shows a gain of Hk.Tls. 1.073.677 over the last year's figures.

The Tariff Autonomy agitation together with the collection of surtaxes in this month is much perplexing the merchants who deem it advisable to withhold their goods pending the announcement of a definite policy. Revenue, both Maritime Customs and Native Customs, is exceptionally poor now. Up to this date the Maritime Customs collects not more than Hk.Tls. 2,500

F. EDWARDES, ESQUIRE,

Etc., Etc., Etc.,

P E K I N G.

2.

683

trative
lars
d by
tendent
w despatch
5).

2,500 while the Native Customs only gets Hk.Tls. 700 odd. However I hope to be able to get sufficient funds for our office and Superintendent's allowances without applying to you for revenue grants.

As no reply has been received to my telegram of the 12th instant I believe that you must have been fully occupied with more important matters than this. On receipt of the Shanghai Commissioner's reply yesterday that he has not been requested by his Superintendent to furnish these particulars, I am now telling the Superintendent that these particulars being wanted by the Nanking Government from his offices only, I regret that I cannot give him such details as have not been asked for from the Shanghai and Ningpo Commissioners. I am sorry that I have unduly worried you with such an unimportant matter.

s Medical
r.

In accordance with the instructions of your S/O. letter dated 2nd August I am forwarding Dr. Ch'ên Mei-hao's application to you officially with recommendations as outlined in your letter.

Telegram

3.

64

n by
i Customs
tion to
Government
ing Tariff
y.

I again read a telegram to the Nanking Government by the Shanghai Customs Association from the Shanghai Shun Pao (申報) of the 11th instant. It says inter-alia that the Staff are prepared to forfeit all their privileges in the Customs to support the Nanking Government in this action. I wonder whether this is the unanimous desire of the Shanghai Staff. I learn the Chairman of this Association is only a Chinese Tidewaiter of one year's service. This man must be a strong agitator backed up by the Kuomintang to suppress the rest of the Staff in the Customs.

The Staff here has nothing to do with this Association. Further the Union here has been voluntarily dissolved.

ion in
y.

The news that the Northern troops have arrived within 60 miles of Nanking is circulated here. A Nanking official with his family arriving by the "Haean" yesterday stated to someone that Nanking cannot stand any longer.

It

4.

625

It is also rumoured here that the Railway communication between Shanghai and Hangchow has been interrupted.

The Kuomintang are busily engaged in their propaganda regarding Tariff Autonomy and Abrogation of Unequal Treaties. Blue cloths with catch-phrases written with nitric acid are hung in all streets. A curious order has been issued by the Kuomintang directing that bills, envelopes, invitation cards, etc. must be printed with catch-phrases adopted by them. Special men will be sent to the Post Office to stamp catch-phrases on letters which do not bear same.

Yours truly,

Ng Shiu Lung

CUSTOM HOUSE,

631

426.

[INDEXED]

Wenchow 16th August 1927.

Dear Mr. Edwardes,

:rative
.ars
l by
tendent.

Your telegram of the 15th instant in reply to mine of the 12th reached me late yesterday afternoon and by that time my letter had already gone out. If the Superintendent would not raise the question any more I would leave the matter alone.

Autonomy.

It now looks as if the Superintendent himself is anxious over this question. His Ko-chang came to me this morning and asked me if I got any definite instructions from you. He said the Nationalist Government already sent the Superintendent many notifications for posting but he suggests not to put them up until the 31st August if the situation will remain unchanged. He persuaded me to ask your instructions by telegraph. It therefore sounds as if the Superintendent also wishes to have foreign intervention in the matter.

If

F. EDWARDES, ESQUIRE,

Etc., Etc., Etc.,

P E K I N G.

2.

If the scheme be in force the Superintendent would have no receipts at all. This causes his anxiety.

I understand the Likin Offices have received instructions from the Chekiang Ts'ai-chêng T'ing directing the people there to carry on.

Yours truly,

Ng Shin-hang

125

INSPECTORATE GENERAL OF CUSTOMS,

S/O

PEKING, 17th August 1927

Dear Mr. Ng,

Your S/O letters of the 1st and 5th August have been wrongly numbered 413 and 414. Will you please change the numbers of these letters to 422 and 423 respectively.

Yours truly,

Stanley F. Wright

...iu hung,

...NCHOW.

INSPECTORATE GENERAL OF CUSTOMS, 626

PEKING, 19th August, 1927

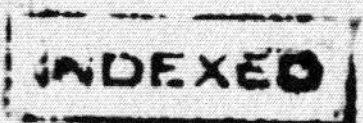

Dear Mr. Ng,

I have duly received your S/O letter No. 423(?) of the 5th August: Superintendent's interference with Outdoor Officers.

I hope that the steps which have been taken through the Shanghai Commissioner to restrain the encroaching activity of the Superintendent will prove effective. The downfall of the Nanking Government ought also to help you.

Yours truly,

[signature]

Ng Shiu hung,

WENCHOW.

CUSTOM HOUSE,

643

N. 427. Wenchow 23rd August 1927.

INDEXED

Dear Mr. Edwardes,

N. Autonomy.

The Superintendent already caused the notifications posted in front of both the Maritime and Native Custom Houses informing the public of the operation of this scheme from the 1st September next last Friday, the 19th instant. This was done contrary to what his Ko-chang informed me as reported in my S/O. No. 426. The Kuomintang also have decided to hold a mass meeting on the 1st September to celebrate the occasion.

However in view of the fall of General Chiang Kai-shek and the alleged capture of Nanking by General Sun Chuan-fang, things may undergo a complete change and this question may drop automatically.

From the Hangchow Commissioner's comments dated the 17th August on Shanghai despatch No. 21,447 I gather that up to that date

Mr. EDWARDES, ESQUIRE,

Etc., Etc., Etc.,

PEKING.

2.

604

date his Superintendent has not yet officially notified him of the enforcement of the scheme. Very probably Hangchow may take no regard of the Nanking Government's instructions. The Superintendent here is a blockhead who never seeks advice from his colleagues in Ningpo and Hangchow and does all things at his own will. I hope he will quit the post if the Northern power extends to this province. He was the man who stirred up the late Civil Governor Hsia Ch'ao to rebel against General Sun Chuan-fang.

[illegible]itch With reference to my S/O. No. 423, on behalf of his relative the Superintendent has written me several letters claiming that the napkins should be free from Native Customs duty, supporting also the accusation against our Examiner Ch'ên K'o-p'in (陳可品) for detaining these napkins on account of failure to obtain a squeeze. To all these letters I have given my strong arguments. Finally he had nothing to say but demanded me to return the napkins to his relative at once on the ground that the Shui-wu Ch'u's

instructions

3.

648

instructions were very explicit that cross-stitch work is exempt from all kinds of duties. Your S/O. of the 11th August was then to hand and I replied that I already referred the question to you and that you ruled that Native Customs duties on this article are leviable. Copies of the correspondence will be incorporated with the Non-urgent Chinese Correspondence for this month. I shall watch with interest what more he will have to say.

...s ...ed by ...tendent.

A very wonderful policy has been adopted by the Superintendent in collecting the Native Customs surtaxes. No surtaxes are collected in his extra 50-li stations. The aim is therefore to turn our trade to his end. If the surtaxes were to continue next month I shall query him officially on the subject. No documents are issued to goods shipped from Wenchow to his stations such as Yotsing, Pingyang, etc., the junk people being only given slips of papers chopped by the Superintendent's men for surrender to those stations. Therefore the Superintendent is

pocketing

4.

pocketing the sums thus collected with his Staff.

…rative …ars. The question has not been further raised by the Superintendent since I replied him on the 15th as reported in my S/O. No. 426.

…-li …ons. In reply to my letter conveying your instructions that these collections being pledged for the 5th and 7th year domestic loans should continue to be remitted to me, the Superintendent says that his office being under the control of the Nationalist Government the collections must, according to its instructions, be remitted to Nanking and that he regrets he cannot remit these sums to me as requested. A further letter was written him requesting him to ask the Nanking Government not to appropriate these moneys already ear-marked for loan service. He then sent his Ko-chang round to inform me verbally that I cannot expect to get these collections from him as the June and July collections have already been remitted to Nanking. When the situation clears up I will forward him further claims. In the meantime

5.

meantime I shall keep silent.

Weather has been very unpleasant and cholera has already made its appearance in the City.

40 retreating soldiers (Wenchow recruits) from Nanking returned here by the S. S. "Haean" yesterday. They had to be carried gratis by this vessel as they were stripped of everything.

A telegram from Hangchow was received by the Likin office directing that collection of Likin is to continue on the 1st September.

Yours truly.

Ng Shin Leung

INSPECTORATE GENERAL OF CUSTOMS, 631

S/O

PEKING, 25th August 1927

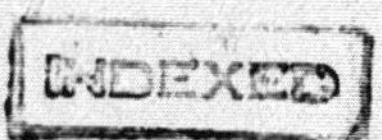

Dear Mr. Ng,

I have duly received your S/O letter No.424 of the 9th August:

Staff worried over situation owing to proposed tariff changes.

Although the future is far from clear, nothing is to be gained from giving way to pessimism. The Service has come through many crises, and I believe that we shall emerge safely from this one.

Tariff Autonomy: (Post-script to letter):

Thanks for this bit of information, which I have quoted verbatim to the Legations. At present it seems very likely that the introduction of Tariff Autonomy will have to be postponed.

Yours truly,

..iu hung,
WENCHOW.

(49)

CUSTOM HOUSE,

[INDEXED]

428.

Wenchow, 27th August 1927.

Dear Mr. Edwardes,

...utonomy.

I received a telegram from the Shanghai Commissioner on the 25th informing me that the Nanking Government has ruled that Native Customs within 50-li limit and 2½ % surtax offices will continue to function without change. The Superintendent has also received telegraphic instructions from Hangchow to postpone the scheme. We can therefore carry on as usual after worrying over the matter for a month or so. But the Superintendent has so far not issued fresh notifications regarding the postponement of the scheme yet.

...iture P... ...to ...: is ...iable ?

With reference to my despatch No. 4044, the Asiatic Petroleum Company is removing the furniture from the leased house and shipping it to Shanghai per the motor vessel "Hai

... EDWARDES, ESQUIRE,

...c., Etc., Etc.,

P E K I N G.

649.1

2.

"Hai Kwang". In the absence of any instructions as to whether old furniture is exempt from duty I am charging a deposit of Hk.Tls. 50 - the value of the furniture being declared as Taels 1,000 - pending your instructions.

[...]endent's [...] Customs [...]s.

The Superintendent's men are collecting surtaxes on import cargoes covered by Exemption Certificates from Shanghai and also on kerosene oil which has already paid 2½% surtax at the same port. The local Agent of the Standard Oil Company came to me the other day and informed me of this illegal levy. I told him that I was not concerned in the matter and that if he wanted to protest he better go to the Superintendent. Yesterday the Asiatic Petroleum Company's oil arriving by the "Hai Kwang" was also taxed similarly.

The contemplated policy of the foreign merchants at Shanghai in refusing to pay such extra-Treaty taxes by depositing the Tariff duty with their respective Consuls and getting their goods delivered without Customs permits will therefore not be workable as these goods

when

3.

651

when shipped to other ports will be liable to such surtaxes.

[Ch]olera epidemic [at Shan]ghai.

The Shanghai Commissioner wired me on the 24th that cholera is epidemic at Shanghai. I at once wrote to the Superintendent and the Consuls requesting their consent to declare Shanghai cholera infected. The Superintendent has signified his agreement and as soon as I receive replies from the Consuls I will enforce the Sanitary Regulations to the Shanghai vessels.

Yours truly,

Ng Mi ... [illegible]

626

INSPECTORATE GENERAL OF CUSTOMS,

S/O

PEKING, 29th August 1927

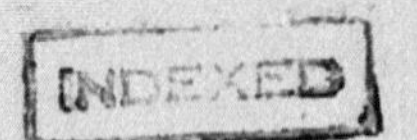

Dear Mr. Ng,

I have duly received your S/O letter No.425 of the 15th August:

Tariff Autonomy.

Tariff Autonomy, at any rate for some time to come, would seem to be a dead letter. I sent you on the 25th, through the Shanghai Commissioner, instructions as to the line of action you are to take in this connection.

Staff and Shanghai Customs Association.

I am glad to hear that your Staff is keeping aloof from this semi-political Association.

Yours truly,

hiu hung,
NCHOW.

CUSTOM HOUSE,

65[illegible]

Wenchow, 2nd September 1927.

Dear Mr. Edwardes,

f autonomy
ond sine

On receipt of a copy of your confidential telegram dated the 25th August from the Shanghai Commissioner I simply wrote to the Superintendent to say that I will collect the same Maritime Customs and Native Customs duties on and after the 1st September in accordance with your telegraphic instructions for I understood he already received instructions both from Nanking and Hangchow. He issued a notification on the 30th August informing the public that the intra and extra Native Customs and his surtax offices are to continue to function as usual but that the tonnage dues have been reduced to one-fourth of the value collected by us. In order to upholding our position I issued a notification to say that in accordance with your instructions the Maritime Customs and

Native

EDWARDES, ESQUIRE,

&c., Etc., Etc.,

P E K I N G.

2.

Native Customs offices are to collect the same duties as heretofore on and after the 1st September without change. Although the Shanghai Commissioner in reply to my telegram enquiring whether he would issue any notification informed me that a notification was unnecessary, nevertheless in this port it would be wise to issue one to show that we are not under the orders of the Superintendent who recently has posted any kinds of notifications in our premises without my knowledge.

[..]ment on [..] authority [..]intendent.

The downfall of the Nanking Government has given the Superintendent more chance to interfere with Customs work for he need not care of either the bankrupt Nanking or the Hangchow Provincial Government. He has employed 40 Watchers to board steamers and passengers have suffered a great deal from them. These men are making open squeezes. In collecting passenger baggage duties our value is not accepted by them. I have told the Senior Out-door Officer not to raise any question provided we have satisfied

ourselves

them. These men are making open squeezes. In collecting passenger baggage duties our value is not accepted by them. I have told the Senior Out-door Officer not to raise any question provided we have satisfied ourselves

1959

3.

65-7

ourselves but let the Superintendent suffer the consequences from the merchants himself. I understand a meeting was held by the Chamber of Commerce yesterday carrying out a resolution to prosecute the Superintendent to the Hangchow Government for obstructing trade and unduly annoying merchants.

In the Native Customs his men occupy whatever rooms not having been occupied by us and even made alterations to the rooms without consulting first with either the Clerk-in-charge or myself. This naughty Superintendent almost regards our property as his own. His aim is to force into any building that is left vacant.

[illegible]property [illegible]st [illegible]d [illegible]rs' [illegible] in [illegible]use.

Hearing that the Superintendent is going to occupy the Tidewaiters' Quarters forcibly and also the property on Conquest Island I at once informed the Chinese Staff that they may move in to any of these houses to prevent their being molested by these lawless people. The Chinese Clerks are not willing to live on the Island and these houses are being occupied by the Chinese Tidewaiters.

As

4.

158

As regards the Tidewaiters' Quarters nobody finds the rooms sufficient for him and I am nominally making it as Customs Club to show that it is inhabited. This is the only way to prevent the Superintendent's greedy action as I believe no outside influence can bear upon him to stop his encroaching activities. I hope my action will meet with your approval. The present occupants of the houses have been told that if at any time the foreign staff be sent back they must vacate them at once. I may say that all these intrigues have been planned by the Native Customs Weiyüan Wu Chi-tse. At present to get rid of him means to create more trouble and as soon as conditions become normal I will officially ask you to discontinue his 10 taels allowance and finally to remove him from the office.

...Customs ...Yang ...o.

The Superintendent being dissatisfied with Mr. Yang's ignoring of his document for fresh eggs from Chili (七里) talked of arresting him to Court for trial.

Mr. Yang who is in charge of the North Gate Station made an egg shop merchant who

5.

659

who held a duty document from the Superintendent's Chili Station to pay duty, assuming that the status of Chili is the same as Kuantou (琯頭), only a checking barrier. The fact that eggs covered by Chili documents had never before passed that station made him to take this step. He was over-zealous but in fact aimed at the protection of the Service revenue interests. This incurred the great displeasure of the Superintendent who asked me to reprimand him severely, record his fault once and send him to his office for eventual handing him over to Court for trial if he dared to disobey.

In order to avoid trouble I replied to him politely but at the same time maintained our position saying that this was due to his document being not chopped with the words "Native Produce". I understood that if I argued the case strongly - which I at first intended to do - he would surely arrest Mr. Yang. To avoid the ridiculous position which we may be driven in should this wild man initiate such action I put the matter off mildly.

66 6.

mildly. You will find the correspondence in the Non-urgent Chinese Correspondence for August.

Quite unexpected our revenue for the month shows promising increases for both the Maritime Customs and Native Customs. The Maritime Customs revenue is about Taels 1,400 more than last year's, and the Native Customs Taels 300.

I regret to say that our old and faithful Native Customs Examiner Mr. Lin Yin-li (林銀梨) died yesterday morning after having been ill from diarrhoea for about 2 weeks. In his lifetime he had shared most of the difficulties we were passing through and his death at this juncture is still more deplorable. I am sending one Maritime Customs Weigher to fill his vacancy in the Native Customs and with regard to other replacements I am addressing you an official despatch.

Yours truly,

Ng Shin-lung

(162)

CUSTOM HOUSE,

. 430.

Wenchow, 9th September 1927.

Dear Mr. Edwardes,

ion.

I am glad to say that we have been able to carry on our revenue collection as usual without a hitch since 1st September although the Kuomintang attempted to stir up trouble on that day. With the dissolution of the Anti-Japanese Association here a good revenue is expected this month for rape seed and wood oil, the export of which was restricted by that Association, are beginning to go out in big quantities. Trade is brisk in the Native Customs too. As a result of the hardship imposed by the surtax offices on the merchants we have gained much popularity from the latter who are willing to help us in every way.

om
er y.

No question has been raised by the Superintendent claiming occupation of our property

H. F. EDWARDES, ESQUIRE,

Etc., Etc., Etc.,

P E K I N G.

2.

664.

property since the action as reported in my despatch No. 4054 and S/O. No. 429 was taken. I believe he would be quiet for the time being.

[...]il oil [...]l [...]intendent's [...]office.

The Asiatic Petroleum Co. wrote me on the 30th August protesting against the levy of surtax on their oil which had paid the 2½% surtax at Shanghai. I replied that this office had never been concerned in the collection of any surtaxes and that they should lodge their protest with the Superintendent here who collected it.

[...]ta[...] [...]lations [...] to [...] vessels.

I duly received your telegram of the 2nd September sanctioning the appointment of Dr. Ch'ên Mei-hao (陳梅豪) as Port Health Officer from the 1st September at a monthly remuneration of Hk.Tls. 30.00. On receipt of replies from the Consuls concerned signifying their approval of declaring Shanghai cholera-infected I enforced the Sanitary Regulations to the Shanghai vessels as from yesterday.

Situation

3.

665

[...]ion in [...]

The Kuomintang, in spite of the postponement of the Tariff Autonomy Scheme having come to their knowledge, still attempted to summon the merchant guilds and labour unions to hold a big demonstration on the 1st September with the view of stirring up trouble. Luckily their call was responded by very few people. On account of very warm weather prevailing then and of the participants being not many, no demonstration was held, these people dispersing themselves after uttering slogans in the Shih Chung School Compound.

Both the S.Ss. "Kaean" and "Hua Feng" were fired on by soldiers stationed at the Lungwan Fort on their inward trip last Sunday, the 4th September. While these ships anchored there 3 soldiers came along and asked the Captains of these ships if operation had begun in Shanghai or not. The action was joky but luckily no passengers were hurt.

Yours truly,

Ng Shin-leung

CUSTOM HOUSE,

No. 431. Wenchow, 14th September 1927.

Dear Mr. Edwardes,

[illegible]l of [illegible]'s office [illegible]rary.

On the afternoon of the 9th instant the Superintendent sent his Ko-chang to see me and again claim the Library for his men. He said the Superintendent had received a letter from his Ningpo colleague stating that the Commissioner there had been kind enough to give 5 or 6 rooms to the Superintendent for surtax collection and asked me to give similar favour to the Superintendent here. The Shanghai Hsin Wen Pao (新聞报) did publish the fact but the rooms given by the Ningpo Commissioner appear to be in the Customs Club. A plan suddenly struck me at the time. I then pointed out to the Ko-chang that the rooms in our building were only just sufficient for our Staff, but that if the Superintendent aimed at our Library only

F. EDWARDES, ESQUIRE,

Etc., Etc., Etc.,

PEKING.

2.

668

only I could turn the said room into a Banker's office where his men might go and work there. He expressed satisfaction at my proposal, and said that this was the best plan to smooth all sides. The removal was duly effected on Monday. The former Banker's office has been turned into a Library.

I think this is the best way to smooth matters. On the one hand we maintain our position without yielding to the Superintendent's claim for a separate room, as we simply change a room for our banker, and on the other the Superintendent's men are satisfied at working in a more spacious place. By this removal our General Office gets more privacy too for the former Banker's room was just opposite our General Office and the entrance was often crowded with all sorts of people who often argued with the surtax men making unpleasant noises. The Library now turned into Banker's office is on the side of the Chinese Post Office thus separating these men from our side.

In my despatch No. 4054 I said I

was

3.

was proposing to remove our Banker to the General Office but after some thought this is not feasible. If our Banker be shifted to the General Office these surtax men would go there frequently and more interruption of our work would be caused thereby. Of course our Banker does not like to work together with these people and now a little compartment has been made for him in his present office to which the surtax men cannot get in. His work therefore cannot now be interrupted by them. I hope my action will surely meet with your approval.

Mr. Lu Si Huo, 3rd Class Tidewaiter B, has applied to me for 4 weeks' leave on account of his mother being seriously ill in Foochow. I have granted him 3 weeks' leave to proceed there from today's date.

a .on in
h .

The Kuomintang have sent men to the Post Office to impress catch-phrases on letters. They stamp even the official letters most of which bear the words "Down with Imperialism".

Owing to the alleged defeat of Marshal

Sun

4.

692

Sun Chuan-fang the trouble-makers are now breathing bolder. For a time they had kept silent.

Yours truly,

Ng Shin-hung

CUSTOM HOUSE,

625

No. 432.

Wenchow 20th September 1927.

INDEXED

...ntendent's ...shments on ... ...stration: ... ...ment's ...; received.

Dear Mr. Edwardes,

Yesterday afternoon the Superintendent's Ko-chang, now in temporary charge of the Superintendent's Office in the absence of the Superintendent who has gone to Shanghai, came to me and showed me a despatch from the Ministry of Finance of the Nanking Government which has apparently been re-established just recently, instructing the Superintendent not to interfere with the Commissioner's duties in future. The Ko-chang asked me why I should accuse the Superintendent of having interfered with my duties. I was greatly delighted of reading the Nanking Government's instructions and took the full opportunity of pointing out to the Ko-chang the irregularities such as occupation and alterations of rooms in the Native Customs without my knowledge, detailing

F. Edwardes, Esquire,

Etc., Etc., Etc.,

PEKING.

2.

676

detailing watchers to board steamers and junks, collection of passenger baggage duties, detention of inland waters steamer by the Native Customs Weiyüan, etc., etc., done by the Superintendent. I emphatically told him that only Customs Officers can board steamers and that the boarding of vessels by his men is an open breach of our authority. He could not reply a word when I narrated all the Superintendent's illegal doings. I further said I feel it a shame myself to allow things which do not occur at other ports go on in this way here and that I could see no reason why watchers should be employed by the Superintendent. Finally he said he would transmit the despatch to me and request my reply to it. I at once accepted his proposal for I can take the full opportunity to put all the Superintendent's wild acts on official record and at the same time lodge a strong protest against the search of vessels and occupation of our Native Customs premises by his men without my permission. Indeed it is foolish for him to transmit me that

despatch.

3.

677

despatch. Perhaps after thinking over he may not do it but I will grasp the chance to lodge an emphatic protest with the Superintendent anyhow.

As regards how things will go as result of this warning by the Nanking Government it depends upon whether the Superintendent will listen to its orders. We will see the policy after the return of the wild man. I omitted to mention to you that when the Superintendent's men occupied the rooms in the Native Customs they took armed men with them preparing evidently for a fight.

...of steamer ...garettes by ... Cigarette ...reau and ...rs.

Recently on the arrival of the China Merchants Company's steamers men of the Cigarette Tax Bureau and soldiers all board vessels and seize any cigarettes not having borne stamps. Our Officers prevent them to do so and small friction often takes place. I have written to the Superintendent protesting against the action of the Cigarette men and soldiers. The Superintendent may not be able to control the soldiers but as the Garrison

Commander

4.

618

Commander here is a Cantonese I am taking the opportunity to make acquaintance with him. By this way I think the soldiers can be checked from doing this.

t..y
..ions
..d against
..i vessels.

Since the enforcement of the Sanitary Regulations against the Shanghai vessels on the 8th instant all have gone on smoothly until last Sunday when some of the missionaries returning here for a visit per the "Haean" were reluctant to submit to medical inspection and when the doctor boarded the vessel they purposely scattered about on the deck. The Chinese passengers were dissatisfied at their attitude and insisted that Chinese and foreigners must be treated alike. These men should have behaved themselves especially in such a time when anti-foreign feeling is running high. The Senior Out-door Officer then asked them one by one, altogether three, to submit to medical inspection which they finally obeyed. The Captain of the "Haean" has been warned that in future foreign passengers must be asked to gather in the saloon (which has been the practice in past years) when the medical officer boards the vessel. The Superintendent has

3.

679

has also been requested to issue a joint proclamation to the effect that while the Sanitary Regulations are in force all passengers irrespective of nationality must be submitted to medical inspection.

I duly received your telegram of the 14th conveying your sanction to the filling of the vacancies of Weigher in the Maritime Customs and second T'ingch'ai in the Native Customs. These positions have duly been filled.

...sion in ...hiv

The Japanese steamer "Nanyo Maru" made her trial trip here on the 17th and it has been intended by the Ito and Company to ship charcoal, rape seed, tea oil and wood oil by her to Japan. Duty to the value of about Hk.Tls. 800 has been collected on these commodities when the local Kuomintang suddenly disallow these goods to be shipped. Their intention is to get a sequeeze from the merchants. Negotiations are still going on and the ship is still in port. If no settlement can be arrived at we have to issue a drawback for the duties already collected.

Yours truly,

Ng Shi-huay

INSPECTORATE GENERAL OF CUSTOMS, 648

S/O

PEKING, 21st September 1927

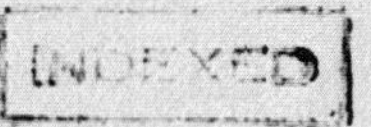
INDEXED

Dear Mr. Ng,

I have duly received your S/O letter No.427 of the 23rd August:

Tariff Autonomy.

My telegram of the 25th August, sent to you through the Shanghai Commissioner, indicates the line of action you are to take in this regard.

Collection of Likin to continue on the 1st September.

A very clear indication that Tariff Autonomy is shelved for the time being.

Yours truly,

[signature]

...S]u hung,
...EN[OW.

INSPECTORATE GENERAL OF CUSTOMS, 169

S/O [MARKED]

PEKING, 21st September, 1927

Dear Mr. Ng,

I have duly received your S/O letter No. 429 of the 2nd September:

Interference by Superintendent: his watchers board steamers, etc.

Your policy of refraining from active intervention with these minions of the Superintendent is the correct one. At the same time you should warn the Superintendent that he alone must accept full responsibility for any untoward consequences that may arise from the activities of these underlings.

Occupation of Customs Property.

You seem to be doing your best to preserve our property from being interfered with, and I approve of what you report as having done.

Please

M. Ng Shiu hung,
WENCHOW.

162

Please make sure, however, that the Quarters and their contents are not damaged in any way, and that the properties are kept as clean as formerly.

Yours truly,

181

CUSTOM HOUSE,

[S/O]. 433. Wenchow 27th September 1927

INDEXED

[Supe]rintendent's [enc]roachments on [Cus]tom [Adm]inistration.

Dear Mr. Edwardes,

The Ko-chang in temporary charge of the Superintendent's Office has at last not fulfilled his words of transmitting the Tsai-chêng Pu's instructions to me. My prediction contained on the top part of page 3 of my S/O. No. 432 therefore comes true. On the 24th September I addressed the Superintendent a letter protesting against his establishment of a separate Customs in our Native Customs buildings and the boarding of vessels by his men and requesting him to withdraw his out-door Staff and leave the collection of the surtaxes in the Banker's hands.

The Superintendent's position is now insecure owing to military conflict in the Chekiang province. It is now rumoured that General Chou Fêng-ch'i has been captured by General

F. EDWARDES, ESQUIRE

Etc., Etc., Etc.,

PEKING.

2.

682

General Ho Ying-ch'in's (何應欽) men. If this is true the Superintendent would have to go.

or N.C. new office: fencing as ted in despatch 456.

I hope you will see your way to granting this small expenditure. It will prevent junks from using this spot thus protecting the property from being spoiled.

caught for ing smuggled ttes from r.

On the arrival of the "Haean" on the 19th instant a sampan was noticed to moor alongside the vessel taking cigarettes from her. Both the cigarettes and the sampan were seized by our Officers. A fine was accordingly inflicted on the cigarettes and the sampan was fined Tls. 2.00. This sampan belongs to the local loafers who refused to pay the fine and on the sampan being pulled ashore by our boatmen the rascals challenged our boatmen to fight. They also threatened the Senior Out-door Officer. A letter was at once written to the Superintendent informing him of the affair and requesting him to get the police to arrest these loafers. The rascals hearing that action was to be taken hurried to pay up

3.

683

a on in
h .

up the fine. The Ko-chang promised to get some of them arrested and punished.

The Japanese steamer "Nanyo Maru" finally succeeded to load cargo and left port on the 23rd instant.

The Japanese destroyer "Kawakaze" arrived from Formosa on the 22nd instant, the intention of this visit being to help the "Nanyo Maru" to get the cargo loaded. Before her arrival, however, the Kuomintang had ceased to interfere with this vessel's loading. She left here on the 25th.

Yours truly,

Ng Shin Kung

CUSTOM HOUSE,

675

No. 434. INDEXED Wenchow, 29th September 1927.

Dear Mr. Edwardes,

[Superi]ntendent's [enc]roachments on [Cus]toms [admi]nistration.

The Superintendent has not yet returned and my protest is still lying in his office unattended. However I understand that the Ko-chang will induce the Superintendent not to withdraw the searching staff, because such withdrawal will deprive of much income from the Superintendent and the Ko-chang. It has now revealed that the whole scheme was planned by the Ko-chang. The vacancies of Examiners and Watchers were openly sold. The in-door staff consists entirely of men who have been the Ko-chang's fellow card-players while the watchers come from the street hawkers, shoe-makers, etc. class. These men only receive $5 to $6 a month and their salaries are put down in their accounts as $15 to $20 per head per month. They also put down their initial expenditure for furniture, fittings,

H. F. EDWARDES, ESQUIRE,
Etc., Etc., Etc.,
PEKING.

2.

fittings, etc. for their surtax offices as $700 but really the real outlay did not exceed $50.00.

In order to maintain their searching staff they are trying to find some plea for submission to the Nanking Government. They are therefore keeping watch on our fault. Unfortunately in the midnight of the 27th instant their watchers seized a sampan with smuggled goods from the "Haean" in the stream. These goods were smuggled by the ship's crew and concealed in places unknown to our Officers, when they boarded the vessel on her arrival. It has been a practice here of not stationing officers on board vessels at night unless they take out Special Night Permits. These goods therefore slipped through without our knowledge. In view of this I have instructed the Senior Out-door Officer to station watchers on board vessels at night. The seized goods were conveyed to the Superintendent's Office and confiscated there. This is therefore a good plea grasped by the Ko-chang for the maintenance of

3.

687

of their searching staff, since he can say that our staff are inefficient. He is still trying to collect other material to substantiate his ground for having instituted a searching staff. I may mention that the surtax men spoke to our Writer after my protest has gone that it would be better for the Customs and the Superintendent's Office to work together with mutual benefit to each other with regards to money affairs i.e. squeezes. The conduct of these people may be judged from these daring words.

There is absolutely no intention on their part to abolish the searching staff for only day before yesterday a telephone was installed in the Native Customs. There is therefore no alternative for me but to keep my eyes shut for the time being.

[F]urniture of [A.P.] [C]o. shipped to [Shan]g[ha]i: is [duty l]eviable ?

In my S/O. No. 428 I asked your instructions as to whether duty was leviable on the old furniture shipped to Shanghai by the Asiatic Petroleum Company but I got no answer from you beyond an acknowledgment of the receipt of this letter by the Personal Secretary.

4.

628

Secretary. As the deposit of Tls. 50.00 is still lying in our General Office I shall be obliged if you will send me instructions in the matter.

d[oo]r Staff
a[r]y.

Mr. Finch, the Honorary Treasurer and Secretary of the Library, has handed over the accounts of the Library to me. Although it is an Out-door Staff Library subscriptions are also paid by the Indoor Staff. It is my intention to run the Library on the old lines but the balance now in hand is only $101.50. I wish to ask whether the grant sanctioned in I.G. Circular No. 53 of 1875 may be drawn in order to meet the expenses for magazines, etc. ordered from London, following the procedure of previous years. The grant which should have been drawn in June Quarter has not been issued so far.

[s]a[t]ion in
[C]h[t]y.

There are big troop movements in the City. More than 2,000 soldiers have come from Chuchow en route to Chinhai and Ningpo. The S.Ss. "Haean" and "Yung Ning" have been commandeered since the 26th instant but have

not

5.

not left yet. Today the S.Ss."Kwangchi" and "Pingyang" arrived and were commandeered too. More soldiers are expected to come. The City is now swarmed with military people. The Yungchia Magistrate has been kind enough to put a notification in front of the Commissioner's House warning the soldiers not to molest the property and not to force into the house. The troops are expected to leave tomorrow.

A fish tax Bureau has recently been inaugurated here. Fish merchants and hawkers have to obtain licences from the Bureau first before they can trade. These licences are to be renewed twice a year, in Spring and Autumn. There are five kinds of licences, the fees chargeable being $16, $4, $3, $2 and $1 respectively. In addition the goods have to be taxed at 5% *ad valorem.*

Yours truly,

Ng Shin-heng

166

INSPECTORATE GENERAL OF CUSTOMS,

S/O PEKING, 30th September, 1927.

Dear Mr. Ng,

I have duly received your S/O letter No. 430 of the 9th September: Attitude of Merchants towards Customs.

I hope that the present friendly feelings of the merchants may long continue, and that nothing may happen to impair these good relations.

Yours truly,

[signature]

Mr. Ng Shiu hung,
WENCHOW.

671

INSPECTORATE GENERAL OF CUSTOMS

S/O

INDEXED

PEKING, 3rd October 1927

Dear Mr. Ng,

I have duly received your S/O letter No.431 of the 14th September:

Removal of Banker's Office to Library.

Your action in allowing the Banker to have the Customs Library as an office is, in the circumstances, approved. It would not have been at all wise to have allowed the Surtax deputies to carry on their work in the General Office.

Yours truly,

[signature]

Siu hung,
WENCHOW.

CUSTOM HOUSE,

No. 435. INDEXED Wenchow 7th October 1927.

892

Dear Mr. Edwardes,

intendent's
achments on
ns
istration.

The Superintendent is still away and judging from the present situation I think he cannot return to his post. The seizure of the sampan containing smuggled goods from the "Haean" on the 27th September by his watchers as reported in my last S/O. letter has provoked a strong opposition from the mercantile public who petitioned him to the Kuomintang pointing out that the surtax men had no right to make seizures. There was therefore no offer made for the confiscated goods. The Ko-chang threatened the goods owners that if they did not buy back their stuff he would send the whole cargo to me to be confiscated altogether. A representative of the Kuomintang and one of the (商民協會) came to see the Senior Outdoor Officer and asked whether if the goods be sent over by the

F. EDWARDES, ESQUIRE,

Etc., Etc., Etc.,

P E K I N G.

2.

692

the Superintendent the Commissioner would have them confiscated. The Senior Outdoor Officer replied that he did not think so. They then informed him that a mass meeting would be held to deal with the Superintendent. They had done their first step, i.e. they had asked the Superintendent's office to give them a copy of the surtax regulations and simultaneously asked for one from Hangchow and Ningpo respectively. When comparison shows that the Wenchow procedure is an exceptional one a mass meeting will be called to urge the Superintendent to cancel his illegal system.

I am keeping wide from their doings but should be pleased to see the Superintendent and his Ko-chang in trouble with the public. I warned the Ko-chang the other day when he came to show me the despatch from the Nanking Government that his office should alone be responsible for all the trouble created by his underlings to the public. He told me he did ask the Superintendent not to institute the searching staff at the very beginning but that the Superintendent did not listen to his words.

694

:)

words. In reality he was the man plotting the whole scheme to enrich himself.

nue.

The September revenue of both the Maritime and Native Customs shows an increase of over Tls. 1,000 respectively over the last year's figures. Had not the latter part of the month been disturbed by military movements the increases would have been greater.

pation of
oms property.

I duly received your S/O. letter of the 21st September approving of my action in getting the property occupied by the Chinese Staff. There is no official furniture in all the houses on Conquest Island and I have warned all the occupants to keep their Quarters absolutely clean. The Senior Outdoor Officer has been instructed to inspect them periodically. The furniture in the Tidewaiters' Quarters has never been used and has been kept in good order.

ation in
now.

The S.Ss. "Haean", "Yung Ning" and "Pingyang" left with troops to Ningpo on last Friday, the 30th September. Since the departure of S.S. "Kwangchi" on the 2nd instant we have been up to now receiving no mails.

The

4.

195

The S.S. "Pingyang" which ought to have arrived yesterday was, I understand, commandeered at Haimen for conveying troops to Ningpo. There must have been trouble in the province. It is rumoured that the crew of the China Merchants Steam Navigation Company's steamers are on strike. If this be so this port would be isolated for sometime.

Yours truly,

Ng Shi-huang

INSPECTORATE GENERAL OF CUSTOMS,

S/O PEKING, 11th October, 1927

Dear Mr. Ng,

I have duly received your S/O letter No. 432 of the 20th September: Sanitary Regulations enforced against Shanghai vessels.

That's right! It is for the Captain of the vessel to instruct passengers to be ready for medical inspection by the Sanitary authorities. We must never forget that although the Customs lend their aid, we are not the Sanitary authorities.

Yours truly,

Ng Shiu hung,

WENCHOW.

697

CUSTOM HOUSE,

No. 436.

INDEXED

Wenchow 13th October 1927.

ıntendent's
ıchments on
ıs
ıstration.

Dear Mr. Edwardes,

I duly received your despatch No. 1469/114,295 instructing me to go direct either to General Chou Feng-ch'i or the heads of the Chekiang Provincial Government with request to stop the Superintendent from unnecessary interference with Customs functions and property. The situation has now been changed as General Chou has resigned and the executive members of the Chekiang Provincial Political Committee have all gone. There is really not a Superintendent here and all the office routine is being managed by the Ko-chang. Until a new man comes the Ko-chang declines to withdraw the searching staff. He promises to let me have a reply to my letter urging the Superintendent to cease his interference with the Customs functions. I am waiting for this letter

. F. EDWARDES, ESQUIRE,

Etc., Etc., Etc.,

P E K I N G.

2.

698

letter before taking another step. I think the proper way is to approach the Nanking Government again through the Shanghai Commissioner. When situation permits I will do so.

With regard to the seizure of some smuggled goods at night by his watchers (vide my previous S/O.) I wrote an official letter to the Superintendent protesting against his action and pointing out that even when these goods be seized by his men they should be handed over to the Customs for disposal. I queried him also whether he has been explicitly ordered by the Nanking Government to establish a seperate Customs for surtax collection and, if so, he better put it in writing in order that I may report the fact to you. The reply made by the Ko-chang in the name of the Superintendent was very cunning. He said that he understood these goods had already paid Customs duty but since they evaded surtax they had been seized and fined according to the regulations formulated by the Ts'ai-chêng Pu. Finally he blamed our Tidewaiters for having

3.

699

having not brought the duty to account. These are all irrelevant matters and he cleverly left the most important query unanswered. I am watching with interest how he answers my first letter of protest.

tude of hants rds Customs.

Since my taking over charge I have been aiming at the cultivation of good feeling with the merchantile public and every legal facility has been given them in their transaction of business with us. The General Office always does things promptly, so the merchants all appreciate our working. I believe nothing can impair their friendly feeling towards us as our staff all realise the necessity of maintaining pleasant relations with the commercial community.

less ratus to be ied by vessels o.No.3781).

The Superintendent, in reply to my enquiry whether he agrees to put the rules into effect, says that he must obey instructions from the Ministry of Communications of the Nationalist Government and that these rules should not be put into force.

ation in now.

For 13 days this port has not been visited by the China Merchants Steam Navigation Company's

4.

700

Company's steamers. The "Haean" is expected here on the 15th. At present cargo is piled up in the Examination Shed waiting for shipment.

More than 20,000 persons participated in the lantern procession on the 10th October in celebration of National Festival.

Posters are up in the streets objecting to the assumption of office by the new Chekiang Political Committee. A majority of the officials here are Chou Feng-ch'i's men and if General Ho Ying-ch'in assumes office the whole body would have to go.

Yours truly,

Ng Shin Kuang

CUSTOM HOUSE,

701

. No.437.

INDEXED

Wenchow 19. October 1927.

)

uki
d Acting
oner.

Dear Mr. Edwardes ,

Many thanks for your relief of my burden and for transferring me to Canton. I feel highly honoured by your placing on official record your appreciation of my services in my tenure of charge in Wenchow . Indeed I am happy to find myself able to maintain the administration in its present wholesome condition with the attendant high increase in revenue in spite of all difficulties having confronted us.

Mr. Suzuki will arrive tomorrow but I only received your despatch late on Saturday last , the 15th instant, so there is rather a hurry to get things through for handing over charge . I intend to sail on the 26th and may stop in Shanghai for a few days taking the opportunity to pay a visit to Hangchow which scenic place I had longed for for years .

ff.

I take this opportunity to record my

H. F. EDWARDES , ESQUIRE ,

ETC., ETC., ETC.,

P E K I N G.

- 2.

702

my appreciation of the good services and loyalty of the whole Staff throughout the trying period which we were passing through , especially to Messrs. Lau Kieng Hing, Wong Cok Man and the Writer Mr. Tsao Kuang-chao. Mr. Ling Chan Ngau , 3rd Clerk, B., has done exceptionally well in the Native Customs and is deserving of a good recognition. Mr. Sia Liang , the Senior Outdoor Officer , has also done excellent work in his capacity and I hope you will see your way to granting him an allowance as such (vide your S/O. of the 6th July 1927.

Mr. Lau Kieng Hing has again asked me to solicit your kindness to appoint his son Liu Chi Tuan as a Service Clerk if a vanancy be open at any time. As his son was found by Mr. Bernadsky to be quite suitable (vide his S/O. No. 396, page 5) for such a post and as Mr. Lau has given good services all the time I venutgre to put his request for your fabourable consideration.

ntendent's
hments.

The Kochang has already replied to my letter of protest in the name of the Superintendent in which he carefully hides the fact

fact that the Superintendent has instituted a searching staff and that he has commandeered the Native Customs property. The plea is that as we had refused to collect surtax for him he must send deputies to collect it forgetting that at the time when the Tariff Autonomy agitation was at its height he had aimed to commandeer the whole N. C. property. He argues that the collection of surtax by his men does not in any way interfere with our revenue and therefore the question of encroachments on the Commissioner's authority does not exist. He has submitted this pretext to the Nanking Government.

On the 17th instant I addressed him another protest pointing out all his irregularities with the warning that he continues to interfere with our duties the Nanking Government will be again approached on the matter. His reply may be dealt with by my successor.

Yours truly,

Ng Shi-hung

INSPECTORATE GENERAL OF CUSTOMS, 684

S/O

PEKING, 22nd October 1927

Rec'd 28/Nov. 1927
through Canton.

INDEXED

Dear Mr. Ng,

I have duly received your S/O letter No. 433 of 27th September:

Site for N.C. new Head Office: expenditure for fencing of bund.

✓ This expenditure is being sanctioned by despatch.

Yours truly,

[signature]

Sz u-hung,
WUCHOW.

INSPECTORATE GENERAL OF CUSTOMS, 69

S/O PEKING, 22nd October 1927

INDEXED

Rec'd 28/Nov. 1927 through Canton

Dear Mr. Ng,

I have duly received your S/O letter No. 434 of 29th September:

Duty on old furniture of A.P.C. shipped to Shanghai.

Ascertain from the A.P.C. whether this furniture is of foreign or native manufacture, and, if foreign, at what time it was imported and paid duty. If it turns out to be duty-paid foreign stuff, you may allow it to be exported free of duty. If on the other hand it is of local native manufacture, you are to levy duty. Throw the onus on the A.P.C. of proving - with all details necessary - that the furniture is entitled to exemption from duty.

Out-Door Staff Library.

You should try and meet out of the funds in hand the liabilities already incurred as subscriptions to foreign newspapers and periodicals and not draw on the

Annual

N Shiu-hung,

WENCHOW.

(9)

Annual Grant for this year, unless these liabilities are in excess of the funds you hold. Do not incur any further expenditure either for renewals or other subscriptions without first referring to me.

Yours truly,

696

INSPECTORATE GENERAL OF CUSTOMS,

PEKING, 22nd October 1927

Recd 28/Nov. 1927. through Canton.

INDEXED

Dear Mr. Ng,

I have duly received your S/O letter No. 435 of 7th October:

Superintendent's trouble with public on Surtax question.

You are quite right in keeping clear of the activities of the public in this matter, and thus obviating the possibility of becoming involved in any trouble that may arise between the public and the Superintendent over the surtax question.

Yours truly,

Ng Shiu-hung,

WENCHOW.

725

CUSTOM HOUSE,

10. No. 438. Wenchow 22. October 1927.

Dear Mr. Edwardes ,

I have this day handed over charge of this office to Mr. T. Suzuki, who arrived here on the 20th instant. I feel exceedingly happy to have been able to hand over the administration to Mr. Suzuki in such a wholesome manner , and as things have now practically returned to their normal condition I believe nothing hard will face him .

We called on the Superintendent this afternoon and he was very courteous to us. He said that the complications formerly existing between his office and the Customs were due to misunderstanding owing to the existence of two governments and that he hoped a central authority would soon be established thus rendering our working much easier.

I will sail on Thursday , the 27th

. F. EDWARDES , ESQUIRE ,

ETC., ETC., ETC.,

P E K I N G .

2.

106

27th per the S.S. HAEAN . On arrival at Shanghai I will take the opportunity to visit Hangchow for 3 or 4 days and then take a steamer to Canton direct . I thank you once more for this transfer and for the dignity you have given me here.

Yours truly ,

Ng Shi-hung

CUSTOM HOUSE, 708

O. No. 439. INDEXED Wenchow 22nd October 1927

Dear Mr. Edwardes,

I arrived here from Shanghai on the afternoon of the 20th instant, taking the first direct steamer -- S/S "Kwangchi" -- and took over charge from Mr. Ng this afternoon. I tender my sincere thanks for the new appointment and also feel very glad to come to this port after the most trying time was over.

Mr. Ng and myself called on the Superintendent this afternoon and I am very pleased to say that his attitude towards us was very friendly.

Mr. Ng, who carried out his work in a very efficient manner during the most troublous time, is leaving for Canton via Shanghai per S/S "Hacan" on next Thursday.

Yours truly,

[signature]

. H. F. EDWARDES, Esquire,

Etc., Etc., Etc.,

PEKING.

716

CUSTOM HOUSE,

INDEXED

Wenchow, 4th November 1927.

No. 440.

Dear Mr. Edwardes,

...e of ...intendent.

The former Superintendent, Mr. Hsü yo-yao (徐樂堯) hurriedly left for Shanghai on the 26th October by the S.S. "Haean" on receipt of a telegram from his family in Shanghai informing him that an attempt has been made on the 24th ultimo to kidnap his young son by armed men, who entered his house while his family was luckily out for shopping. The new Superintendent, Mr. Chuang Chih-huan (莊智煥), arrived here on the 30th October from Shanghai and took over charge on the 1st instant. He is a Ningpo man and looks not older than twenty six in his appearance and manner.

...ation in ...how.

Dr. E. T. A. Stedeford, our former Medical Officer, returned here from Shanghai

on

F. EDWARDES, ESQUIRE,

Etc., Etc., Etc.,

P E K I N G.

2.

711

on the 16th October, also Rev. J. W. Heywood of the United Methodist Mission on the 30th ultimo. Dr. Stedeford told me that he is not in a position to apply for his re-appointment in the Service as the H. B. M. Consul General in Shanghai gave him permission to visit here only temporarily, although he brought all his personal effects with the intention to stay here permanently.

Local situation is very quiet except the appearance of numerous placards on the streets yesterday morning denouncing the newly inaugurated fish tax and fish shop license.

Yours truly,

[signature]

709

INSPECTORATE GENERAL OF CUSTOMS,

S/O

PEKING, 10th November, 1927

Dear Mr. Suzuki,

I have duly received your S/O letter No. 439 of the 22nd October:

Assumption of charge.

I hope you will like your new port, and that your tenure of it may be a happy and prosperous one.

Yours truly,

T. Suzuki, Esquire,

WENCHOW.

?/11/27.

7/2

INSPECTORATE GENERAL OF CUSTOMS,

S/O

PEKING, 18th November 1927

Recd 28/11/27.

Dear Mr. Suzuki,

I have duly received your S/O letter No. 440 of 4th November:

Change of Superintendent.

You are well rid of Mr. Hsü. He has been the reverse of helpful to the Customs ever since his appointment. It is to be hoped that the new incumbent will take up a different attitude.

Yours truly,

. Suzuki, Esquire,

WENCHOW.

CUSTOM HOUSE,

713

No. 441.

INDEXED

Wenchow, 21st November, 1927.

intendent stoms.

Revenue de 50 li s.

Dear Mr. Edwardes,

I have duly received your S/O letter dated the 10th instant and thank you for your complimentary words. I will do my best to carry out work to your satisfaction.

After a short stay of fortnight in this port Mr. Chuang Chih-huan (莊智焕), Superintendent of Customs, left for Nanking via Shanghai on the 12th instant, leaving his routine work in the hands of his newly appointed secretary, Mr. Chang Ling-fêng (張令芳).

This money up to the end of May, 1927, was handed over to us on the 29th June (vide S/O No. 414), but no payment has been made since that time A letter written to the Superintendent on the 6th August by my predecessor acting under your instructions (I.G. Despatch No. 1460/113,497) was met with a flat refusal, and no answer has yet been received

F. EDWARDES, ESQUIRE,

Etc., Etc., Etc.,

PEKING.

2.

714

received to our second letter of protest dated the 13th August (vide Non-urgent Chinese Correspondence, August, Native Customs Subject No. 2). As it would be futile to raise the question while the Superintendent is away, I shall take up the matter on his return from Nanking.

[...]lishment of [...]l Controlling [...]1 (管理船舶事務所).

A proclamation has recently been issued announcing the establishment of this new tax office, calling for the registration of all vessels and payment of registration fee ranging from $1.50 to $8.00 half-yearly according to size of boat. So far this office has taken no action in enforcing these rules.

[...]lishment of [...]ang Opium [...]bition Bureau 部浙江禁煙局).

A branch office of this Bureau was opened here a few days ago under instructions received from the Ministry of Finance, Nanking, and a precis of the rules is as follows:

(1) Unauthorised cultivation of poppy is strictly prohibited.

(2) People under 25 years old are not allowed to smoke opium.

(3)

3.

915

(3) After three years opium smoking will be absolutely forbidden.

(4) Opium smokers are divided into undermentioned three classes:

(a) Ordinary smokers

(b) Indigent smokers

(c) Travellers.

and opium smoking licenses will be issued on payment of following fees:

1st year	Annually	Monthly	Daily
(a)	$54.00	$ 4.50	. . .
(b)	$14.40	$ 1.20	. . .
(c)	. . .	. . .	$ 0.30
2nd year			
(a)	$81.00	$ 6.75	. . .
(b)	$21.60	$ 1.80	. . .
(c)	. . .	. . .	$ 0.45
3rd year			
(a)	$162.00	$13.50	. . .
(b)	$ 43.20	$ 3.60	. . .
(c)	. . .	. . .	$ 0.90

lishment of opium Medicine oly Bureau (.藥品專賣處).

Following the inauguration of the Opium Prohibition Bureau the establishment of this Bureau has been proclaimed. No anti-opium medicines

medicines are sold at present, but only native raw and prepared opium are sold at the rate of $4.50 and $5.90 per tael respectively. I understand that all native opium sold by this bureau comes from Fukien overland under official protection.

[I]ncrease of [Keros]ene Oil

An enormous increase of kerosene oil tax to take effect as from today has just been announced by the Oil Tax Office. According to the new regulations duties on lubricating oil, gasolene, paraffin and stearine remain unchanged while fuel oil is passed duty free. A comparative table showing the old and new rates is appended hereunder:-

Description	per	Old rate $	New rate $
Lubricating oil	10 gallons	0.158	0.158
Gasolene	"	0.173	0.173
Fuel oil	Ton	0.728	Free
Paraffin	Picul	0.285	0.285
Stearine	"	0.675	0.675
Kerosene oil (under Kiangsu oil tax certificate)	10 gallons	0.078	1.000
Kerosene oil (no document)	"	0.108	1.000
Kerosene oil (under Customs inward Transit pass)	"	0.054	1.000
Kerosene oil (passing through Chêkiang province for consumption in other provinces)	10 gallons	0.054	1.000

Staff.

5.

717

Staff. Mr. Chi Pao-yuan (戚報元), 4th (Chinese) Assistant A, reported for duty on the 7th instant. He is a quiet and intelligent man and is doing well at the General Office. He was told to revise the Memorandum on the working of the General Office and on its compilation to study carefully the Memorandum on the working of the Native Customs with a view to eventually taking over charge of that Department. Other staff are doing well.

Local news. Fires: We have had no rain since October 12th and nearly all creeks and wells in the city were dried up and a timely rainfall yesterday relieved us considerably. Four large fires broke out in the city quite recently and in one of them a famous temple Fei Hsia Tung (飛霞洞) outside the South Gate was completely reduced to ashes including a 1,000 year-old camphor tree in its yard. Every precaution against fire is being taken by our men. Our fire engines both at the Maritime

6.

718

Maritime and Native Customs were tested and found in good working order.

Communists: Five communists were arrested by the local military authorities a few days ago on their arrival from Shanghai and Ningpo, and it is reported that their plot to destroy principal buildings in the city was discovered in the nick of time. Three of them were shot yesterday.

Celebration of late Dr. Sun Yat-sen's birthday: A mass meeting in the morning of the 12th instant was followed by a lantern procession in the evening. The crowd was very orderly and dispersed without any incident.

Yours truly,

725

CUSTOM HOUSE,

#0 INDEXED Wenchow, 26th November, 1927.

Dear Mr. Pritchard,

While clearing up the drawers of the General Office safe Mr. Chi Pao-yuan, newly appointed Chinese Assistant, came across among valueless papers three native orders issued by the Bank of China aggregating — Hk.Tls.25 + 15 + 10 — Hk.Tls. 50.00 in all. These orders were initialled by late Mr. Assistant R. W. Cholmondeley, then in charge of the General Office, but nothing was mentioned thereon as to their particulars. After taking great pains Mr. Chi found out that these orders represent the proceeds of three cases of fines inflicted during the 265th/December Quarter, 1926, but not entered in the Confiscation Report for that quarter as well as in succeeding quarter's Reports. It is not known why the seizure reports were not made out and these moneys were not handed

over

E. A. Pritchard, Esquire,

P E K I N G.

2.

726

over to the Accountant, but it is presumed that they were entirely overlooked owing to local troubles prevailing at that time. As late Mr. R. W. Cholmondeley was sick for sometime before he hurriedly evacuated this port for Shanghai in April last it appears that these orders were not properly handed over to his successor.

This is an extraordinary case and I am in a quandary how to adjust the matter. I think there is no alternative but to report these cases in the Confiscation Report for this quarter with two dates — the original date of seizure and the date of reporting — in the English version and one date only, the latter, in the Chinese version. Before bringing in these moneys into account I should be very much obliged if you would let me know your opinion on the subject.

Yours truly,

INDEXED

INSPECTORATE GENERAL OF CUSTOMS,

727

PEKING, 6th December 1927.

Recd 19-12-27.

S/O

Dear Mr. Suzuki,

Thank you for your S/O of 26th November. The matter will have to be adjusted in the Confiscation Report but will, I am afraid, have to be officialised first. So would you please ask for instructions by despatch and defer any action pending receipt of those instructions. Credit is due to Mr. Chi for tracing the money.

Yours truly,

Edwin A. Pritchard

T. Suzuki, Esquire,

WENCHOW.

CUSTOM HOUSE,

728

No. 442.

INDEXED

Wenchow, 7th December, 1927.

erintendent of
toms and the
rganization of
Surtax Office.

Dear Mr. Edwardes,

Mr. Chuan Chih-huan, the new Superintendent, returned to this port from Nanking on the 24th November, and after his return he was busily engaged in reorganization of the Surtax Office. He asked me to send him a daily report of collection instead of that of 10 days' which I did. After a few days he sent his Secretary for a loan of Maritime and Native Customs Duty Memo butts from the 1st November in order to compare with his own records. I sent him all the counterfoils as requested, and as a result of checking, so I was told, a discrepanc of over Hk.Tls. 700.00 was discovered in the Maritime and Native Customs revenues from the date of his assumption of charge, consequently the

H. F. EDWARDES, ESQUIRE,
Etc., Etc., Etc.,
PEKING.

729

the Superintendent discharged the majority of his men and arrested several of them and handed over to the local court for trial and punishment. On the 30th November the Superintendent sent me a letter stating that he intends to instruct his men attached to the Bank of China to chop all Maritime and Native Customs Duty Memos from the 1st December and asking me to release import and export cargo on production of Customs Duty Memos, bearing the Surtax Office chop in addition to the Bank of China's seal following the practice of the Ningpo Customs, etc. I understand that the collection of Surtax is entrusted by the Superintendent to the Bank of China in other Southern ports, and as this looks like the thin end of the wedge I politely answered him on next day saying that the Customs and the Surtax Office are of entirely different concern, that each department should look after its own business, that the Customs cannot share any responsibility in the matter of collection of surtax and requesting him to devise some other means to prevent the leakage

3.

730

leakage of his revenue. In the same evening when I met the Superintendent at a dinner party I explained the matter verbally and he told me that my refusal is quite reasonable. He also told me that he did not know that the surtax is independently collected by his own men at Wenchow and that he is going to propose to the Nanking Government to adopt the Shanghai practice in order to save his office expenses, etc. On the 3rd instant he wrote me a nice letter acknowledging receipt of mine of the 1st and asking me for our co-operation in future. I hope the Superintendent will soon withdraw his men and abolish the present obnoxious system of double examination of cargo and passengers' luggage. I wrote to Mr. Cubbon to verify the Superintendent's statement as to the alleged acceptance of Duty Memos with two seals, but so far I have received no reply from Ningpo.

loor Staff
:ary.

The balance in hand at the end of November was $98.90 without any outstanding liabilities. Strict economy will be

exercised

4.

731

exercised as instructed.

a Tax and Fish
p Licenses.

Early in the morning of the 25th November there was a big row in front of the Custom House between fishermen and the guards of the newly inauguarated Fish Tax Office over the payment of new tax and the unloading of fresh and salt fish was stopped by the latter. The case was immediately reported by the former to the Kuomintang Headquarters and after its intervention fish was allowed to be landed. Local wholesale fish merchants closed their doors in the afternoon to emphasize their dissatisfaction. The collection of tax was postponed pending instructions from Nanking and the shops recommenced their business on next day.

um Monopoly
eau.

Following the drastic measures taken by the Nationalist Government in the case of bribery offered by the opium tenderers and the decision of abolition of the opium monopoly system, the local Opium Monopoly Bureau was closed on the 4th instant, causing a heavy loss of nearly $20,000 to a few local

enterprising

5.

72

enterprising merchants who made advance in getting this job.

|al news. Wild rumours of attempted disturbances by communists were circulated towards the end of last month and the city was under Special Martial Law from the 26th November. Nothing untoward had happened and the Law was lifted on the 4th instant.

Yours truly,

Hayashi

INSPECTORATE GENERAL OF CUSTOMS, 715

S/O INDEXED PEKING, 12th December 1927

Rec'd. 22. Dec. 1927.

Dear Mr. Suzuki,

I have duly received your S/O letter No. 441 of 21st November:

Establishment of Vessel Controlling Bureau.

Leave it to the local authorities to enforce this registration. Should the Superintendent apply to you for assistance, point out that the Customs has no right to detain steamers once they have complied with all treaty obligations.

Yours truly,

[signature]

Suzuki, Esquire,

WENCHOW.

CUSTOM HOUSE,

INDEXED

No. 443. Wenchow, 20th December, 1927

734

Dear Mr. Edwardes,

nge of
erintendent.

Mr. Ho Chia-yu (何家猷) was appointed the Superintendent of Wenchow Customs by the Nanking Government vice Mr. Chuang Chih-huan (莊智煥) transferred to Hangchow to take charge of the Cigarette Tax Office. Mr. Chuang left very hurriedly for Shanghai per S.S. "Kwangchi" on the 17th instant. The new Superintendent is a younger brother of Mr. Ho Chia-chü (何家駒), the present Shanghai Superintendent, and he is expected to arrive here on next Thursday.

llection of
rtax by the
nk of China.

Acting under instructions received from Nanking the former Superintendent entrusted the collection of both Maritime and Native Customs surtax to the Bank of China as from the 18th instant, but he still retains his watchers, etc. All surtax-paid Maritime Customs

H. F. EDWARDES, ESQUIRE,
Etc., Etc., Etc.,
PEKING.

2.

735

Customs duty memos bear the impression of 甌海關內地稅局附稅收訖 chopped by the surtax deputies attached to the Bank. When the Superintendent's Secretary called on me last Tuesday I protested against this practice and he explained to me that this is only a temporary measure. I told him that I take no notice of these chops and repeated to him what I have written to the Superintendent on the 1st instant, the gist of which was mentioned in my S/O letter No. 442. Native Customs duty memos are not chopped by the surtax men. As regards the alleged practice of chopping duty memos in Ningpo, mentioned in my last S/O letter, I have received a reply in the negative from Mr. Cubbon.

[Nat]ive Customs [Rev]enue outside [50] li radius.

As stated in my S/O letter No. 441 this question has been taken up with the former Superintendent, and in reply to my written request to hand over the collection from the 1st June this year I have received a letter from him stating that:-

(1) extra 50 li Native Customs Revenue has never been hypothecated to foreign loan

3.

736

loan and indemnity payments,

(2) the Inspector General's arguments are not based on Treaties,

(3) no further remittance can be made according to Nanking Finance Ministry's instructions, and

(4) suggesting to request the Inspector General to take up the case directly with the Finance Ministry, Nanking.

I am afraid that further protests would be futile, but I would like to be instructed whether I shall keep on protesting or leave the matter in abeyance until more favourable time comes.

racy at Middle
Land.

Mr. Sia Liang, Senior Outdoor Officer, who went down river yesterday to inspect the unofficial Sanpwan Lighthouse (I. G. Despatch No. 1076/88,344), reported to me today that a gang of well-armed pirates, over 100 in number, visited Middle Island on the 17th instant and looted all villages on the Island and took away two men for ransom. The Lighthouse was also visited by them but no damage was done. The case has been reported to the Superintendent.

737

Superintendent.

Weather is ideal and the place is very quiet at present. All the Staff are doing well and join me in sending you best compliments of the season.

Yours truly,

[signature]

INSPECTORATE GENERAL OF CUSTOMS, 733

S/O

INDEXED

PEKING, 21st December, 1927

Rec'd 3-1-1928.

Dear Mr. Suzuki,

I have duly received your S/O letter No. 442 of the 7th December:

Surtax Office: reorganisation of.

Get your port practice, if possible, into line with that of Shanghai, where the Surtax collector receives the Duty Memo after the Customs Banker has finished with it.

Yours truly,

T. Suzuki, Esquire,

WENCHOW.

1928 年

INSPECTORATE GENERAL OF CUSTOMS, 738

S/O

PEKING, 4th January 1928

Recd 14-1-28.

Dear Mr. Suzuki,

I have duly received your S/O letter No. 443 of 20th December:

Collection of Surtax by Bank of China.

You should endeavour to move the Superintendent to cease using the chop, which is undesirable, especially the prefix of 甌海關

N.C. Revenue outside 50 li radius.

As my standing in this matter is based entirely on a Presidential Mandate, which is not recognised by the Nationalist authorities, and as all protests have been, and are, unavailing, you may let the matter rest till a more favourable season.

Yours truly,

Suzuki, Esquire,

WENCHOW.

CUSTOM HOUSE,

INDEXED

S/O No. 444.

Wenchow, 6th January, 1928

Dear Mr. Edwardes,

Revenue, 1927.

The Maritime Customs Revenue for 1927 was Hk.Tls. 114,031 and that of Native Customs was Hk.Tls. 63,197 showing an increase of Hk.Tls. 7,695 and Hk.Tls. 1,426 respectively over the figures for 1926.

Superintendent of Customs.

Mr. Ho Chia-yu, the new Superintendent of Customs, arrived from Shanghai on the 23rd December and took over charge on next day. According to your telegraphic instructions Superintendent Allowance was issued to him on the 28th December. Mr. Ho is not related to Mr. Ho Chia-chu, the present Shanghai Superintendent, as reported in my last S/O letter. He was stationed in Peking for some time in the National Loans Department.

Kerosene Oil Special Tax.

I have received a letter from the Superintendent yesterday transmitting the

instructions

A. H. F. EDWARDES, ESQUIRE,

Etc., Etc., Etc.,

P E K I N G.

2.

2

instructions from the Finance Ministry of the Nationalist Government to the effect that all kerosene oil imported by firms and merchants other than Standard Oil Co., Asiatic Petroleum Co. and Texas Co., who enjoy privilege of discharging cargo into their godowns under special arrangement with the Ministry, should be reported to the Tax Office for examination and payment of tax, and that marks, quantity and date of importation should be notified by the Superintendent to the local Tax Office. As this appears to be the question to be enforced by the Chinese Authorities concerned I have taken no steps in the matter and should the Superintendent make further request to co-operate I intend to inform him that import-duty-paid foreign goods cannot be detained by the Customs.

Yours truly,

[signature]

3

INSPECTORATE GENERAL OF CUSTOMS,

S/O

PEKING, 17th January 1928

Recd 2. February, 1928.

Dear Mr. Suzuki,

I have duly received your S/O letter No. 444 of 6th January:

Special tax on Kerosene Oil.

Your attitude in this matter is correct. Kerosene Oil arriving at Wenchow under E.C. cannot be detained by the Customs. It is up to the Superintendent to make his own arrangements for the collection of this tax independently of the Customs.

Yours truly,

T. Suzuki, Esquire,

WENCHOW.

7

Inspectorate-General of Customs,

INDEXED

PEKING. 20th January, 1928.

Rec'd 2. February, 1928.

Dear Mr. Suzuki,

More than a year has passed since the so-called Washington Surtaxes were first put into operation at Canton, and since that time practically every Port in the country has followed suit, although not always on the same lines in regard to amount and method of levy and to classes of goods taxed. References have been made to these surtaxes in both official and semi-official correspondence at the time of their inception, but as it is essential that I should be in possession of as reliable and as complete information as possible on this subject, I have to request you - even although you may have already done so in part - to supply me as quickly as possible with detailed replies to the following queries.

1. What is the name, English and Chinese, of the Office in your port levying the so-called Washington Surtaxes ?

2. Are surtaxes collected by this Office on Imports only, or on both Imports and Exports - (a) abroad and (b) coastwise ?

3. Are surtaxes collected on Native Customs duties ?

4. When was the collecting of these surtaxes commenced ?

5. What are the exact rates charged ? Are

luxuries

T. Suzuki, Esquire,

WENCHOW.

8

luxuries specially taxed, and, if so, at what rate or rates ? What articles are classed as luxuries ?

6. What is the tax treatment of Wine, Tobacco, and Kerosene Oil ? What rates are levied on these articles in addition to the Customs Import duty ? Are the taxes on these articles collected by a special Office or by the ordinary Surtax Office ?

7. To whom, or to what Government department, is the revenue collected by the Surtax Office remitted ?

8. Leaving out special levies on Wine, Tobacco, and Kerosene Oil, what is the average annual collection raised from these surtaxes at your Port ? (N.B. Separate totals should be shown for Imports, Exports, Native Customs, etc.)

9. What is the average annual collection from special taxes on Wine, Tobacco, and Kerosene Oil ? In the case of Tobacco, is there any discrimination made against foreign firms as compared with Chinese firms ?

10. How is the Surtax Office run at your Port ? What staff is employed, and what is the general modus operandi ?

11. Is there a surtax on Postal Parcels at your Port ? If so, what are the rates levied, and what is the estimated annual income ?

The answers to the above queries should be typed on foolscap, headed "Report on Surtax Collected at ...... " and should be sent here under cover of a semi-official letter.

In

9

In procuring this information you are to be very careful not to convey an impression that the Customs is seeking it in order to use it against the Offices concerned. There is no such intention.

Yours truly,

4

CUSTOM HOUSE,

Wenchow, 28th January, 1923.

S/O No. 445.

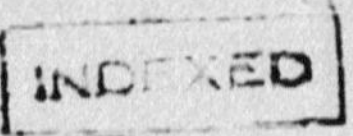

Dear Mr. Edwardes,

Superintendent of Customs:

Mr. Ho Chia-yu left for the Provincial capital on the 11th instant and returned to this port on the 19th. At his special request and following the precedent the Superintendent Allowance was issued on the 14th instant to tide him over the Chinese New Year.

2½ % Surtax on Postal Parcels:

On the 10th instant I received a letter from the Superintendent requesting me to collect surtax on postal parcels by the Customs on his behalf. I answered him that I cannot comply with his request explaining that duties on parcels are collected by the Post Office and remitted to the Customs once a month. I was informed by the Postmaster that an identical letter

A. H. F. EDWARDES, ESQUIRE,

Etc., Etc., Etc.,

P E K I N G.

5

letter was received by him who referred the matter to the Postal Commissioner, and I understand that an arrangement will shortly be made to collect surtax by the Superintendent's deputies attached to the Bank of China.

The weather during the Chinese New Year holidays was wet except one day. Only a few cases of bankruptcy among Chinese merchants and bankers were reported and the city was very quiet and peaceful during the holidays.

Yours truly,

J. Hayashi

INSPECTORATE GENERAL OF CUSTOMS, 6

S/O

PEKING, 10th February, 1928

Rec'd 17-2-28.

Dear Mr. Suzuki,

I have duly received your S/O letter No. 445 of the 28th January:

Superintendent's Allowance:

It is not at all desirable that the Superintendent's Allowance should be issued in advance at China New Year, and this practice is to be discouraged.

Yours truly,

R. Shimoso

For Officiating Inspector General.

T. Suzuki, Esquire,

WENCHOW.

CUSTOM HOUSE,

INDEXED

S/O No. 446.

Wenchow, 11th February, 1928.

Dear Mr. Edwardes,

Report on Surtax collected at Wenchow:

I am sending you, herein enclosed, my report on the Surtax as instructed in your circular S/O dated the 20th January. The S/O letter reached me on the 2nd instant having been considerably delayed owing to new year holidays, Shanghai-Wenchow steamers ceased running for 18 days. The preparation of the report was also delayed on account of prevalence on new year holiday atmosphere, making it very difficult to obtain information required.

Fundamental re-organization of the Customs administration: (Wenchow Despatch No. 4072):

On receipt of the letter in question I intended to wire you for instructions but after consideration I decided to call on the Superintendent to sound his opinion on the subject. I kept quiet all the time and asked him to excuse me to commit my reply on

A. H. F. EDWARDES, ESQUIRE,

Etc., Etc., Etc.,

PEKING.

on paper. In the course of our conversation he told me that he is going to propose to the Nanking Government to close the Superintendent's Office and remove it to the Custom House to exercise full control of the Customs affairs by him lowering the position of the Commissioner to that of an adviser.

I have just received two more letters from the Superintendent, one about the Wuhu Commissioner and the other stating that the Nationalist Government control 16 out of 22 provinces, collect[illegible] 70 % of Customs revenue, and denouncing Peking Government's nominees to control Customs administration, both of which have recently been published in Shanghai papers. I expect I will be bombarded by this kind of letters in future. Shanghai vernacular papers are full of recent occurrences and several inflammatory pamphlets are pouring in from Shanghai Customs Union, causing great uneasiness among our staff. I told them to stick to the post as hard time will soon be over.

General: Two Japanese Destroyers "Tanikaje" and

3.

12

and "Kawakaje" arrived from Foochow on the 3rd instant and left for Formosa on the 5th. During their stay the Commander exchanged calls with local officials who were very friendly.

Three C. I. M. missionaries and a French Sister returned to port from Shanghai on the 8th and more are expected shortly.

Yours truly,

INSPECTORATE GENERAL OF CUSTOMS, 13

S/O INDEXED PEKING, 23rd February 1928

Rec'd 3. March, 1928.

Dear Mr. Suzuki,

I have duly received your S/O letter No. 446 of 11th February:

Reorganisation of Customs.

You acted correctly in not committing yourself with the Superintendent. You should refrain from expressing an opinion to him on the subject, leaving it to him to make such report to the Nanking Government as he sees fit.

Yours truly,

K. Kishimoto

For Officiating Inspector General.

T. Suzuki, Esquire,

WENCHOW.

CUSTOM HOUSE,

14

S/O No. 447.

INDEXED

Wenchow, 24th February, 1928.

Dear Mr Edwardes,

Superintendent of Customs.

Mr. Ho Chia-yu (何家猷), the present Superintendent of Customs, is transferred to Hangchow to be in charge of the Kerosene Oil Tax Office there, and Mr. Pei Tsu-hsiang (貝祖祥), who is the elder brother of the Manager of the Bank of China in Shanghai, is appointed to succeed him. I have just received a telegram from Mr. Maze notifying the departure of the new Superintendent from Shanghai on the 25th. Mr. Pei is the fourth Superintendent since my arrival at this port in October last and I hope he will stay here longer than his predecessors.

Bandits at Haimen:

On the 14th instant the port of Haimen was attacked by a gang of armed bandits numbering about 400. According to

information

A. H. F. EDWARDES, ESQUIRE,

Etc., Etc., Etc.,

P E K I N G.

15

information to hand they systematically looted the city and steamers in port and cleared out with a booty of over $200,000 in silver and valuables. Threatening letters were sent by them to attack the town of Kanmen (坎門), 15 miles from the mouth of Wenchow River, and many refugees are arriving daily from that town to this city.

Juian Canal steam-launch accident.

On the 19th instant a passenger boat towed by the steam lauch "Hsin Kwai Lee" was capsized through carelessness of the lowdah and about 40 people were drowned.

Staff: Mr. Sia Liang, 3rd Class (Chinese) Tidewaiter A.

In his S/O letter No. 410 of the 10th June, 1927, Mr. Ng suggested the issue of an allowance to Mr. Sia for the extra work thrown upon him after the evacuation of foreign staff, and in your reply dated the 6th July it was stated that "the question as to whether Mr. Sia should draw an allowance as Senior Outdoor Officer will be decided later on". Although Mr. Sia was reported at one time to have instigated a campaign to undermine the interests of foreign staff,

3.

16

staff, yet during my stay here for four months I have found him to be an intelligent, obedient and hardworking man and has given satisfaction in performance of his duties, and I recommend that an allowance of say Hk.Tls. 20.00 a month, equivalent to Acting Assistant Boat Officer's allowance, be issued to him with retrospective effect from the date of his taking over charge of outdoor work in April 1927. May I officialize this matter ?

General. Three more British missionaries returned to this port but their families are still staying in Shanghai under Consular advices. All mission buildings were returned to their legitimate owners with the exception of the Methodist Mission College which is still retained by the local authorities and its name was changed to Ou Hai Chung Shan College (甌海中山中學).

Yours truly,

INSPECTORATE GENERAL OF CUSTOMS,

S/O   INDEXED   PEKING, 8th March, 1928

Rec'd 15-III-28.

Dear Mr. Suzuki,

I have duly received your S/O letter No.447 of the 24th February:

New Superintendent of Customs.

Please report the change officially.

Suggested Allowance for Mr. Sia Liang.

This matter will be considered in the near future, when instructions to officialize and apply for a small bonus will be sent you.

Yours truly,

[signature]

T. Suzuki, Esquire,

WENCHOW.

CUSTOM HOUSE,

S/O No. 448. INDEXED Wenchow, 12th March 1928.

18

ae

Superintendent of Customs.

Dear Mr. Edwardes,

Mr. Pei Chih-hsiang (貝志翔) (not Mr. Pei Tsu-hsiang as reported in S/O No. 447), the new Superintendent of Customs, arrived here from Shanghai on the 26th ultimo and took over charge on the 1st instant. Mr. Ho Chia-yu (何家猷), the former Superintendent, left for Hangchow *via* Shanghai on the 29th ultimo. The first problem for the new incumbent to solve is to float 2½ % Surtax bond for \$20,000.00 among local merchants who have already subscribed \$30,000.00 through the magistrate some time ago. Mr. Pei asked me to use my influence over shipping people, especially junk owners, to subscribe to this loan, but I cordially refused and told him to refer the matter to the junk owners' guild.

Revenue

A. H. F. EDWARDES, ESQUIRE,

etc., etc., etc.,

P E K I N G.

2

Revenue stamps on Bills of lading, etc.

The Weiyüan in charge of the local Revenue Stamp Bureau called on me a few days ago with a letter of introduction from the new Superintendent, and told me that he intends to send a representative to the Customs House to inspect bills of lading, shipping orders, etc. and requested me to detain all these documents for his deputy's inspection. This is another humbug but in view of your instructions contained in I. G. Despatch No. 2346/115,446 to Kiukiang, copy of which has been circulated for information and guidance, I asked him to refer the former question to the Superintendent and politely refused to comply with his latter request. I received a letter last Saturday from the Superintendent transmitting a letter from the Stamp Bureau notifying the appointment of a representative to the Customs.

In the meantime I obtained information from the Chinese Chamber of Commerce, Chinese shipping companies and Customs brokers to the effect (1) that they have purchased at a discount large quantities of revenue stamps

issued

3.

issued by the old Chekiang Provincial Government from the former notorious Superintendent, Mr. Hsü Yo-yao (徐樂堯); (2) that it is the intention of the new Weiyüan to invalidate them and enforce the affixing of new revenue stamps issued by the Nationalist Government; and (3) that several merchants and shipping companies requested the Stamp Bureau to exchange old stamps to new ones and upon refusal the Chamber of Commerce is going to have a meeting to take strong action against the Bureau.

As it is not at all desirable to be involved in this question, which might drag us into a difficult position, I pointed out to the Superintendent in writing that we have no foreign steamers engaging in general carrying trade ---- one British and one American for carrying Kerosene oil and a few Japanese charcoal steamers ---- and it would be more effective and economical for the Revenue Stamp Bureau to deal individually with Chinese shipping companies instead of stationing a representative in the Customs. As I also verbally explained the

circumstances

4.

circumstances to the Superintendent I do not think he will go further, but should he insist on stationing a representative in the Customs I shall act according to your instructions mentioned in the Despatch quoted above.

General. Six more missionaries, including three ladies, returned from Shanghai recently.

About 800 soldiers belonging to 32nd Army under the command of General Ch'ien Ta-chün (钱大钧) arrived from Swatow per S/S "Hua Hsin" on the 6th instant on their way to join the Northern Expedition Army, and they are temporarily staying in this port. They are behaving fairly well and the time of their departure to the front is not yet known.

Yours truly,

INDEXED

CUSTOM HOUSE,

S/O No. 449.

Wenchow, 27th March 1928.

Dear Mr. Edwardes,

Revenue Stamps on bills of landing, etc. (S/o No. 448) :

As a result of further request of the Revenue Stamp Bureau through the Superintendent to station a representative in the Customs, I acquiesced in putting him in the banker's room. So far he appeared to the Customs only once and I have not heard anything either from the Superintendent or the Stamp Bureau on this subject. Merchants are still using old stamps freely.

Outward transit dues to be collected by the first inland barrier:

I have received a letter from the Superintendent transmitting the instructions from the Finance Ministry to the effect that in order to safeguard revenue outward transit dues will

A. H. F. EDWARDES, ESQUIRE,
etc., etc., etc.
PEKING.

2.

24

will in future be collected by the first inland barrier to be met with instead of by the Customs at the port of destination. As no san lien tan is issued by this office no action has been taken by me in this matter.

General :

All soldiers of 32nd Army temporarily stationed at this port left for Ningpo yesterday.

The French gunboat "Craoune" arrived from Ningpo on the 21st and departed for Chinhai on the 26th instant.

Yours truly,

[signature]

INSPECTORATE GENERAL OF CUSTOMS, 22

S/O 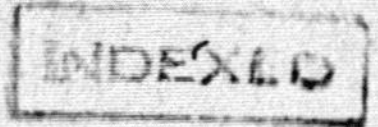 PEKING, 3rd April 1928.

Rec'd 12-4-28.

Dear Mr. Suzuki,

I have duly received your S/O letter No. 448 of 12th March:

Revenue stamps on Bills of Lading.

You are safe so long as you follow the lines indicated in my despatch to Kiukiang No. 2346/115,446. Do not allow yourself to be mixed up in any dispute between the Chinese Chamber of Commerce and the stamp-taxing authorities.

Yours truly,

T. Suzuki, Esquire,

WENCHOW.

CUSTOM HOUSE, 26

S/O No. 450. INDEXED Wenchow, 17th April 1928.

Dear Mr. Edwardes,

Transit Dues in lieu of Likin on Postal Parcels:

On the 29th March I have received a letter from the Superintendent conveying a letter from the newly-established Chêkiang Postal Parcel Tax Bureau (浙江邮包税局) notifying the opening of its office on the 1st April and requesting me to surrender the function of collection of Likin on parcels by the Customs to that office (Vide March Non-urgent correspondence, Subject No. 4).

On the 11th instant Mr. Ho Ch'i-ch'ü (何其樞), the Weiyüan in charge of the local Parcel Tax Bureau, called on me and requested me to cease the collection of Likin as he intends to send his own men to the Post Office to collect it.

I

A. H. F. EDWARDES, ESQUIRE,

etc., etc., etc.,

P E K I N G.

2.

27

I explained to him that the Customs used to remit the Likin collection (less 10 % for cost of collection) to the local Likin Office (温州洋广货捐徵收局) and that I cannot take the matter of changing the office practice into consideration before I get a letter from the Director of the Likin Office stating that he has given up the claim for this money.

On the 13th another letter was received from the Superintendent informing me that at the request of the Parcel Tax Bureau he has consulted with the Bank of China to allow the Bureau's representative to be stationed in the banker's office along with the Surtax men (a small table and two chairs were brought into the banker's office on the 12th without my knowledge). On the 14th I have again received a letter from the Superintendent on this subject stating that as the Wenchow Postmaster has not received any letter from the Customs he cannot change his practice and requesting me to notify the Postmaster to discontinue the collection of Likin as from the 13th April.

I

3.

28

I called on the Superintendent in the same afternoon and pointed out to him that I cannot very well give up the collection of Likin before I get a letter from the Likin Office, either directly or through his hands, asking me to change the office practice. I also drew his attention to the fact that the banker complained to me several times that his office is already crowded with Surtax people (seven men in all), that I have granted to station Revenue Stamp Bureau's men in the banker's office (although they have not turned up yet) and that further admission of outsiders in his office would inconvenience him intolerably. The Superintendent tacitly admitted his fault and asked me to settle the matter amicably.

On the 15th instant Mr. Chu Ting-hsin (朱鼎新), the Director of the Wenchow Likin Office, came to see me and, as I expected, lodged a protest against the change of the practice and asked me to wait until I hear officially from him in writing, which I agreed.

The amount at stake is insignificant, the total collection during 1927 being

Hk.

4.

29

Hk.Tls. 353.171, but according to the new rules, which are very vaguely worded, all import and export parcels over $5.00 in value (educational books and articles and household sundries excepted.) are liable to Chêkiang Provincial Likin at the rate of 5% *ad valorem*. It is reported to me that local piece goods merchants, etc. held a meeting and passed a resolution to oppose this new tax.

Should the Likin Office and the Parcel Tax Office compromise and request me officially to change the practice I shall wire you for instructions.

Accident to Ningpo-Wenchow I.W. steamer:

On the 9th instant on her arrival from Shanghai the Lowdah of the Motor Vessel "Shun Li" reported to the Customs that she brought in 60 Chinese passengers rescued from one of the Ningpo-Wenchow I.W. steamers, S/S "Hsin San Kiang", which went ashore at Lao Shu Shan (老鼠山) near Tau Pang Island on the night of the 7th. He also reported that before taking passengers on board her crew

had

30

had a severe fighting with a gang of pirates who attempted to seize the ill-fated steamer. No lives were lost and the vessel is still aground being guarded by a Chinese gunboat.

Piracy:

The Water Police Cruiser "Hai Ping" left here on the 15th and returned in next afternoon with three wounded sailors on board and one Fukien junk in tow. According to information she engaged severely with a large number of pirates on four junks at Sanpwan Pass (near the Unofficial Light on the Middle Island) and after six hours' hard fighting finally succeeded in dispersing marauders and recapturing a junk from their hands.

Transit Dues in lieu of Likin:

While I was writing this letter another letter was received from the Superintendent stating that as the Likin collecting functions have been completely handed over by the Hangchow Customs this office should follow the precedent immediately. I sent my Writer to the Likin Office to see the Director, who

told

6.

31

told the former that he will withdraw his protest and write me officially to that effect, hence I wired you for instructions.

Yours truly,

Hayashi

Recd 1-5-28.

[A.—42]

25

ES/O

INSPECTORATE GENERAL OF CUSTOMS,

PEKING, 23 April 1928

Dear Sir,

I am directed by the Inspector General to inform you that your S/O Letter No. 449, dated 27th March, has been duly received.

Yours truly,

Stanley F. Wright

Personal Secretary.

T. Suzuki, Esquire.

Wenchow.

2000 / 12.26.

CUSTOM HOUSE,

S/O, No, 451. INDEXED Wenchow, 26th April 1928. 37

Dear Mr. Edwardes,

Likin on Postal Parcels:

According to your telegraphic instructions of the 18th instant I have handed over the work of collecting Likin on postal parcels to the Chêkiang Postal Parcel Tax Bureau on the 19th. A full report on this subject will be submitted in due course of time.

Exemption of foreign and Chinese cigarettes from Transit Dues and Native Customs duty, Finance Ministry's instructions in re:

As stated in my comments on Ningpo Commissioner's Despatch No. 5444/I.G. (N.C. No. 412) I discussed the matter with the Superintendent before taking any action. I told him that according to the new order not only the Transit Dues or Native Customs duty on foreign cigarettes

A. H. F. EDWARDES, ESQUIRE,

etc., etc., etc.

P E K I N G.

should

2.

58

should not be levied but the collection of regular Maritime Customs export and coast trade duties as well as Native Customs duty on native cigarettes should be ceased, which is a very important question. I also pointed out to him that no complaints have ever been made by merchants here against all the existing Maritime and Native Customs duties and dues, so that there is no reason for the Ministry to interfere with the present Customs duty treatment. Several despatches on this subject received from the Finance Ministry were shown to me by the Superintendent, who concurred with my opinion that the new ruling has nothing to do with the Customs and it is not necessary to change the present practice, therefore no action was taken in this matter.

Superintendent's Surtax Office levies ½ of the Customs Transit Dues on foreign cigarettes which is paid by local tobacco merchants under protest, and I understand that they complained to the Finance Ministry against this imposition, as the term of 復子口税 is used in the first part

3.

19
71

part of the Ministry's Despatch. Should I receive further instructions which affect our revenue I shall refer the case to you for instructions.

Customs official language:

I have received a letter from the Superintendent yesterday transmitting instructions from the Kuan Wu Shu of the Finance Ministry to the effect that in order to maintain China's dignity as an independent nation, etc., etc., Chinese language must be used in future in all Customs documents, notifications and pishih, and that the use of Chinese language should gradually be introduced into all office correspondence, books, accounts, etc. As a reply is wanted I simply acknowledged receipt of the letter stating that the case will be reported to the Inspector General.

Yours truly,

INSPECTORATE GENERAL OF CUSTOMS. 32

S/O

PEKING, 5th May, 1928

Recd 14-5-28.

Dear Mr. Suzuki,

I have duly received your S/O letter No.450 of the 17th April:

Transit Dues on Postal Parcels.

I sent you my instructions by telegram on 18th April to hand over collection of likin on Postal Parcels, but to continue as before to collect Customs duty on all parcels liable to such.

Yours truly,

T. Suzuki, Esquire,

WENCHOW.

CUSTOM HOUSE,

S/O. No. 452.

Wenchow, 11th May 1928.

Dear Mr. Edwardes,

Consolidated Cigarette Tax and Maritime and Native Customs duties:

Mr. C. Cance, the travelling agent of the British-American Tobacco Co. who is making a tour of inspection of various system of taxation in Kiangsu and Chêkiang provinces, called on me a few days ago and endorsed my opinion mentioned in my S/o letter No. 451, viz, the company, in addition to the Consolidated Cigarette Tax, recognise the following impositions on foreign and native cigarettes.

Foreign cigarettes: Maritime Customs import duty
Import surtax
Transit dues (or Native Customs duty)

Native

A. H. F. EDWARDES, ESQUIRE,
etc., etc., etc.,
P E K I N G.

Native cigarettes: Maritime Customs export duty
Export surtax
Coast trade duty
Native Customs duty.

I understand that he went to see the Wenchow Superintendent, who promised him to instruct the Surtax Offices to discontinue the collection of surtaxes on Native Customs duty and Transit dues.

<u>Additional import and export applications for the Surtax Office:</u>

I have received a letter from the Superintendent conveying an order from the Finance Ministry to the effect that when applying for import and export cargo the merchant should be told to hand in two additional applications to the Customs for transmission to the Surtax Office. No action was taken by me except acknowledging receipt of the letter and informing him that the case will be reported to the Inspector General.

<u>Staff:</u>

3.

49

Staff:

Mr. T.J. Broderick, Tidesurveyor B, arrived here from Foochow on the 28th April and took up his quarters on the Conquest Island. Mr. H.A. Thalberg, Assistant Examiner B, reported for duty on the 1st instant, and at his request he was temporarily quartered in the Tidewaiters' rooms on the top of the Post Office.

House coolie for the Tidesurveyor's House:

There is only one old gatekeeper for the three houses on the Conquest Island, and Mr. Broderick wishes to engage a coolie for his house for carrying water, etc., as his house in Pagoda Anchorage was provided with three official servants. I would like to know whether such proposal will meet your approval if applied for officially.

General:

Various memorial days passed off very peacefully. With the exception of appearance of a few anti-Japanese Shantung Expedition posters the city remains quiet, and so far anti-Japanese boycott movement is not on foot.

Schoolboys

4.

50

Schoolboys are attending to their lessons by order of the Provincial Authorities in Hangchow.

Yours truly,

[signature]

Recd 24-5-28.

[A.—42]

40

S/O

INSPECTORATE GENERAL OF CUSTOMS,

PEKING, 17 May 1928

Dear Sir,

I am directed by the Inspector General to inform you that your S/O Letter No. 451, dated 26 April, has been duly received.

Yours truly,

Stanley F. Wright

Personal Secretary.

T. Suzuki, Esquire

Wenchow.

000 / 12.26.

INSPECTORATE GENERAL OF CUSTOMS,

S/O

PEKING, 25th May, 1928

Recd 4-6-28.

INDEXED

Dear Mr. Suzuki,

I have duly received your S/O letter No.452 of the 11th May:

Proposal to engage coolie for Tidesurveyor's House.

A watchman seems to be the only official servant supplied in the past: the present proposal would therefore entail an increase in staff, which can only be allowed if really justified. What is your own opinion ?

Yours truly,

T. Suzuki, Esquire,

WENCHOW.

CUSTOM HOUSE,

S/O No. 453.

Wenchow 25th May 1928.

Dear Mr. Edwardes,

Outdoor Staff Library:

In your S/O letter dated the 22nd October last you instructed my predecessor not to draw the annual grant for 1927 and also not to incur any further expenditure either for renewals or other subscriptions without first referring to you. In reply to this letter I stated in my S/O letter No. 442 of 7th December last that the balance in hand at the end of November was $98.90 without any outstanding liabilities and that strict economy will be exercised. The subscriptions to 14 English papers for the period January to December 1927 amounting to £19: 12s: od was paid in advance to Mudie's Library in September 1926, and although no request for their renewals has been made these papers for 1928

are

A. H. F. EDWARDES, ESQUIRE,

etc., etc., etc.,

PEKING.

are arriving continually, due, perhaps, to some misunderstanding on the part of Mudie's Library. We have now $108.77 in hand and the members' monthly subscriptions amount to $7.00, so that should we receive a bill from Mudie's Library for roughly £20 our fund will not be enough to meet this liability without drawing on the annual grant.

In his memorandum to me the Tidesurveyor states that should the Inspector General renew the annual grant to the library it is the intention of the members to call a meeting for the purpose of cancelling some of the publications ordered and to substitute periodicals and books pertaining to China in accordance with I.G. instructions. Our foreign Outdoor Staff have been appointed again, and I hope you will authorise me to issue the annual grant to the library for this year.

Anti-Japanese boycott:

The anti-Japanese boycott was started on the 17th instant and many male and female students are patrolling the wharves and the

Customs

3.

Customs Examination Shed in search of "enemy" goods, but so far they are orderly and did not interfere with the Customs work. The Japanese destroyer "Tanikaje" arrived from Amoy on the 17th instant and is anchoring in port. The time of her departure is not known at present. The city is very quiet and the business is carried out as usual.

Yours truly,

56

CUSTOM HOUSE,

S/O No. 454.

Wenchow, 8th June, 1928.

INDEXED

Dear Mr. Edwardes,

Pilotage: shelter for boatmen-pilots on White Rock:

In I.G. Despatch No. 1481/115,441 you instructed me to look into the matter of providing a shelter for our boatmen-pilots on White Rock to improve local pilotage conditions. Accordingly I have selected a suitable site, obtained estimates from local contractors, and drafted a Despatch sometime ago. In the meantime I was informed privately that our boatmen, especially No. 1, are not keen in this scheme, so I asked Mr. Tidesurveyor Broderick to investigate the matter, and according to his report our boatmen outwardly appreciate the idea but inwardly they are not in favour of it owing to rampancy of pirates in down river districts. They told Mr. Broderick that when they pass a night or nights on board sampan near White

Rock

A. H. F. EDWARDES, ESQUIRE.

Etc., Etc., Etc.,

PEKING.

2.

57

Rock they are obliged to change her anchorage several times in order to avoid detection by pirates, and he is of opinion that should a permanent shelter be erected on shore it would not be utilised by our boatmen until more peaceful conditions prevail in down river districts. Under these circumstances I think it would be better to leave the question in abeyance until more favourable time comes.

Staff:

Your telegram of the 5th instant notifying me the transfer of Mr. Hsei Hui (謝煇), 2nd Clerk A, to Mengtsz has been duly received and he was ordered to leave the port for Shanghai by next steamer on the 13th.

House coolie for Tidesurveyor's Quarters:

The time is not opportune to raise the question and, moreover, as it does not seem very difficult to arrange locally to meet requirements without engaging additional hand I told Mr. Broderick that the matter will be dropped for the time being.

General:

3.

58

General:

Everything is quiet locally. The Japanese destroyer "Tanikaze" is still in port.

Yours truly,

[signature]

45

INSPECTORATE GENERAL OF CUSTOMS,

S/O

PEKING, 11th June, 1928

Rec'd 28-6-28.

Dear Mr. Suzuki,

I have duly received your S/O letter No.453 of the 25th May:

Outdoor Staff Library.

You should write at once to Mudie's Library and point out that the periodicals which are being sent to you were not renewed, and arrange to pay for all those received up to a fixed date, and renew only such as can be afforded. You may draw a library grant of Hk.Tls.50 for the current year, but please make application by despatch.

Yours truly,

[signature]

T. Suzuki, Esquire,

WENCHOW.

59

INSPECTORATE GENERAL OF CUSTOMS.

S/O

INDEXED

PEKING, 28th June, 1928

Rec'd 9-July-1928.

Dear Mr. Suzuki,

I have duly received your S/O letter No.454 of the 8th June:

Pilotage: shelter for boatmen-pilots.

Yes! Leave this question of a pilotage shelter over for the time being.

Yours truly,

T. Suzuki, Esquire,

WENCHOW.

CUSTOM HOUSE,

S/O No. 455.  Wenchow, 29th June, 1928. 60

Dear Mr. Edwardes,

Native Customs duty and Transit Dues; Nationalist Government instructs special-tax-paid kerosene oil and gasolene are to be exempted from:

I have received a letter from the Superintendent transmitting a letter from the local Kerosene Oil Tax Bureau stating that according to the instructions received from the Ministry of Finance of the Nationalist Government kerosene oil and gasolene imported by Asiatic Petroleum Co., Standard Oil Co., and Texas Co., after payment of a special tax (now raised to $1.00 per unit) are permitted to be sent anywhere in China without further taxation as per agreement entered into by the Nationalist Government with the three oil companies, and requesting me to instruct the Native Customs to discontinue

A. H. F. EDWARDES, ESQUIRE,

Etc., Etc., Etc.,

P E K I N G.

61

discontinue the practice of either demanding the production of transit pass or collecting Native Customs duty on such oil.

As this is exactly the same case with Consolidated-Tax-paid cigarettes, which was reported to you by the Ningpo Commissioner in his despatch No. 5,444 (N.C. No. 412) in April last, I have replied to the Superintendent quoting your instructions contained in your Despatch No. 2134/116,934 to Ningpo, and copies of correspondence will be forwarded in non-urgent Chinese correspondence for June.

Outdoor Staff Library:

Your S/O letter dated the 11th instant in answer to my S/O No. 453 reached me yesterday. A meeting will be held in a day or two and Mudie's Library will be notified to discontinue sending periodicals with the exception of a few which will be decided by the meeting. Strict economy will be exercised to make our library self-supporting without drawing I.G. grant. A despatch will be sent in a few days' time.

Superintendent

3.

62

Superintendent of Customs:

Mr. Pei Chih-hsiang left for Shanghai on the 24th instant to attend the Financial Conference to be held in Nanking. He will be away for about three weeks and during his absence his secretary will carry out the routine work.

General:

Everything is very quiet here. Owing to stagnant tea trade our revenue for this month decreased roughly by Hk.Tls. 5,000.00 as compared with that for June last year. H.I.J.M.S. "Kawakaje" arrived from Formosa on the 15th instant and her sister ship "Tanikaje" left for Formosa on the 17th.

We congratulate heartily that Peking and Tientsin have been peacefully transferred to Southern party.

Yours truly,

CUSTOM HOUSE,

S/O.

Ningpo 4th June, 1928.

Recd. 10th July, 1928

Dear Suzuki,

With reference to my despatch No.89/909 to Wenchow, the Superintendent has written to me and informed me that the Ningpo Chamber of Commerce has already petitioned the Government for an extension of the privileged treatment of sugar shipped on inland water vessels from Ningpo. In view of this fact, and of the impossibility of receiving a reply from the Government within this short space of time, the Superintendent has asked me to permit of an extension of this concession until a reply has been received from the Government. I have accordingly arranged for the Superintendent's request to be complied with.

\- - - - - - - - - - - - - - -

I hope you are not having it too hot, and that you find Wenchow to your liking.

With kind regards.

Yours sincerely,

J. W. Hubbard

T. Suzuki, Esquire,

W E N C H O W.

INSPECTORATE GENERAL OF CUSTOMS,

S/O

PEKING, 13th July 1928

Recd 23-7-28.

63

INDEXED

Dear Mr. Suzuki,

I have duly received your S/O letter No. 455 of 29th June:

Kerosene Oil Tax.

You acted correctly.

Yours truly,

T. Suzuki, Esquire,

WENCHOW.

CUSTOM HOUSE,

S/O No. 456. 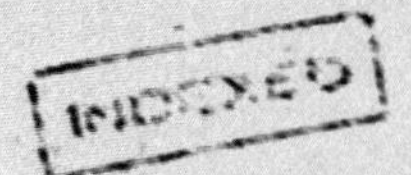 Wenchow . 13th July, 1923.

Dear Mr. Edwardes,

Staff: Mr. Sia Ing K'ing (谢承钦), 3rd Assistant A, reported for duty on the 7th instant on transfer from Chinkiang and was placed in charge of the General Office. Mr. Chi Pao-yuan (戚葆元), 4th Assistant A, will be detailed for duty at the Native Customs from the 16th instant after the quarterly Returns and Reports have been finished. Mr. T. J. Broderick, Tidesurveyor B, is now on sick leave having been bitten by a three-inch-long centipede in his leg a few days ago. He is under medical treatment and I hope he will be able to come on duty again shortly.

General. All the Staff are anxiously watching what action will be taken by

A. H. F. EDWARDES, ESQUIRE,

Etc., Etc., Etc.,

PEKING.

2.

68

by the new Government towards the Customs, but they are calmly carrying out their work as usual.

Mr. Chang I-ming (張一鳴), newly appointed manager of the C.M.S.N. Co., arrived from Shanghai yesterday and called on me this morning. He told me that he is going to apply to the Head Office to send more ships to take general cargo to Shanghai and I hope his proposal will materialize.

H.I.J.M.S. "Kawakaze" left for Formosa on the 10th instant.

Yours truly,

[signature]

INSPECTORATE GENERAL OF CUSTOMS. 37

S/O

PEKING, 21st July 1928

INDEXED

Recd 2nd August, 1928.

Dear Mr. Suzuki,

Consolidated Cigarette Tax and Maritime and Native Customs Duties:

With reference to your comments on Ningpo despatch No.5444 and to your S/O letters Nos.451 and 452, the attitude adopted by the Superintendent at Ningpo has been such that I have been compelled to authorise the Commissioner there to give effect to the instructions of the Nationalist Government as interpreted by the Superintendent - under protest of course - and to exempt cigarettes which have paid the tax from Native Customs duties. During this period of transition it is a matter of the utmost difficulty to keep the practice at the various ports uniform, and in many cases, especially those in which departures from recognised procedure are involved, the only possible way is to treat with each port according to the circumstances locally. It was for

this

T. Suzuki, Esquire,

WENCHOW.

88

this reason that I did not send a copy of my despatch authorising the Ningpo Commissioner to act in accordance with the Superintendent's request. From the view taken by your Superintendent, it would appear that an urgent situation in regard to these exemptions from Native Customs duty is unlikely to arise, but, should it do so, please telegraph immediately for instructions as, although it is absolutely necessary for us to uphold our position in regard to duties collected according to Treaty and duties assigned to the service of Foreign Loans and Indemnities, I do not wish to place Commissioners in an invidious position vis-a-vis their Superintendents and the Nationalist Government.

Finally, in view of the fact that your Superintendent is of opinion that duties hitherto collected by us (M.C. and N.C.) are unaffected by the consolidated taxation policy of the Nationalist Government, which view would appear to be supported by the Agent of the British American Tobacco Company referred to in your S/O No.452, it appears possible that the Ningpo Superintendent has misinterpreted the instructions of the Nationalist Government and forced

the

89

the issue by an unyielding attitude. I would be glad, therefore, if you could raise the question discreetly with your Superintendent - omitting all reference to Ningpo of course - and obtain through him an official intimation as to whether the Nationalist Government intends that Native Customs duty should be exempted or levied in the case of cigarettes etc. paying Consolidated Taxes.

Yours truly,

CUSTOM HOUSE,

S/O No. 457.

Wenchow, 31st July, 1928.

Dear Mr. Edwardes,

Nankeens; exemption from Native Customs duty:.

In the beginning of this month a letter has been received from the Superintendent transmitting the instructions from the Ministry of Finance, Nationalist Government, to exempt Nankeens from Native Customs duty. Since the receipt of this letter three lots of Nankeens arrived by I.W.S.N. steamers from Haimen (海門), where Ningpo Superintendent's extra 50-li barrier is established, and as these lots were covered by Duty free documents issued by that barrier, they were released on deposit of duty pending arrival of your circular instructions.

Superintendent of Customs:

Mr. Pei Chih-hsiang returned to port from Nanking on the 19th instant.

Staff:

A. H. F. EDWARDES, ESQUIRE,
Etc., Etc., Etc.,
PEKING.

2.

82

Staff:

Mr. T. J. Broderick, Tidesurveyor B, who had been laid up as a result of centipede bite, reported for duty after nine days' sick leave.

Yours truly,

[signature]

Rec'd 13-8-28.

[A.—42]

69

INSPECTORATE GENERAL OF CUSTOMS,

I/O

PEKING, 3 August 1928

Dear Sir,

I am directed by the Inspector General to inform you that your S/O Letter No. 456, dated 13th July, has been duly received.

Yours truly,

Stanley F. Wright

Personal Secretary.

T. Suzuki, Esquire,
Wenchow.

100 / 12.26.

INSPECTORATE GENERAL OF CUSTOMS,

S/O PEKING, 13th August, 1928

Rec'd 23-8-28.

Dear Mr. Suzuki,

I have duly received your S/O letter No.457 of the 31st July:

Nankeens: exemption from Native Customs Duty.

Give effect to the instructions of the Government and exempt from N.C. duty, but please officialise for purposes of record.

Yours truly,

T. Suzuki, Esquire,

WENCHOW.

CUSTOM HOUSE,

S/O No. 458. INDEXED Wenchow, 17th August 1928 97

Dear Mr. Edwardes,

I have duly received your S/O letter dated the 21st July.

Consolidated Taxes and Maritime and Native Customs duties:

It was rather awkward for me to take up the matter again and to urge on the Superintendent for a reply to my letter of the 30th June (vide Non-urgent Chinese Correspondence, June, Subject 1; and S/O No. 455) in which I pointed out that the case of kerosene oil is identical to that of cigarettes and that the Ministry's instructions cannot be complied with. On the 8th instant the Superintendent's chief secretary, Mr. Chang Kuei yung (張桂榮), — who had served under Mr. Hsü Yo-yao, former Superintendent, and was recently re-appointed by the present incumbent — called on me and informed me that the Ministry's

A. H. F. EDWARDES ESQUIRE,

Etc., Etc., Etc.,

PEKING.

2.

91

Ministry's definite instructions regarding cigarettes and kerosene oil have arrived and asked me to comply with instructions promptly without referring to you as I may get into trouble if I lay the matter over. I told him that I have no authority to change office practice of such importance without first obtaining your approval. I also pointed out that in former days these instructions have invariably been sent to port Commissioners through the Inspector General, and that the Ministry should be approached to re-establish this time-honoured practice as soon as possible for the sake of uniformity, economy, time-saving, smooth-working, etc., etc. The Ministry's instructions regarding cigarettes, kerosene oil and nankeens have been given effect to and these cases were reported to you officially as instructed in your telegram.

Wheat bran for export abroad: exemption from Maritime Customs export duty:

On the 7th instant I have received a letter from the Superintendent conveying Kuan Wu Shu's instructions to the effect that the Shanghai

3.

92

Shanghai Commissioner and the Superintendent have been instructed to exempt wheat bran produced by flour mills, on which consolidated tax had been paid to the Flour Special Tax Bureau (麦粉特税局), from Maritime Customs export duty (both 出口關税 and 出口正税 are used) and 2½% surtax when exported abroad, and that this practice is to be extended to all ports in Kiangsu, Chêkiang and Anhui provinces. This does not concern the Wenchow Customs as we have no flour mill in this district and there is no export of this article from this port. So far only Native Customs duty has been encroached by the Consolidated Taxation policy, and this is the first attempt of the Ministry to interfere with regular Maritime Customs duty. Should this new system put into practice I am afraid that many more Consolidated Tax Bureaux for other important articles would be established at the expense of the Maritime Customs revenue.

Activities of local Likin Office (or Yang Kuang Chü 洋廣局):

Towards the end of July the local Likin Office requested me through the Superintendent

4.

93

Superintendent to grant permission to send its men on board steamers for examination of cargo, and also to allow its deputy to come to the General Office to copy all import and export applications. Upon my refusal (vide Non-urgent Chinese Correspondence, July, Subject 7) the Likin Office established a branch office near the C.M.S.N. Co.'s wharf and its plain-cloth watchers are holding up passengers' luggage on the street outside the wharf compound and watching examination of cargo by our Examiner in the godowns. So far they did not interfere with our work, but this does not seem to be a good sign for the early abolition of likin.

Yours truly,

CUSTOM HOUSE,

S/O No. 459. INDEXED Wenchow, 24th August, 1928. 95

Dear Mr. Edwardes,

Consolidated Tax on wheat bran and exemption from Maritime Customs export duty: (S/O No. 458):

On the 20th instant I have received another letter from the Superintendent on this subject transmitting definite and strongly-worded instructions from the Ministry of Finance to put them into practice without delay. Wheat bran for export abroad only was mentioned in the previous letter, but new instructions include coastwise shipments as well. As stated in my last S/O these instructions do not concern this office as there is no trade in this article, but I would like to know the Inspectorate's attitude towards this important question for my information and guidance.

Consolidated Tax on foils and exemption from other duties and taxes:

Another Consolidated Tax, this time on all

H. F. EDWARDES, ESQUIRE,
Etc., Etc., Etc.,
P E K I N G.

all kinds of foils! The Wenchow branch office of the Foil Special Tax Bureau for Kiangsu and Chêkiang Provinces (江浙箔类特税局) was opened on the 15th March, 1928, but its establishment has not been notified to me either directly or through the Superintendent. The quantity of tin foil and other kinds of foils which pass through the Wenchow Maritime and Native Customs is insignificant. According to information obtained from reliable sources tin foil generally comes from Fukien overland, and as the quantity is not large enough to cover office expenses the local office attempted to levy tax (12½ % ad valorem) on joss paper and joss paper dollars, but it has not been carried out owing to strong objections raised by merchants.

According to instructions issued by the Ministry of Finance transmitted through the Superintendent on the 20th instant, all kinds of foils after payment of special tax are to be exempted from other duties and taxes (其他税捐), which, I think, include the Native Customs duty. No mention of Maritime Customs

3.

91

Customs export duty is made therein as in the case of wheat bran. I have heard no complaints from the merchants for the payment of Maritime and Native Customs duties since the opening of this office, so that I shall wait for further development of the case and will wire you for instructions if more pressure is bear upon me.

Yours truly,

[signature]

[A.—42]

94

INSPECTORATE GENERAL OF CUSTOMS,

/0

PEKING, 3rd September 1928
Rec'd 13-9-28.

Dear Sir,

I am directed by the Inspector General to inform you that your S/O Letter No. 458, dated 17th August, has been duly received.

Yours truly,

H. Williamson

For Personal Secretary.

T. Suzuki, Esquire

Wenchow.

0/12.26.

INSPECTORATE GENERAL OF CUSTOMS,

S/O [INDEXED] PEKING, 8th September 1928

Recd 20-9-28.

98

Dear Mr. Suzuki,

I have duly received your S/O letter No. 459 of 24th August:

<u>Wheat Bran: exemption of, from export duty</u>.

If wheat bran is exported from your port, you may give effect to the instructions of the Ministry of Finance.

Yours truly,

[signature]

for O. I. G.

Suzuki, Esquire,

WENCHOW.

INDEXED

CUSTOM HOUSE,

/o No. 460.

Wenchow, 11th September, 1928.

Dear Mr. Edwardes,

Organization of the Association for the Severance of Economic Relations with Japan:

Under the auspices of the Kuomintang, local military and civil officials, Chamber of Commerce, etc. the Wenchow branch of the Association was organised on the 23rd August, and a set of regulations, similar to that published in papers, has recently been issued for the registration of Japanese goods and punishment of "traitors". The Association established its office in the China Merchants Steam Navigation Company's premises, and its members, principally students, are very active in searching passengers' luggage and examining "enemy" goods, but so far they did not interfere with the Customs work.

Typhoon:

H. F. EDWARDES, ESQUIRE,

Etc., Etc., Etc.,

PEKING.

2.

10

Typhoon:

On the 6th instant a fairly severe typhoon visited the port during the afternoon and throughout the night, but luckily no serious damage was done to properties both afloat and ashore. A pontoon at the Yung Chüan Wharf, outside the East Gate for berthing Wenchow-Ningpo Inland Waters steamers, was sunk, and a slight damage was done to the chicken house in the Commissioner's house compound.

Staff, Long leave:

Mr. T. J. Broderick, Tidesurveyor B, sent in an application for six months' leave from the 16th April, 1929, and it was forwarded under cover of Wenchow Despatch No. 4088. His leave is due in October, 1929, but he is very anxious to be at home in next spring to look after his children as stated in his application, which, I hope, will receive your favourable consideration.

Yours truly,

[signature]

102

INDEXED

CUSTOM HOUSE,

S/O No. 461.

Wenchow 29th September, 1928.

Dear Mr. Edwardes,

Typhoon:

The second typhoon visited the port on the 14th instant but it was milder in force than that on the 6th and practically no damage was done.

Shipping:

Contrary to an announcement of the new manager of the C.M.S.N. Co. on his arrival that a new steamer will be added to the Shanghai-Wenchow run, the S.S. "Kwangchi" was withdrawn for the Tientsin-Tangku service from the beginning of this month. As the S.S. "Haean" is the only regular vessel carrying mails weekly between Shanghai and Wenchow at present, interport communications were very badly cut off; a letter recently arrived from Peking took twelve days and from Amoy seventeen days.

General:

A. H. F. EDWARDES, ESQUIRE,
Etc., Etc., Etc.,
P E K I N G.

2.

103

General:

The Cigarette Special Tax Bureau and The Kerosene Oil Special Tax Bureau have been amalgamated on the 26th instant under instructions received from the Ministry of Finance.

The anti-Japanese boycott is still going on, but students are forbidden to go about, their place having been taken by shop-assistants, etc. who are hired by the committee and paid out of "Registration Fees".

The Mid-Autumn settling day passed off very quietly, no important failures having been reported.

Yours truly,

[signature]

Rec'd 15-10-28. 161

[A.—42]

INSPECTORATE GENERAL OF CUSTOMS,

PEKING, 3rd October 1928

Dear Sir,

I am directed by the Inspector General to inform you that your S/O Letter No. 460, dated 11th September, has been duly received.

Yours truly,

Stanley F. Wright

Personal Secretary.

Suzuki, Esquire,

WENCHOW.

/ 12.26.

Recd 25/10/28.

[A.—42]

104

S/O

INSPECTORATE GENERAL OF CUSTOMS,

PEKING, 15th Oct. 1928

Dear Sir,

I am directed by the Inspector General to inform you that your S/O Letter No. 461, dated 29th September, has been duly received.

Yours truly,

E. T. Williams

for Personal Secretary.

Suzuki, Esquire,

WENCHOW.

30/12.26.

CUSTOM HOUSE,

S/O No. 462. INDEXED Wenchow 23rd October, 1928. 105

Dear Mr. Edwardes,

I much regret for my delay in writing this S/O letter for several days, owing to pressure of work caused by the seizure of piece goods as mentioned below:-

Seizure of large quantity native factory piece goods declared as foreign under E. C.: The case was reported in Wenchow Despatch No. 4089. As stated therein the seizure was effected under exceptional circumstances and I cannot understand why local merchants attempted to save duty amounting to Hk.Tls. 384.795 running such a large risk of being caught red-handed. After the seizure was made some merchants told me that all goods are of Japanese origin, but I think this is merely an excuse as all boxes are plainly marked and some of them sealed by the

factories

A. H. F. EDWARDES, ESQUIRE,

Etc., Etc., Etc.,

PEKING.

2.

108

factories concerned and every piece bears the factory's label. This being a record case in this port I was bombarded by petitions, and incessant calls of "friends" occupied a lot of my time in and out of the office. The local Chinese Chamber of Commerce has been indifferent in this case from the beginning and did not appear on the stage until last moment, when the Chairman called on me and, having admitted the merchants' fault, requested me to reduce a fine, which I did after prolonged argument. All local Customs brokers, nine in all, are not guaranteed, therefore I am taking this opportunity to enforce the execution of bond (C.-107) by them, which will not be encountered with much opposition.

General:

A very large fire broke out on the night of the 21st and over 150 houses, including many large shops on the main street, have been reduced to ashes.

Wenchow-

3.

[0]

Wenchow-Shanghai steamers —— "Haean" and "Kaho" —— are now running regularly.

Yours truly,

INSPECTORATE GENERAL OF CUSTOMS, 188

S/O

INDEXED

PEKING, 7th November, 1928.

Rec'd 19-11-28.

Dear Mr. Suzuki,

I have duly received your S/O letter No. 462 of 23rd October:

Seizure of Factory Cotton Piece Goods.

You report in your despatch No. 4089 that the Superintendent has requested you to detain the goods, if you decide to confiscate them, as his surtax office also intends to fine the merchants and that you have refused to comply with his request, saying that you will let him know of your decision after the case has been settled. While you would appear to have successfully dealt with this case, you were not quite right in not informing the Superintendent of your decision till after the case has been settled. In this connection, I have to refer you to I.G. Circular No. 3491, §5, which lays down that, in important cases, involving heavy penalties,

the

T. Suzuki, Esquire,

WENCHOW.

109

the Superintendent should be consulted. It is, however, hoped that we shall hear no more from him about the case.

Yours truly,

CUSTOM HOUSE,

S/O No. 463.

Wenchow, 7th November 1928.

Dear Mr. Edwardes,

Export of charcoal to Japan:

In 1927 the first charcoal steamer left here for Japan on the 23rd September, but owing to the activities of the Anti-Japanese Boycott Association none entered the port so far in this year. At the end of last month the Association, assisted by some students, sealed up all the charcoal godowns owned by Chinese merchants in order to prevent charcoal being sold to Japanese firms for export to Japan. There are three kinds of charcoal on the market viz.: (1) hardwood charcoal for export to Japan, (2) softwood charcoal for local consumption and export to Shanghai, and (3) pinewood charcoal mostly used by local blacksmiths. It is reported in local papers that a proposal was made by a few members of the Boycott

H. F. Edwardes, Esquire
Etc., Etc., Etc.,
PEKING.

Boycott Association to force all Chinese merchants to ship their stocks — soft and hard — to Northern ports to be disposed of in China, but this, being a great sacrifice, was strongly opposed by the latter. It is also reported that owing to the strong attitude taken by Mitsui Bussan Kaisha, who stock over 150,000 bags in their godowns, the Boycott Association finally agreed to allow shipment of charcoal purchased before the 3rd May this year. While writing this letter Mitsui Bussan Kaisha handed in an export application for 36,000 bags to be shipped to Yokohama by the S.S. "Fujisan Maru" which is expected to arrive here tomorrow, and what action will be taken by the Association after the steamer's arrival is watched with great interest by local merchants.

Superintendent of Customs:

Mr. Pei Chih-hsiang went to Shanghai on the 27th ultimo to attend the Extraordinary Financial Meeting and returned to this port on the 5th instant.

Yours truly,

[signature]

CUSTOM HOUSE, 113

S/O No. 464. INDEXED Wenchow, 22nd November, 1928.

Dear Mr. Edwardes,

Your S/O letter dated the 7th instant reached me on the 19th.

Seizure of Factory Cotton Piece Goods:

I regret that I did not report the case in details. While the overhauling of boxes was going on, Mr. Pei Hsüeh-ts'ên (貝雪岑), Superintendent's Secretary, and Mr. Chang Kuei-jung (張桂榮), Chief Inspector, came to my office and told me that they were sent by the Superintendent to ask me to pay special attention to this case as it is very important. I told them that I will do my best and when I asked them to inform the Superintendent that I shall call on him as soon as the seizure report is made out, they hesitatingly told me that Mr. Pei Chih-hsiang, the Superintendent, went to Shanghai on the 1st September on some private affairs and

H. F. Edwardes, Esquire,
Etc., Etc., Etc.,
PEKING.

2.

and the date of his return is uncertain. I took extra precaution in dealing with the case, I.G. Circulars, including No. 3491, have been read carefully, my staff's advices freely listened to, and I have had several interviews with the piece goods merchants who asked me to give my decision as early as possible owing to approach of the winter sale season. At 10 a.m. on the 17th October Messrs. Pei and Chang of the Superintendent's office, as mentioned above, called on me again to ask my decision which has not yet been given. I told them that I originally intended to declare a heavy penalty, say Hk.Tls. 10,000, and to give "face" to various parties by reducing it piecemeal but that I gave up this cumbersome policy and am at a point of deciding the case to confiscate the goods and sell to owners at one-half of the Customs value, viz: Hk. Tls. 8,000.00. They thanked me for my personal attendance to this case for several days and told me that my decision is quite fair and reasonable. Then they began to talk about fines to be inflicted by the Surtax Office and asked me to detain the goods after the fine has been paid

to

to the Customs as requested in the Superintendent's first letter. I objected to this proposal stating that any goods, whether ordinary or confiscated, which have gone through our formalities cannot be detained by the Customs. I gave them a hint, however, that fines are paid by the merchants to the Bank of China in the same way as duties on ordinary goods on presentation of "fine memos" issued by the Customs instead of "duty memos", so that the Superintendent's office is at lberty to instruct the banker to detain the Customs "fine memos" until the payment of Surtax Office's fine, should it be inflicted. They were satisfied with my explanations. As stated in my S/O letter No. 462 the fine was reduced to Hk.Tls. 7,000.00 at the special request of the Chairman of the Chamber of Commerce, who managed to have Surtax Office's fine waived. The fine was paid on the 23rd October and the goods were released on the same date. The Superintendent returned to Wenchow on the 22nd October but his arrival was kept so secret that it escaped the notice of our Boarding Officers, who have standing

instructions

116

instructions to report the movements of high Chinese Officials. He again left for Shanghai on the 27th October on official business and returned here on the 5th instant as mentioned in my S/O letter No. 463, and on this occasion his movements were reported to me by despatches. I mentioned this case to the Superintendent after his return from Shanghai and he was pleased with my action.

Informants' fees on Factory Piece Goods Seizure:

The first information on this case has been received by me on the 6th October, the day after the arrival of the S.S. "Haean", in the form of a petition signed by five piece goods merchants, and on the 7th and 8th one of the signatories, a Wang Jun-chüan (王潤泉), came to my office on several occasions. Since my advice was given to keep away from the Customs for the sake of his personal safety he did not turn up to the office but came to my house twice to give further information. After his temporary disappearance from the vicinity of the Customs six petitions

from

5.

from four different parties have been received stating all sorts of stories agaist the original informers mainly accusing them for their compromise with the merchants by receiving a graft. No notice was taken to these petitions but after the settlement of the case they again sent in petitions claiming informants's fees. As I was told that these petitioners are local loafers who might give us troubles in future, I went to see the Superintendent and after showing him all the petitions received we decided to issue informants' fees to the first informers, Wang's party, ignoring the claims of all others. The informants' fees were issued yesterday evening in my house before several witnesses.

Chinese-owned S.S. "Cassum" under British flag, the former H.M.S. Woodlark:

This much-talked-of steamer arrived here at 8.45 a.m. on Sunday, the 11th instant, from Shanghai on her way to Hongkong taking five days en route owing to heavy seas and bad coal. When assistance was asked for by Captain W. C. H. Knight I told him that it would be difficult to get

6.

get good steaming coal as not only Wenchow is not a coaling port but the importation of good Formosa coal has been stopped as a result of anti-Japanese boycott, and in case of his failure I would try to get some from the local Electric Light Co. Our Harbour Master and Captain Randby of the S.S. "Kwangchi" also told Captain Knight to take in only a few tons of coal here and to proceed to Foochow where good coal for the rest of her voyage can be obtained. They also advised him to engage experienced firemen acquainted with special kind of boilers fitted on the vessel in Foochow. Several attempts have been made and finally 29 tons coal, which have been pronounced as satisfactory by the Engineer, were loaded on the 14th and the ship hove her anchor at 7.10 a.m. on the 15th. On the 16th the Coast Inspector wired me to ask for her news and in the same night a telegram has been received from the Hongkong Admiralty asking me to inform Captain Knight that $700.00 had been remitted by telegraphic transfer by the owner of the ship in Hongkong. I wired back informing her departure, the latter through the Kowloon Commissioner.

7.

119

Commissioner. According to our boatman-pilot, who took her down as far as to Rocky point, she took six hours for a distance of 14 miles with occasional slowing down. I hope she will reach Hongkong without accident.

Export of charcoal for Japan:

The first steamer of the season, the S.S. "Fujisan Maru" of Mitsui Bussan Kaisha, as mentioned in my last S/O letter, left here on the 15th with 40,000 bags of charcoal. While she was loading cargo a few of the boycott men went on board to tally cargo, but nothing untoward has happened. It is reported that no more export of charcoal is allowed and there is no news of arrival of more Japanese steamers.

Yours truly,

[signature]

Recd 3-12-28.

121

Shanghai Office of the

Inspectorate General of Customs,

S/O

SHANGHAI, 28th November 1928.

Dear Mr. Suzuki,

ANNUAL REVENUE TELEGRAM.

To serve its purpose this must reach me not later than the 1st January. If necessary, you should close your Revenue Accounts several days in advance.

You should address your Revenue telegram to "Inspection Shanghai."

Yours truly,

[signature]

uzuki, Esquire,

WENCHOW.

Rec'd 7-12-28.

[A.—42]

S/O

INSPECTORATE GENERAL OF CUSTOMS, 117

PEPING

~~PEKING~~, 30th Nov. 1928

Dear Sir,

I am directed by the Inspector General to inform you that your S/O Letter No. 463, dated 7th November, has been duly received.

Yours truly,

G. F. Williams

for Personal Secretary.

. Suzuki, Esquire,

WENCHOW.

0 / 12.27.

Rec'd 14-12-28.

[A.—42]

178

INSPECTORATE GENERAL OF CUSTOMS,

PEPING

~~PEKING~~ 6th Dec. 19 28

Dear Sir,

I am directed by the Inspector General inform you that your S/O Letter No. 464, ted 22nd November, has been duly ceived.

Yours truly,

E. T. Williams
for Personal Secretary.

. Suzuku, Esquire,

WENCHOW.

/ 12.27.

CUSTOM HOUSE, 132

S/O No. 465. INDEXED Wenchow, 18th December, 1928.

Dear Mr. Edwardes,

Export of charcoal to Japan:

The Mitsui Bussan Kaisha's 2nd and 3rd charcoal steamers arrived here on the 27th and 29th November and took away 63,000 bags to Japan, but it is very doubtful whether the firm will make further shipments owing to local opposition. A Chinese merchant who alleged to have sold charcoal to a Japanese firm was caught by the Boycott Association and paraded through the streets in fancy cloth on the 25th November. This trade, which yields quite a good revenue to us, is completely at a standstill for the time being.

Chinese-owned S/S "Cassum" under British flag: formerly H. M. S. "Woodlark": (vide S/O No. 464):

I am very glad to hear that this vessel arrived at Hongkong on the 1st December, taking

17

H. F. Edwardes, Esquire.
Etc., Etc., Etc.,
SHANGHAI.

2

123

17 days from Wenchow.

Installation of wireless apparatus on board Chinese vessels over 500 tons:

The Chinese tramp steamers "Tongshan" and "I Li" have been fitted with wireless, while preparations are being made to install on board the C.M.S.N.Co.'s regular coasters "Haean" and "Kwangchi".

Wenchow Chinese Post Office, lowering of rank of:

The rank of the Chinese Post Office at Wenchow has been lowered from 1st to 2nd Class as from the 16th instant. Mr. Li Pao-ch'ang (李寶昌), Acting First Class Postmaster, has been transferred to Hangchow and succeeded by Mr. Hsiang Ting (項鼎).

Comments on Mr. T. J. Broderick's second application for long leave: (Wenchow Despatch No. 4097):

Since the receipt of the sad news of his third son's death and especially after the refusal of his application for long leave, Mr. Broderick became very melancholy despite efforts

have

3.

124

have been used to cheer him up. I repeatedly advised him to resign himself to the inevitable and to dispose of his son's body, either cremate or otherwise, instead of keeping it in the hands of an undertaker at considerable expenses, and also to make some arrangements with the school masters to look after other children until he goes home in next autumn when his leave is due. He seems to have a different idea undoubtedly influenced by his wife (Chinese), who is very anxious to see her children as soon as possible, hence this application. Although I have a full sympathy with him in his recent bereavement yet it is getting well-nigh intolerable for me to see his inactive and sentimental manner in and outside the office. The reasons given in his second application are entirely private affairs and I am of opinion that he is not entitled to get leave in next spring.

With best compliments of the season,

Yours truly,

[signature]

S/O

SHANGHAI OFFICE OF THE
INSPECTORATE GENERAL OF CUSTOMS,

125

SHANGHAI, 28th December, 1928.

Recd 31-12-28.

Dear Mr. Suzuki,

I am directed by the Offiwiating Inspector General to acknowledge the receipt of your S/O letter No.465 of 18th instant.

Yours truly,

Staff Secretary.

SUZUKI, Esquire,

W e n c h o w.